Resurgent India

Resurgent India

The Economics of Atmanirbhar Bharat

JAGADISH SHETTIGAR
POOJA MISRA

OXFORD
UNIVERSITY PRESS

OXFORD
UNIVERSITY PRESS

Great Clarendon Street, Oxford, ox2 6dp,
United Kingdom

Oxford University Press is a department of the University of Oxford.
It furthers the University's objective of excellence in research, scholarship,
and education by publishing worldwide. Oxford is a registered trade mark of
Oxford University Press in the UK and in certain other countries

© Oxford University Press 2022

The moral rights of the authors have been asserted

First Edition published in 2022

Published in the United States of America by Oxford University Press
198 Madison Avenue, New York, NY 10016, United States of America

British Library Cataloguing in Publication Data

Data available

Library of Congress Control Number: 2022937635

ISBN 978–0–19–286648–6

DOI: 10.1093/oso/9780192866486.001.0001

Endorsements

The Covid pandemic shocked India, as it did the rest of the world. While uncertainty about the virus may have ebbed, there is still global uncertainty, political and economic. By any metric, not just vaccination coverage, India has performed remarkably well and resurgence has recouped losses of 2019-20 in 2020-21. How has Indian policy reacted to the shock and what more should be done to move to a higher growth trajectory? Economic Survey 2021-22 and Union Budget 2022-23 have answered these questions. But those are government views. It is always useful to have someone from outside and Jagadish Shettigar and Pooja Misra have authored a comprehensive book, documenting not only the descriptive, but also the prescriptive. Under the normative head, in the template of future reforms, not only is there a discussion of obvious elements (taxation, privatization, land, labour, agriculture, health), but relatively neglected areas (administrative and judicial reforms). A very timely and useful book.

—Bibek Debroy, Chairman of the Economic Advisory
Council to the Prime Minister of India.

The book promises to be an interesting read for all those interested in learning more about the Indian economy, its past performance, the challenges we face and the prospects that lie ahead. I expect that this book will be useful to academics, policymakers, economists and other stakeholders alike.

—Rajiv Kumar, Former Vice Chairman, Niti Aayog

As Atmanirbhar Bharat is a new concept and is expected to stay for a long time, the book provides a better understanding of the concept.

—Dr. N.R. Bhanumurthy, Vice-Chancellor, Dr. B.R. Ambedkar
School of Economics, Bengaluru

The book proposes to encapsulate and provide a realistic perspective of the issues at hand. In this direction, the book makes an insightful contribution by emphasizing the need of a roadmap to bring the dream of Atmanirbhar Bharat to fruition. It is one of the kind initiatives which delineates the options which the government can exercise to help achieve the dream of doubling farmer's income and making India into a global manufacturing hub-both of which contribute towards an Atmanirbhar Bharat. The work is topical and timely as it comes at a time when the government is actively engaged with the task of promoting an atma nirbhar Bharat to bring the shine back to the Indian economy. The authors take a deeper dive into reform agenda in diverse areas such as land and labour reforms, tax, administrative and judicial reforms, corporate social responsibility, among others.

—Shobha Ahuja, Former Senior Director, Confederation of Indian Industry

डॉ. राजीव कुमार
उपाध्यक्ष
DR. RAJIV KUMAR
VICE CHAIRMAN
Phones : 23096677, 23096688
Fax   : 23096699
E-mail : vch-niti@gov.in

भारत सरकार
नीति आयोग, संसद मार्ग
नई दिल्ली - 110 001
Government of India
NATIONAL INSTITUTION FOR TRANSFORMING INDIA
NITI Aayog, Parliament Street,
New Delhi - 110 001

Foreword

The COVID pandemic is surely one of the most severe challenges faced by humankind. The costs of the pandemic have been huge, first in terms of lives lost and the economic costs associated with lockdowns and uncertainty. The impact of the pandemic will be studied for years to come. And so will the response to the pandemic, both from a health and an economic perspective, to be better prepared for the future. The need to invest in healthcare systems has been highlighted by the pandemic. Building a strong foundation on which the economy can take off and enter a high growth trajectory is one of the key challenges we face today. Sustaining growth, in turn will require investments, both private and public, not just in physical infrastructure, but also in social infrastructure.

In this context, this book by Jagadish Shettigar and Pooja Misra is a timely publication. They discuss not only the economic impact of the pandemic, but place it in cotext of a detailed, long term trend analysis. Through multiple chapters, the authors both succinctly, analytically and thoroughly appraise India's economic performance in the years preceding COVID and then examine and quantify the impact of the pandemic. Along with economic analysis, the book also offers a criticle analysis of policies aimed at making India *Atmanirbhar* (Self-reliant). Monetary and fiscal policiess announced by the Government are analysed, along with economic reforms introduced under the umbrella of 'Atmanirbhar Bharat'.

Of particular interest are the policy suggestions contained in Section III of the book. Returning India to a high growth trajectory path will require policy interventions, which this book discusses in considerable detail. The suggestions cover the entire gamut of the Indian economy, ranging from agriculture, rural development to manufacturing and services. Crucially, the book also provides a set of suggestions to improve governance as well. This rich body of work will no doubt contribute greatly to the public discourse around the course of action we adopt to take forward India's economic transition – during the Atma Kal – meets 2047 when we celebrate the centenary of our Independence.

The book promises to be an interesting read for all those interested in learning more about the Indian economy, its past performance, the challenges we face and the prospects that lie ahead. I expect that this book will be useful reference to academics, policymakers, economists and other stakeholders alike.

I congratulate Jagadish Shettigar and Pooja Misra on putting together this fascinating read

Rajiv Kumar
February 24, 2022

Preface

In the backdrop of the Coronavirus having wreaked havoc on nations across the world and adversely impacting the economic growth of countries the world over, the Government and monetary authorities, ie Reserve Bank of India, stepped forward with conventional as well as unconventional stimulus measures.

In times of such an unprecedented crisis, the pertinent questions in the minds of not only economic analysts but also the common man were: Should the Government be providing the stimulus to the economy in small doses (with an industry-specific stimuli) or announce a big bang stimulus? Should the Government have adopted the Keynesian theory of economic growth? Were there any lessons to be learnt from the Great Depression of the 1930s?

During the first and second waves of the COVID-19 pandemic, was it more of a demand-side problem or was it the supply side? Should the Government focus more on demand-side measures as against supply-side measures or was there a need for both?

Was this the right time for the Government to worry about a widening fiscal deficit? Should monetization of deficit be done? If yes, what about its implication on future inflation and interest rates and consequent cost to investors and consumers?

This was the time for the Government and fellow Indians to reboot, re-draw and reinvent the wheel of progress and paint a new standing in the World Economic Order. Had the process already begun with countries such as the United States and the United Kingdom asking for India to be included in the G7 group of countries?

Thus, in light of the abovementioned macroeconomic scenario existing in India in June 2020, the authors decided to continuously examine the important policy measures announced by the Government and evaluate its impact on the country.

Part 1 of the book traces the preceding trends in the economic growth of the country during 2010–20, the impact of the virus on the Indian economy, the macroeconomic perspectives, economics of farm crisis, inputs for the Budget for 2021–22, economic impact of the second wave of the virus and what did the surge in GDP in Q1FY22 show?

Part 2 critically analyzes policy initiatives undertaken by the Government for achieving an Atmanirbhar Bharat which includes short-term and long-term structural reforms, agricultural reforms, six pillars on which the Union Budget 2021–22 had been based, Government's re-think on the retrospective tax, asset monetization and many other measures.

Part 3 lays out a roadmap of policy suggestions that warrant Government focus and attention to make India into a self-reliant nation. These initiatives can help achieve the dream of doubling farmers' income and making India into a global manufacturing hub, an Atmanirbhar Bharat. It discusses that for India to be a major manufacturing destination, technology upgradation is needed. Keeping in mind the importance of universal vaccination, a balanced approach is needed on IPRs for crucial medicines. Lastly, this section discusses the importance of cooperative federalism and challenges before the Government in making India into an Atmanirbhar Bharat.

This book would be highly useful to policymakers and political leadership interested in economic matters, corporate leaders and chambers of commerce, financial institutions and research institutes, and postgraduate programmes.

Acknowledgements

We would like to express our deep gratitude to Dr. Harivansh Chaturvedi, Director, Birla Institute of Management Technology (BIMTECH), Greater Noida for his encouraging words and utmost support. The conducive atmosphere prevalent in BIMTECH has made it possible for us to pen down our thoughts and delve deep into an analysis of the roadmap to making India into an Atmanirbhar Bharat. We would also like to thank Ms. Anika Mittal, an alumna of BIMTECH for helping us with the research on economic growth trends.

We would like to thank Pushpa, Sanchita, and Samata for their invaluable support.

A big thank you to Mayank, Suneela, and Shiven for their innumerous encouragement.

Contents

3. POLICY SUGGESTIONS

PART 1
THE STATE OF INDIAN ECONOMY

In light of the coronavirus outbreak presenting an alarming health crisis for nations all over the world, the Indian economic situation, along with the foundation of India's healthcare system, was shaken up. However, it is important to bear in mind that even prior to the pandemic Indian GDP growth numbers were decelerating with Q4 GDP 2019–20 being 4.2%.

The authors in Part 1 of the book have traced the trends in economic growth for the period 2010–20 and analysed the fiscal and monetary measures adopted by the government and RBI. They have done a detailed analysis of the impact of COVID-19 on the Indian economy and discussed the macroeconomic perspectives. Interestingly, with all sectors of the economy being negatively impacted, the Indian stock market has been buoyant due to incoming foreign portfolio investment (FPI). The authors have discussed the paradoxical trend of the Indian capital markets and analysed the green shoots of economic recovery seen with Unlock happening.

Also, in view of the pandemic having adversely impacted the economy and leading to India witnessing a contraction of 6.6% of GDP in FY21, suggestions for Budget 2021–22 have been given. Not to miss the fact that for building the country into an Atmanirbhar Bharat, the need for a historic budget has been discussed which can lay the road-map in terms of increased government expenditure, increasing purchasing power of the common man who is expected to play a proactive role in demand boosting and building of a robust policy environment. Last but not the least, in view of the fact that the spread of the second wave of the virus in 2021 had resulted in a humanitarian and health crisis, its adverse impact on the Indian economy has been assessed and subsequent Q122 and Q222 GDP numbers have been closely analysed.

1.1

Trend in Economic Growth 2010–2020

India, an emerging economy, is known to be one of the fastest-growing economies in the world. With the pandemic ensuing in a global economic downturn, India too was not spared from the onslaught of the virus. At the onset of the pandemic, India had focused on saving lives which transitioned to saving both lives and livelihoods. Post the first wave of the virus, it was being largely propounded that the Indian economy had witnessed a V-shaped recovery and eventually the country's gross domestic product (GDP) had contracted at 6.6% in FY2020–21. However, with the onslaught of the second wave of the virus resulting in an economic and humanitarian health crisis for the country, it led to economists and analysts going back to the drawing board and reforecasting growth numbers from approximately 10.5% to 9.5% for FY2021–22. While the economic impact of the second wave of the virus was being said to be not as severe as the first, analysts were not sure about whether economic recovery would be U-shaped or W-shaped or K-shaped instead of V-shaped. Interestingly, with the Indian economy growing at a record pace of 20.1% in Q1 FY22, the country was fast paving its path towards economic recovery.

Tracing back history and looking at the state of the Indian economy for the last 10 years (FY2010–20), post the global financial crisis (GFC) of 2008, India had shown remarkable recovery with the services sector coming out to be a major growth driver along with other sectors. Each year had its own challenges in the form of high inflation, high fiscal deficit, high current account deficit (CAD), slowing demand, poor monsoon, etc., which were ably addressed by the government and Reserve Bank of India (RBI) using fiscal policy and monetary policy measures, respectively.

A detailed trend analysis of the Indian economy since 2010 and how it has evolved into one of the fastest-growing economies of the world is discussed in the following section:

Resurgent India. Jagadish Shettigar and Pooja Misra, Oxford University Press. © Oxford University Press 2022.
DOI: 10.1093/oso/9780192866486.003.0001

Table 1.1.1 GDP growth rate (%) FY 2010–20.

Year	GDP growth rate (%)	Base year
2010–2011	10.3%	2004–2005
2011–2012	6.6%	2004–2005
2012–2013	5.5%	2011–2012
2013–2014	6.4%	2011–2012
2014–2015	7.4%	2011–2012
2015–2016	8%	2011–2012
2016–2017	8.3%	2011–2012
2017–2018	7%	2011–2012
2018–2019	6.1%	2011–2012
2019–2020	4.04%	2011–2012
2020–2021	(–)6.6%	2011–2012

Source: Ministry of Statistics and Programme implementation

Post the global financial crisis (GFC) of 2008, FY2010 was a year in which the policymakers' focus shifted from crisis management to recovery and expansionary monetary and fiscal measures were adopted.

India's growth was impressive at 8.5%. This was due to the notable growth depicted by the industrial and services sectors showing a rise in

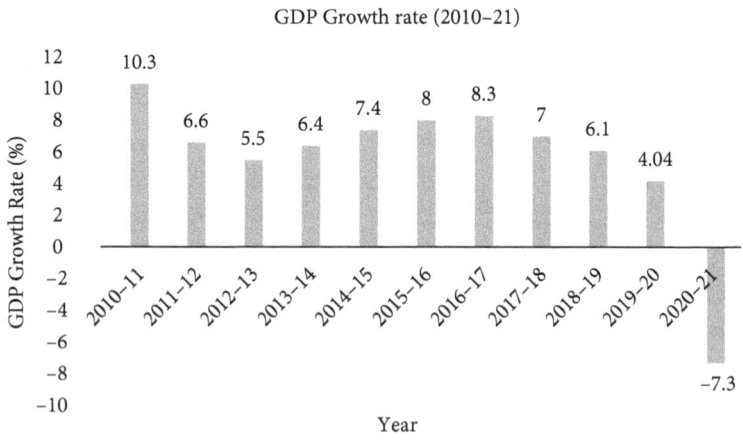

Figure 1.1.1 GDP growth rate (%) FY2010–21

gross capital fixed capital formation, private investments, corporate sales, credit demand, and merchandise exports. However, the year was marked by a delayed monsoon resulting in supply-side shortages of food items which resulted in double-digit food inflation signalling the beginning of policy exit. The fiscal measures initiated were with a viewpoint of providing substantial financial stimulus, whereas monetary policy measures implemented were in terms of lowering repo rate, reverse repo rate, and infusion of liquidity, which helped the Indian economy make a remarkable recovery and achieve a GDP growth rate of 8.5%.

2011 was the final year for recovery from the global financial crisis and economic slowdown, which had negatively impacted the country. Robust economic growth was witnessed with GDP growing at a rate of 10.3% in 2011. The services sector continued to be the dominant contributor to GDP, and the agricultural sector also contributed significantly to GDP growth owing to normal monsoons. Robust private household demand also contributed to the strong economic growth. On the flip side, the economy was still plagued by inflation throughout the year due to high commodity prices, high aggregate demand, and cost-push factors. Increased input costs were passed on to the consumers amidst high consumption demand. High commodity prices shook business confidence and hence led to low investment activity by the industrial sector. Contractionary monetary policy or monetary tightening was used as an anti-inflationary measure. Fiscal support remained limited during this period.

The Indian economy was characterized by a growth slowdown in FY12. From 10.3%, GDP decelerated to 6.6%. Factors responsible for the economic slowdown were high inflation, rising fiscal deficit, and rising current account balance. A steep decline in industrial and service sectors such as construction, hotels, trade, communication were major drivers that drove down economic growth. However, on the whole, the service sector was the major contributor to GDP. Low investment levels and weak external as well as internal demand constituted additional factors affecting growth. Household investments in financial assets, employment, and incomes were adversely affected.

Economic slowdown coupled with high inflation led to the continuation of monetary tightening until October 2011, after which rising policy rates were paused due to growth risks. Scope for monetary as well as fiscal stimulus was limited, keeping in mind inflation levels. Investment in infrastructure was seen as a major source of improving growth levels.

Indian economy experienced an ongoing slowdown in 2012–13, and the GDP growth rate decelerated to 5.5%. High persistent inflation, structural issues, and poor asset quality were the main challenges in the economy. The earlier part of the year was hit by high fiscal and current account deficits (CADs). All the principal sectors, namely, agricultural, industrial, and services sectors suffered with the industrial sector being impacted the most. Economic activity in all the three sectors decelerated with the services sector being the major contributor.

The slowdown in the agricultural sector was due to weak monsoon, whereas a weak demand (domestic and global) and electricity generation decline owing to coal shortage impacted industrial sector activity. Private consumption got adversely affected due to high inflation. It was important to address the structural issues and focus on infrastructure development for economic growth, for which capital formation was essential. A decline in government consumption expenditure as well as fixed investment was also seen. Monetary authorities undertook monetary easing, which helped in checking inflation and fiscal deficit in the latter part of the year.

There was a marginal improvement in GDP growth in FY14 to 6.4% from the previous year's 5.5%. Sectors contributing significantly to growth were the agriculture and services sector with the service sector leading the growth. The industrial sector faced a major downfall. Major challenges for the policymakers were in terms of controlling inflation, twin deficits (fiscal deficit and CAD), volatility in exchange rates, declining investments, and working towards stabilizing the economy.

Growth in private consumption was very slow owing to inflation and resultant weak purchasing power. Government expenditure also fell as compared to the previous year. Fixed capital formation (fixed investments) saw a major fall due to structural as well as cyclical factors. Political uncertainty, low business confidence, problems with infrastructure, and lack of good policy framework were some reasons for the fall in fixed investments.

Rupee depreciation led to improved exports. Imports declined due to low demand and a substantial fall in gold imports because of policy restrictions contributed to the growth and controlling of the CAD, which improved from 4.9% in Q1 to 1.7% full-year CAD. Decreased govern-ment expenditure and increased non-tax revenues, and high dividends from Public Sector Enterprises (PSEs) and Public Sector Banks (PSBs) led to a lower fiscal deficit than what was budgeted.

The economy started stabilizing with better management of fiscal as well as current account deficits and inflation during the second part of the year. There was some success in controlling inflation. It was impor-tant to implement policies in a way that it increased productivity, thereby improving supply.

GDP picked up in FY15 marking growth at 7.4%. India was amongst the fastest-growing economies in the world. An increase in household consumption and a considerable increase in fixed investments were the economic growth drivers. There was a decline in government expend-iture and a considerable fall in net exports. Fall in exports was a matter of concern as it affected aggregate demand. Share of agriculture sector declined due to deficient rainfall and loss of crops due to unseasonal rains and hailstorms. This affected rural demand and also posed a threat of in-creasing food prices.

Sectors responsible for growth were the industrial and service sectors. Growth in manufacturing was mainly due to increased business confi-dence, electricity and coal production, effective capacity utilization, and increased global and domestic demand. There was less volatility in the foreign exchange market and the stock market was on the rise due to in-vestor confidence. Issues to be addressed were declining savings rate, eco-nomic stability, and focusing on structural impediments to growth.

FY16 witnessed an increasing growth rate at 8%. Private consump-tion was the main driver of growth, accounting for about half of the GDP growth owing to higher real incomes due to low inflation levels. Household consumption in urban areas was higher with an increase in sales of passenger vehicles, whereas rural demand was low as rural income was affected due to an inefficient monsoon. Government ex-penditure accounted for a very little share in GDP due to the ongoing efforts of controlling fiscal deficit. Net exports started falling during the first half of the year. However, during the second half of the year, a fall in imports outpaced the falling trend in exports. No major improve-ments can be seen in fixed investments which dragged down economic growth.

The 'Make in India' initiative boosted investor confidence and improved business sentiments. Looking at a sectoral view, the agriculture sector's share was very low due to erratic weather conditions. The industrial and service sectors again were the major contributors to GDP. Disinflation helped in increasing real incomes and interest rates on savings became positive in real terms. Factors attributable to disinflation were falling global commodity prices and policy measures undertaken by RBI. A high amount of foreign direct investment (FDI) and an increase in the number of IPOs were also seen as a sign of growth. The fiscal deficit was also reduced on account of additional revenues.

GDP growth rate in FY17 was 8.3%. The important event in 2016–17 was demonetization announced on 8 November 2016, Q3 2016. The agriculture sector rebounded owing to high horticulture and food-grain production and an increase in minimum support price (MSP) of pulses. The industrial sector's share declined as compared to the previous year due to slow growth in manufacturing. Industrial production was affected severely by demonetization. There was a deceleration in the services sector as construction and real estate sectors were severely impacted after demonetization as they mainly depended upon cash transactions. The share of fixed investments declined due to low business confidence. Net exports were very low and major contributors were private consumption and government consumption. Therefore, it was basically a consumption-led growth.

Inflation, though being high in the first part of the year, turned into disinflation due to falling vegetable prices post demonetization. Deposits saw an increase due to demonetization, however, money supply was moderate. Another reason for the increase in deposits was the income declaration scheme (IDS) and arrears paid by the seventh pay commission.

Spike in deposits created excess liquidity in the banking system, which was controlled through reverse repo rate under liquidity adjustment facility, increased Cash Reserve Requirement (CRR), issuing cash management bills. Credit growth was slow as investments remained subdued. After demonetization, banks did not transfer the full benefit of policy rate cuts to lending rates which in turn caused investments to remain subdued. Fiscal deficit was controlled through increasing revenues through IDS scheme, imposing cess, additional excise duty rather than decreasing expenses. Strong external stability was visible through controlled CAD,

FDI inflows, increasing forex reserves. Investment revival required incorporating structural changes along with monetary measures.

In 2017–18, GDP growth rate slowed down to 7% on account of transitory difficulties due to demonetization and implementation of GST. Implementation of GST was a milestone achieved towards adopting an effective indirect taxation regime.

Drivers of growth were gross fixed capital formation or fixed investments. Household consumption mainly comprised of rural demand owing to a good harvest season and focus on rural housing and infrastructure development. Government consumption had weakened compared to the previous year. There was a loss of domestic demand as it was fulfilled through imports.

Looking at a sectoral view, agriculture production was very high, which was supplemented with imports and resulted in excess supply of rice, pulses, wheat leading to deflation in prices and high levels of buffer stocks. The manufacturing sector started recovering, supported by capital goods and infrastructure goods. The service sector too showed signs of recovery. Growth in the infrastructure sector was remarkable with various developments taking place, such as the construction of roads and national highways, launching Mumbai–Ahmedabad bullet train project, various projects launched by smart cities. Not only this, to achieve the goal of universal household electrification, Pradhan Mantri Sahaj Bijli Har Ghar Yojana was launched.

After various fluctuations, the year ended with a low inflation rate. As demonetization affected liquidity position, the transmission of benefits from policy rates to lending rates improved but was uneven. The position of fiscal deficit was unsatisfactory due to increased expenditures and reduced revenues. On account of the late implementation of GST, there were low indirect tax collections. Apart from that, there was a shortfall in non-tax revenues too. Expenses rose on account of farm loan waivers and the implementation of pay commission recommendations.

The external sector remained positive with CAD staying within controllable limits, robust FDI and FPI inflows, thereby increasing forex reserves and leading to rupee appreciation. Credit growth picked up serving as a source of finance for commercial banks. Personal loans and loans to the service sector spiked significantly. Non-performing assets (NPAs) still remained high, affecting the profitability of banks. RBI came up with a revised prompt corrective action (PCA) framework keeping in mind the falling asset quality and also provided PSBs with capital infusion through recapitalization bonds and budgetary help.

Impressive growth in FY18 was followed by slow growth in FY19, bringing down GDP growth to 6.1%. The economy was basically going through a slowdown as growth suffered various downturns. It might not be incorrect to state that the global economy was going through a slowdown in economic activity and reduced global demand also impacted India.

Certain factors responsible for the weakening of global activity were increasing trade tensions, oil price volatility, Brexit uncertainty, Chinese economy slowdown, and normalization of the US monetary policy. All this caused great uncertainty in financial markets due to weak investor sentiment. There was an adverse impact on the manufacturing sector and net exports. Indian exports declined in spite of Indian currency depreciating and weak domestic demand led to a fall in imports.

Industrial production decelerated, affecting employment and income generation. Moreover, as production of capital goods declined, investments were affected, hence, gross fixed capital formation slowed down. Firms were focusing on using existing capacity as against expanding it. Private consumption, which constitutes the main part of aggregate demand, dropped drastically. The sale of FMCG saw a downfall indicating weak rural demand on account of poor harvest. The share of agriculture also declined leading to low rural demand. Therefore, consumption along with investment affected growth.

The fiscal deficit was at 3.4% of GDP, which was in line with the budgeted fiscal deficit, whereas CAD was more than capital inflows, thereby reducing the reserves. NPAs declined from 11.25% to 9.1%. Insolvency and bankruptcy code provided a boost in recovering NPAs and also tried removing obstacles in the way of investment growth.

With the surge in digital payments, India was moving on the path of a cashless economy where the challenge was to minimize the risk of misuse of data and technology. At this stage, the nature of slowdown was identified as a cyclical one rather than structural. As regards monetary policy, it had to bear in mind both inflation and changing growth patterns. During the first half, high international crude prices and financial market volatility led to inflationary pressures, and therefore monetary tightening was adopted. During the latter part of the year, crude oil prices declined, food prices reduced, thereby bringing down inflation levels in the economy. Along with this, the Indian economy lost momentum amidst the global slowdown. Keeping this in mind, a cut in repo rate was made by RBI.

FY2019–20 was very critical for the Indian economy as well as the global economy due to a persistent economic slowdown. While economies were trying to recover from the slowdown, all countries globally, including India were hit by COVID-19 (in Q4 of 2019–20). GDP growth rate of the Indian economy for FY20 decelerated to an eleven-year low of 4.04% due to the halt of economic activities during the nationwide lockdown amid coronavirus spread. Quarter-wise GDP growth rates at constant prices for FY20 were—Q1: 5.39%, Q2: 4.61%, Q3: 3.28%, Q4: 3.01%.

During 2019–20, a climate of uncertainty was persistent. Index of industrial production (IIP) saw a major downfall on account of a drastic fall in manufacturing owing to low demand. There was weakened construction activity. Consumer demand for non-durables increased somewhat in Q1, but demand for durable goods witnessed a major hit which was visible through deceleration in automobile sales and white good sales. Sales of commercial vehicles and passenger vehicles contracted significantly indicating declining urban demand. Private consumption weakened in both urban and rural areas. Owing to a slowdown in trade across the world, exports and imports were also facing deceleration. Government expenditure also declined as compared to the previous year. Production of cement and steel, which are essentials of construction and hence investment, declined, thereby leading to a fall in gross fixed capital formation. Financial markets were very volatile. Exports and imports, both, contracted. Keeping in mind low levels of investment and inflation levels, the policy rate was reduced.

Due to demonetization, GST, various NBFC crisis, NPAs, there was a lack of liquidity or cash crunch in the economy, which led to a decline in investments and consumption. Consumption or demand registered a drastic fall. There was a contraction in demand for cars. The decline in the sale of cars affects various forward and backward ancillary industries such as tyre producers, steel producers. In terms of forward linkages, a number of auto dealerships were shutting down or contracting. Demand for vehicle loans also declined with a decline in demand for cars.

Similarly, demand for two-wheelers also contracted. Tractor sales which signal rural demand, also declined.

Housing sales had also declined with a mounting number of unsold housing units. Real estate is linked with a large number of ancillary units. Therefore, the performance of the real estate sector determines the performance of other sectors like cement, steel, paint, furniture, etc. Sales of FMCG companies was also witnessing a downward trend.

As consumption declined, suppliers were left with piled-up inventories, thus forcing them to cut back production and hence leading to a deceleration in the industrial sector. This affected fixed investments, too, as producers were not expanding their production capacities. The fall in production led to a fall in employment and people even lost their jobs which affected incomes and savings patterns.

Global slowdown kept exports and imports low. All these factors combined led to the economic slowdown. To further compound the situation of economic slowdown, the nationwide lockdown due to COVID-19 brought almost all economic activities to a halt and further worsened the situation. Prior to COVID-19, the Indian economy was bearing the brunt of a demand slowdown which had worsened with supply chain disruptions and declining discretionary expenditure on the part of consumers due to the havoc that the pandemic had wrought.

1.2

Impact of COVID-19 on the Indian Economy

COVID-19, an infectious disease caused by the coronavirus, had resulted in a global health outbreak. All economies, being primarily open economies, involve free movement of people and goods from one country to another. Being a communicable disease, COVID-19, which had originated in China, spread worldwide. As the number of people being infected and dying kept on increasing, WHO declared the crisis as a pandemic. Pandemic refers to a global spread of an infectious disease.

Governments all over the world had taken concrete steps to limit the spread of the virus, resorting to social distancing, border closures, imposing travel restrictions within and outside the country, nationwide lockdowns, halting almost all types of economic activity. These measures had brusquely brought businesses to a halt, resulting in demand and supply chain disruptions, leading to unemployment and adversely affected economies worldwide.

Global Outlook

The global macroeconomic outlook had been overcast with the COVID-19 pandemic. Disruption of economic activities across the geography was set to intensify in the form of disruptions in demand, production, supply chains, trade, and tourism globally. Global output contracted in 2020. Financial markets worldwide started experiencing extreme volatility and equity markets had witnessed sharp sell-offs. Global commodity prices, especially of crude oil, had declined sharply in anticipation of weakening global demand, and failed negotiations of the Organisation of the Petroleum Exporting Countries (OPEC) and Russia.

Resurgent India. Jagadish Shettigar and Pooja Misra, Oxford University Press. © Oxford University Press 2022.
DOI: 10.1093/oso/9780192866486.003.0002

As per IMF World Economic Outlook, the global economy was projected to contract sharply by (–)3.5% in 2020, much worse than during the 2008–09 financial crisis. In a baseline scenario, which assumed that the pandemic fades in the second half of 2020, the global economy was projected to grow by 5.5% in 2021 as economic activity normalizes, helped by policy support. The report stated that the total loss to global GDP during 2020 and 2021 from the pandemic crisis could be around USD9 trillion, greater than the economies of Japan and Germany, combined.

As per the RBI report, among 'advanced economies' (AEs) that had released GDP readings for Q2-2020, contractions were in the range of 2.7% to 21.5% (q-o-q, annualized), for 'emerging market economies' (EMEs), the growth rate ranged between 3.2% and (–)23.98% (year on year basis). Higher pressure was faced by EMEs in the form of capital outflows and volatility in asset prices.

Among the key AEs, economic activity contracted in the United States, Euro area, Japan, and the United Kingdom in Q2 of 2020. Among EMEs, the Chinese economy went into a pronounced deceleration and subsequently recovered in Q2, 2020.

According to the United Nations Conference on Trade and Development (UNCTAD), world trade contracted by 5.0% in Q3 2020–21 against an initial forecast of a contraction of 3% y-o-y. Depending on how the virus would negatively impact countries worldwide, UNCTAD forecasts stated that the value of global trade would end up at 7%–9% below 2019 levels.

Due to fall in demand amidst lockdowns, commodity prices eased, but pressure of supply chain disruptions on food prices was visible in inflation prints. After facing a difficult time in March with global indices falling drastically, financial markets globally had subsequently calmed down and volatility in financial markets had also gradually decreased.

IMF Global Financial Stability Report stated that the financial system globally had been impacted dramatically, and that a further intensification of the crisis could affect global financial stability. Since the pandemic outbreak, prices of risk assets had fallen sharply.

As India is exposed to the global economy, its exports had been severely hit. Indian exports had been expected to decline to USD290 billion compared to USD313.36 billion in the previous fiscal. The reason for the sharp fall in exports was the ongoing global slowdown which got amplified by lockdown across geographies owing to COVID-19. Due to lockdown, which halted almost all economic activities, there had been a sharp decline in demand from across the world, which led to cancellation of orders and no new orders. Gems and jewellery, leather products, petroleum products, engineering goods, and chemicals, all sectors witnessed negative growth in exports. As per the Federation of Indian Export Organisation, this had been the highest ever decline in monthly exports.

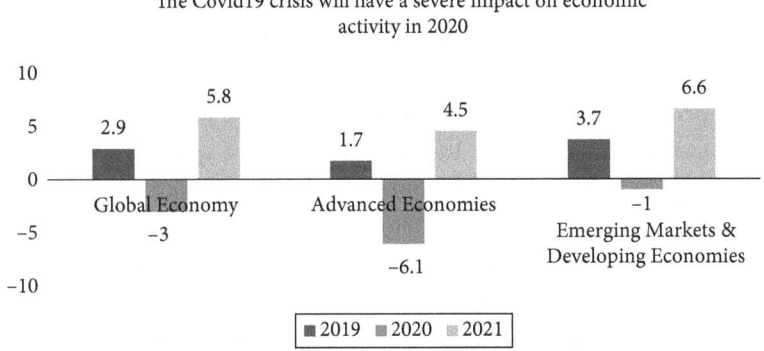

The Covid19 crisis will have a severe impact on economic activity in 2020

Source: https://www.imf.org/-/media/Images/IMF/Publications/WEO/2020/April/Arrows.ashx

Disruption of Supply Chain

Efficient supply chain management is an integral part of smooth running of any business. For manufacturing concerns, a smooth supply of raw material is essential for timely production and to further maintain timely supply of output to wholesalers and retailers. All backward linkages and forward linkages of a business are closely intertwined. Disruption at any one of the stages can adversely affect the business.

The negative impact of the pandemic on supply chain and logistics was spreading across the world. China being the world's largest manufacturing hub and largest exporter of goods with the outbreak of the virus in China, there was month-long closure of production units and shipping ports in China which disrupted the supply chain in all the countries as raw material and finished goods could not be exported to other countries including India. This led to a shortage of raw material for manufacturing units and finished goods for wholesalers and retailers globally. The supply of vehicles, smart-phones, pharmaceuticals, etc., and many more products was severely affected.

Any disruption in supply and demand affects prices of goods. If supply is insufficient to meet demand, prices shoot up. Moreover, if demand falls drastically, unsold inventories will be piled up, which will drive down prices.

Impact on Indian Economy

India, prior to the outbreak of COVID-19, was trying to recover from the economic slowdown but the virus that was fast spreading worldwide had not spared India and made its first appearance in India on 30 January 2020. As cases of coronavirus patients increased in the country, the government implemented a 21-day nationwide lockdown on 24 March 2020 (Lockdown 1.0). All educational institutions, businesses, commercial establishments, places of worship, etc. were shut, except for a few essential services.

Almost all economic activities came to a halt. Subsequently, the Lockdown was further extended till 3 May 2020 (Lockdown 2.0). After this, all cities were divided into red, orange, and green zones depending upon the number of cases of corona positive. Again, the Lockdown was extended until 17 May (Lockdown 3.0), but cities under the orange and green zones were given certain relaxations. Lockdown 4.0 was imposed from 17 May to 31 May but with certain relaxations. Partial opening up of the economy started in Lockdown 4.0. Economic activities such as industrial activities, air travel, e-commerce deliveries of essential and non-essential items, opening up of retail shops had started with precautionary measures. The idea behind opening up the economy was—'*Jaan Bhi Jahaan Bhi*'.

The GDP growth rate of India for the fiscal year 2020 was 4.04% against an earlier estimate of 5%, and the GDP growth rate for Q4 of FY2020 was 3.01%. According to IMF, the GDP growth rate of India for 2020–21 was estimated to be (–)4.2%, and for the following year, 6% growth was projected. However, estimates in the Economic Survey 2020–21 pointed out that India's GDP was expected to contract by (−7.7%) in FY21. India's real GDP was expected to grow by 11.0% in FY2021–22. Subsequently, as per revised estimates in May 2021, with Q4 2020–21 GDP growth being 1.6%, the Indian economy contracted by (−7.3%). However, revised estimates released in February 2022, painted a better picture and showed that the economy had contracted by 6.6% in FY 21. To minimize the negative impact of the virus, India had adopted a four-pillar strategy of containment, fiscal, financial, and long-term structural reforms. There was a calibrated fiscal and monetary support given by RBI in the form of lowering policy rates and quantitative easing etc. and the government, respectively, ensuring abundant liquidity.

As anticipated by experts and economists, Q1, FY2020 results showed a major contraction in the growth of the Indian economy. On 31 August 2020, the Ministry of Statistics and Programme Implementation (MoSPI), Government of India declared the provisional estimates for April–June quarter (Q1) 2020. It posed a grim picture showing that the Indian economy had contracted by 23.9% in Q1 2020, the most drastic contraction witnessed over decades. The worrisome GDP numbers for India were corroborated by the International Monetary Fund (IMF), chief economist, Gita Gopinath who stated that as per IMF estimates, India's internationally comparable q-o-q GDP shrank the highest amongst G20 countries at 25.6%.

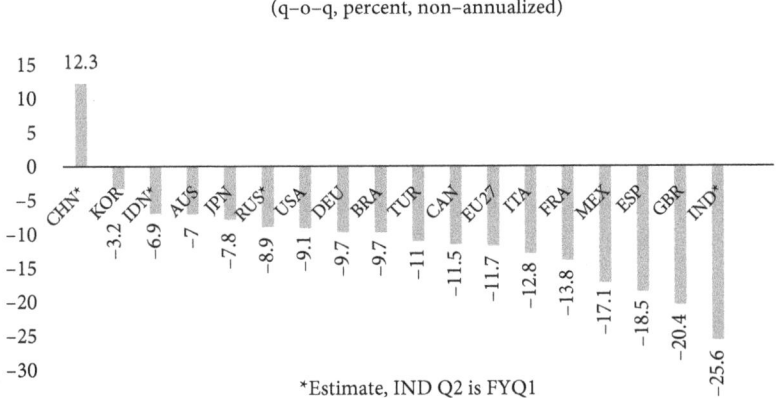

2020 Q2 April–June GDP Growth
(q–o–q, percent, non–annualized)

*Estimate, IND Q2 is FYQ1

Source: www.imf.org

However, Q2 and Q3 of 2020–21 with Unlock happening proved to be better quarters with Q2 2020–21 contracting by 7.5% followed by Q3 2020–21 predicted to grow by 0.1%. In Q2, economic recovery was fairly broad-based. Q3 2020–21 saw shifts in the macroeconomic landscape, brightening the outlook with GDP entering positive territory and inflation levels nearing the inflation-targeting framework. India's strategy of an early lockdown helped flatten the curve with the virus peaking in September 2020, followed by declining daily cases in spite of increased mobility. A V-shaped recovery was seen in Q2 and Q3 of 2020–21, an outcome of structural reforms on the supply side and calibrated demand-side measures. Q4 2020–21 saw a GDP growth of 1.6%.

Lockdown and Impact on Economic Activities

There is no doubt that this Lockdown of nearly two months had adversely affected the economic growth of the country resulting in dismal growth, if not recession. High-frequency indicators pointed out a drastic fall in demand beginning in March 2020 across both urban and rural sectors. Electricity and petroleum products consumption that indicate day-to-day demand showed steep declines. The loss in terms of demand and production had affected fiscal revenues. Investment demand came to a standstill. This was evident by the decline in production of capital goods by 36% and shrinkage of 27% in imports of capital goods in March 2020 and 57.5% in April 2020, fall in 'finished steel consumption' by 91% in April 2020 and a fall of 25% in cement production in March 2020.

The biggest component of aggregate demand affected from COVID-19 was private consumption, which accounts for about 60% of domestic demand. In March 2020, the production of durable goods recorded a fall of 33% and a 16% fall in non-durables.

The preliminary analysis of the impact of lockdown due to COVID-19 on different sectors of the Indian economy follows:

Impact on Agriculture Sector

India is an agrarian country wherein the agricultural sector is considered to be the backbone of its economy. Agriculture sector contributes to approximately 16% of GDP of India. There had been a detrimental effect of the pandemic on the Indian farm economy. Although agricultural activities from harvesting to transportation of output were exempted from lockdown guidelines, the agricultural sector suffered due to two major problems that were related to

a) Labour availability
b) Movement of goods due to halted transportation.

Nonavailability of migrant labourers, as they fled to their hometowns owing to lockdown and fear of coronavirus, halted harvesting activities and posed serious challenges to the harvesting of rabi crop. Over 30% of the crop lay unharvested due to the acute shortage of labour and lack of access to fields.

Shortage of labour led to an increase in daily wages, causing problems for producers as prices of output went up due to supply chain disruptions. In contrast to this, the areas where labourers had returned to, saw an increase in the supply of labour, leading to a decline in wages. The rise in labour costs and lack of access to markets made farmers let their crops rot in fields.

Due to disruption in transportation, the harvested crops remained stacked in the fields and houses of farmers, as they could not transport the grains without logistics support and the agricultural produce could not reach the mandis, thus leading to wastage of produce. The movement of trucks used for carrying essential commodities was hampered because of the lockdown. Even cold storage and warehouses could not function properly due to labour shortage. Workers are essential for both pre-harvest and post-harvest activities, and their shortage caused severe supply chain disruptions in the supply of perishable fruits and vegetables and dairy products, milk, eggs.

Interestingly, it was seen that on the whole India's farm sector functioned smoothly despite COVID-19 lockdown and there had not been much impact on its growth, unlike other sectors. The agricultural sector and allied activities had provided a ray of hope in difficult times with an increase in the production of food grains by 3.7%. Forecast of good southwest monsoon, sufficient water level in reservoirs, increase in kharif sown areas by 85%, all these factors were in favour of farm sector growth. A good harvest of rabi crops had resulted in the full procurement of oil seeds, pulses, and wheat.

Impact on Industrial Sector

The industrial sector, which contributes around 28% to GDP, was significantly impacted with the intensification of COVID-19. The industrial sector had been hit hard with COVID-19 and witnessed contraction amid lockdowns. Industrial production contracted by around 17% in March 2020 and manufacturing activity fell by 21%. Core industries output, constituting about 40% of overall industrial production, recorded a fall of 6.5%. Manufacturing PMI at 27.4 saw its highest fall in April but recovered to 47.2 in May 2020. IIP contracted 55.5% year-on-year in April as against a revised contraction of 18.3% in March and contracted 34.7% in May 2020. Manufacturing output growth contracted 64.3% in April and 39.3% in May compared to a contraction of 22.4% in March. Mining output contracted 27.4% after a contraction of 1.4% in the previous month. Electricity generation contracted 22.6% against a contraction of 8.2% last month.

With the spread of the virus in China, it resulted in supply chain disruptions being faced by foreign suppliers of auto components, electronics, smartphones, chemicals, pharmaceuticals due to border closure. As Indian manufacturers are heavily dependent upon imports for raw materials, the manufacturing sector suffered. (India imports 45% of electronics, around one-third of machinery, about two-fifths of organic chemicals, around 70% pharmaceuticals, 90% smartphones, and more than 25% of auto parts from China.) Not only imports, but exports also decelerated. With regards to exports, China is India's third largest export partner and accounts for about 5% of India's exports.

Gradually as coronavirus started spreading in India, due to lockdown, domestic demand for consumer durable goods and automobiles declined significantly as demand was majorly concentrated towards essential commodities. Migrant labourers flocked to their hometowns which created a shortage of workforce required to carry out production. Thus, due to reduced demand, shortage of labour, lack of transportation facilities, and imposition of lockdown, most of the manufacturing units (except a few) had to shut down their plants, bringing production activities to a complete halt. Owing to backward linkages, suppliers of components and ancillary units had to close their operations as there was no demand from producers.

Impact on Service Sector

Services sector has been a significant contributor to India's economic growth and contributes about 53.66% to GDP. This sector is considered as a lifeblood for economic growth and includes construction, trade, hotels, transport, communication, professional services, tourism, and financial services. Under the services sector, the highest contributors are financial, real estate and professional services and trade, hotels, transport, and communication.

In the second half of 2019–20, there was a moderation in the service sector, especially construction, trade, hotels, transport, and communication. Construction activities showed a slowdown in Q3 and Q4, whereas growth in remaining activities was muted in the second half of 2019–20.

Growth rate of the overall services sector had been continuously declining in 2019–20. Decline in construction activities was majorly due to a decline in cement production. Growth in financial, real estate, and professional services was mainly due to the growth of IT companies.

Due to country-wide lockdown amid coronavirus, the services sector was severely hit and witnessed a sharp rise in unemployment. There had been a contraction in activities due to decelerated demand from domestic as well as the external market. Incoming new businesses were very less and were insufficient to maintain the existing workforce. Companies responded to it by laying off employees and contracting the workforce, which led to huge unemployment.

An all-time low in global services PMI was recorded at 5.4 in April 2020. Export of services had been severely impacted due to global lockdown. As per ICRA, the growth of the services sector was forecasted to fall to 3%–5% in FY21 against previously estimated growth of 6%–8%. It had been very challenging for the sectors which primarily depended upon human interaction, such as hospitality, tourism, banking and financial services, telecommunication, transportation, railways, flights services. Several organizations had taken certain measures like Work from home to continue operations along with practising social distancing.

Impact on Trade with External Sector

Being an open economy, India has trade relations with a number of countries and carries out imports and exports with them. Global economies had been severely hit by the pandemic and were witnessing slowing growth. Major trading partners of India (China, the United States, UAE, Saudi Arabia, Switzerland, Germany) were witnessing a decline in their economic growth, thus India's trade with these nations was adversely affected.

India's merchandise exports and imports recorded their worst fall in the last 30 years as COVID-19 took a toll on world production and demand. India's exports contracted by 60.3% in April 2020 and imports fell by 58.6%. The trade deficit reduced to USD6.8 billion in April 2020 (lowest since June 2016).

Net FDI inflows picked up in March 2020 to USD2.9 billion from USD0.8 billion a year ago. In 2020–21 (till May 18), net FPI in equities had also increased to USD1.2 billion from USD0.8 billion a year ago.

In the debt segment, there were portfolio outflows of USD3.8 billion during the same period as against outflows of USD1.4 billion a year ago. Net investment under the voluntary retention route increased by USD0.7 billion during the same period.

India's foreign exchange reserves had increased by USD9.2 billion in 2020–21 (up to May 15) to USD487.0 billion (equivalent to a year's imports).

To Sum Up

- Indian economy has evolved over the years and emerged as one of the fastest-growing major economies of the world. FY2019 and FY2020 witnessed a slowdown in economic growth which got further amplified by nationwide lockdown owing to coronavirus pandemic.
- COVID-19 adversely affected every sector of the Indian economy along with the global economy.
- Global economy was projected to contract by (–)3.5% in 2020 as per IMF and projected to grow by 5.5% in 2021 and world trade contracted by 5% in Q1 2020–21.

- India faced four phases of lockdown from 24 March 2020 to 31 May 2020, post which the economy started opening up in a staggered way.
- RBI adopted an accommodative policy and undertook various monetary policy measures to inject liquidity into the system such as reduction in repo rate, reverse repo rate, CRR, Introduction of TLTROs, moratorium of loans, deferment of interest on working capital facilities, export credit, to name a few.
- Union government provided fiscal stimulus through various economic packages covering sectors such as MSMEs, farmers, vendors, vulnerable sections.
- Every problem comes with an opportunity. Similarly, India could also have taken advantage of various opportunities in this time of crisis, such as providing impetus to the domestic manufacturing sector and attracting global investors to make India a manufacturing hub, infrastructure development, undertaking structural reforms, attracting FPI.

Economic Survey 2020–21 stated:

- GDP growth rate of India for 2020 was 4.2% against an earlier estimate of 5%, whereas the growth rate for FY2020–21 was (-)7.3% which has been further revised to (-)6.6% in February 2022.
- In FY Q1 2020, the Indian economy contracted by 23.9%, Q2 2020–21 by (–7.5%) and Q3 2020–21 and Q4 2020–21 saw recovery entering the positive territory at 0.1% and 1.6%, respectively.
- Lack of labour availability and restricted movement of goods due to halted transportation were major problems faced by the agriculture sector.
- Agriculture sector provided a ray of hope with an increase in food grain production by 3.4% owing to good monsoon.
- Industry and services were estimated to contract by (–9.6%) and (–8.8%), respectively and exports were expected to decline by 5.8% and imports by 11.3% in the second half of FY21.
- Recovery in the second half 2020–21 was expected to be fuelled by government consumption which was to grow at 17% y-o-y.
- India was forecasted to have a current account surplus of 2% in FY21, a historic high after 17 years.

- India remained a much-preferred investment destination and net FPI inflows recorded an all-time high of USD9.8 billion in November 2020. A buoyant Sensex and NIFTY saw market cap to GDP ratio surpassing 100% for the first time since October 2010.
- A V-shaped recovery was underway as shown by high-frequency indicators such as power demand, e-way bills, GST collection, steel consumption.
- Based on the mega vaccination drive, the Indian economy was moving back towards restoring normalcy.

1.3
Investors' Confidence

The COVID-19 pandemic, also defined as a 'Black Swan' event, resulted in adverse health and economic consequences for nations across the world. It ensued in a complete 'Lockdown' being announced by the Prime Minister, Mr. Narendra Modi, until 14 April 2020 to battle the transmission of the virus and minimize its disastrous impact on citizens' health. The lockdown resulted in demand and supply chain disruptions and a liquidity crisis for countries. A logical outcome of the havoc was its negative impact on stock markets globally.

The market capitalization in Indian stock exchanges prior to the pandemic was approximately USD2.16 trillion and market conditions were largely favourable, with record highs being witnessed in January 2020. With the onset of the pandemic, it brought about a scenario of gloom and uncertainty in the stock markets, with markets crashing to five-year lows and trough points not witnessed ever since the global financial crisis (GFC) of 2008. However, during the GFC, the Sensex had crashed 61% in a year as against 30% in a three-month time during the post-pandemic period.

BSE Sensex: Trend during March–August 2020

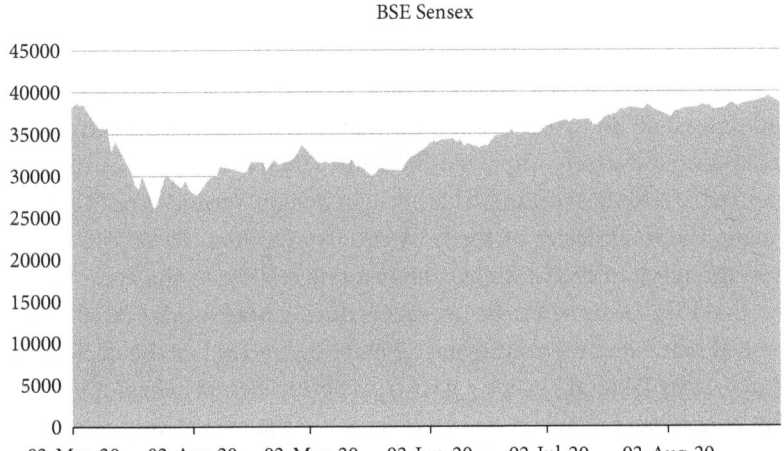

BSE Sensex

Source: https://www.bseindia.com/index.html

Resurgent India. Jagadish Shettigar and Pooja Misra, Oxford University Press. © Oxford University Press 2022.
DOI: 10.1093/oso/9780192866486.003.0003

With the virus pervading the borders of the country in March 2020, the BSE Sensex had crashed to 25,981.24 on 23 March 2020 from 41569.50 on 13 February 2020. The news of Unlock 1.0 did bring some cheer to the markets and it recovered to 33,303.52 on 1 June 2020. Domestic Institutional Investors (DIIs) invested Rs. Fifty-five thousand nine hundred fifty-five crores in this interim period, the highest during the past 15 years. Nifty was not far behind and its numbers too were reflective of a similar trend, with Nifty ending up at 7610.23 on 23 March 2020 and Unlock 1.0, bringing about its recovery to 9826.15 as of 1 June 2020. This fall was in line with global benchmark indices.

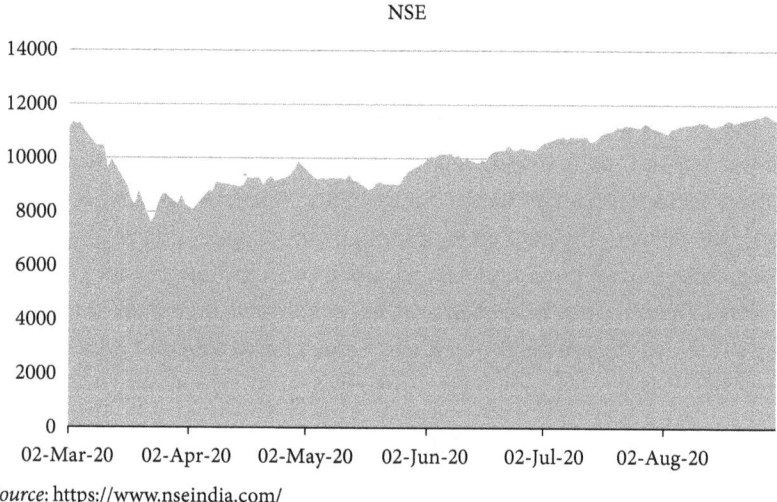

Source: https://www.nseindia.com/

The gloom and doom were indicative of weak sentiments that the virus had unleashed on investors, domestically and globally. Interestingly, the uncertainty adversely impacted the Sensex/Nifty in March as investors resorted to relentless selling. This brought to light a paradox of FII money leaving the boundaries of the host country (approx. Rs 65,816 crores) even though it offered a higher interest rate relative to the Fed rate. The fact that FIIs continued to be net sellers during March–May 2020 despite the Fed rate being reduced from 1.25% to 0.25% (as per the decision on March 15 by Federal Reserve) goes against the normal behaviour of FIIs. This contrarian behaviour was an outcome of the uncertainty caused due to the pandemic. A point of concern for emerging markets including

India was the massive sell-off in global risk assets by foreign portfolio investors and theirs preferring to move back to the safety of dollar-backed assets.

To add fuel to the fire, with news of production being brusquely brought to a halt, fear of retrenchment and layoffs, consumer demand focused on essential items, sectors such as tourism, aviation, hospitality, entertainment receiving a major blow and all economic indicators pointing towards contraction of economies world over, stock prices of companies were adversely affected. RBI and Government did unfold a slew of measures such as infusion of liquidity of Rs. 1.37k crores by bringing down the repo rate and reverse repo rate, Rs. 3 lakh crores automatic collateral-free loan for businesses/MSMEs, three months moratorium on interest payments which was subsequently extended to 31 August 2020, etc.

Interestingly, with the coronavirus spreading both to the urban and rural areas in India, and people having contracted the virus being as high as 20,27,746 as of 7 August 2020, the stock markets had been seen to be going against the tide and witnessing a rise. BSE Sensex had touched 37,929.24 as of 7 August 2020. Localized lockdowns had also not acted as a deterrent to increased buying sentiments in stock markets.

One of the key reasons that this rise in the stock market could be ascribed to was increased FPI in India. Increased liquidity by way of stimulus by Central Banks was finding its way into the stock markets globally. May–June 2020 showed FPI inflows into India touching a 15 month high and receiving net FPI inflows to the tune of Rs. 36,400 crores despite the fact that economic indicators were in the recovery mode but still not strong enough. Even though rating agencies had downgraded India's sovereign ratings (Moody's had downgraded the same to 'Baa3' from 'Baa2' with the outlook 'negative'), foreign investors were still upbeat about the Indian economy.

Macroeconomic fundamentals, government policies, stimulus measures announced being a mixed bag of demand and supply measures with structural reforms and near to medium-term reforms pointed towards a positive outlook for investors. Thus, the return of FIIs since June 2020 may also be ascribed to big-ticket reform measures announced by the Prime Minister, Mr. Narendra Modi. With the PM stating that more structural measures pertaining to land and labour reforms were on the anvil and were being actively discussed in the Ministries, investor confidence in

India's policy measures had risen. It was important that the Government actively moved into an implementation and execution phase so that positive outcomes of these reforms and measures could be seen and felt at the ground level and gave the much needed boost to economic growth and further reinforced investor confidence.

The stock market was influenced and buoyed by investor optimism about the economy in the future. The Macroeconomic Report for July 2020 released by the Finance Ministry was indicative of an uptick in the economy and mentioned signs of green shoots appearing. The report cited a host of high-frequency macroeconomic indicators such as IIP, Purchasing Manager's Index, steel and cement production, e-way bill generation, GST collection, railway freight, generation of power, etc., all showing improvements. This had helped in boosting the confidence of investors and encouraged market sentiments with regard to economic recovery. Yes, the increasing number of COVID-19 cases were alarming, but on the flip side, with steady progress taking place in the research for COVID-19 vaccine, stock markets were hopeful and positively reinforcing buyer sentiment amidst positive global cues.

It must also be borne in mind that FPIs are looked upon as 'Influencers' by Retail Investors. With FPI inflows into India touching a 15 month high in May–June, investor sentiments turned positive, with 10 lakh demat accounts being opened only in June. Drops in BSE Sensex provided investors especially the retail investors the opportunity to enter into the market and earn a higher rate of return especially when they had a long-term perspective in mind. The hope and belief amongst these investors was that COVID-19 should also become history and liquidity would push prices of stocks up. Rather, going by numbers, the new entrants to the stock markets had been blessed with plentiful beginner's luck. The fear in the minds of these retail investors was that with economic recovery, they might not get an opportunity to buy at current prices. With an average annual return of 15%, the stock market did become an attractive option for investors to venture in, partake in the profits and be a part of the growth story.

1.4

Green Shoots of Economic Recovery

The COVID pandemic had brought in a 'New Normal' and largely changed the economic landscape and business environment. As per (KPMG, 2020), the pandemic would change the scenario across the world with cash being the king, business organizations leaning towards variable cost models, supply chains being made more resilient with the call being 'Vocal for Local', policymakers being agile and re-strategizing and redesigning various policies.

Economic activity and market sentiments saw an uptick with the opening of the economy in Unlock 1.0. As per Centre for Monitoring Indian Economy (CMIE), the worst appeared to be over for the Indian economy and the unemployment rate settled at 8.4% as of 15 July 2020, a tad higher than pre-COVID levels as against 27.1% in May 2020 (due to supply chain disruptions and massive job losses). Rural employment numbers were leading the economic recovery for India with a 7.3% unemployment rate as against urban unemployment rate of 10.8% for mid-July 2020. The reasons that could be ascribed to better employment numbers in the rural sector were a better than normal monsoon, availability of water in reservoirs for irrigation, aggressive implementation of the Mahatma Gandhi National Rural Employment Guarantee (MGNREGA) scheme by the government and enhanced sowing activities. As per estimates, the Indian agricultural sector was forecasted to grow at 3% despite COVID-19 lockdown.

Resurgent India. Jagadish Shettigar and Pooja Misra, Oxford University Press. © Oxford University Press 2022.
DOI: 10.1093/oso/9780192866486.003.0004

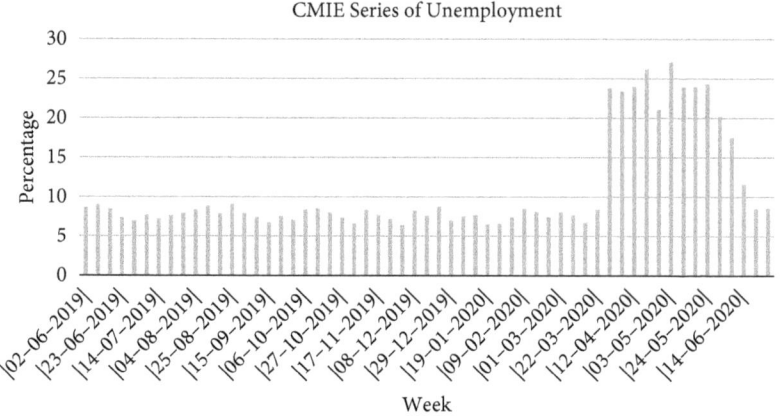

Source: https://unemploymentinindia.cmie.com/

Goods and Services tax collected in June 2020 was Rs. 90,917 crores, ie 90% of the revenues in the same month last year. The collections in April and May 2020 during the period of lockdown were relatively lesser and stood at Rs. 32,294 crores and Rs. 62,009 crores, respectively. Interestingly the collections in June 2020 were closer to those in the month of January 2020, which was at Rs. 1,10,828 crores. These revenue numbers were indicative of the fact that a revival was underway and collections would only improve in the near future with production levels increasing. These were all signs of green shoots of recovery happening in the economy. However, these tax collection numbers needed to be considered with a pinch of salt as they did not necessarily relate to transactions in May alone.

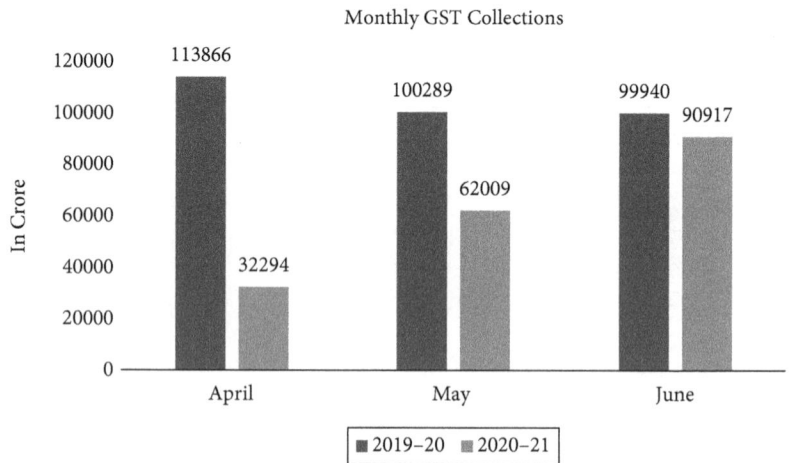

Source: Ministry of Finance https://pib.gov.in/PressReleasePage.aspx?PRID=1635572

E-way bills generated in June 2020 were to the tune of 42.7 million equivalent to Rs. 12.4 lakh crores as against 40 million bills of Rs. 11.43 lakh crores in March 2020, a clear indication of the fact that movement of goods was nearing the ranks of pre-lockdown days. Rather, numbers for power demand also reflected that the slump narrowed to 2.6% in July 2020 as against 9.6% in June. This was again reflective of an increase in commercial and industrial activities across the country. Analysts were hopeful that the demand for power would reach normal levels by August 2020.

CPI Inflation

The consumer price index (CPI) inflation trajectory showed a decline from 7.2% in April to 6.1% in June 2020. Inflation numbers came down due to food inflation declining with the advent of Unlock 1.0. Food inflation, especially for vegetables and fruits, had risen to 23.6% in April due to supply chain disruption, a fallout of the lockdown. In June, the same declined to 1.9%. Moreover, core inflation due to demand destruction had softened to 4.8% in May but showed a rise in June to 5.2%. However, this rise can be attributed to an increase in prices of petrol, diesel, gold, and healthcare. Crude oil prices due to low demand coupled with the price war between the global players, ie Saudi Arabia, Russia, and the United States, had dropped to as low as USD19.34 per barrel in April 2020. With the opening up of economies world-over, crude oil prices had recovered and were trading in the range of USD43.05 in mid-July 2020.

Gold being a safe and less risky investment as per the report titled 'Gold Mid-Year Outlook 2020' had the current business environment of high risk and uncertainty, low opportunity cost, and a positive price momentum working in its favour. These inflation numbers were further expected to soften with a normal monsoon having a favourable effect on the agricultural sector and core inflation to further steady itself with production levels increasing and having a positive impact on consumer sentiments.

Index of Industrial Production

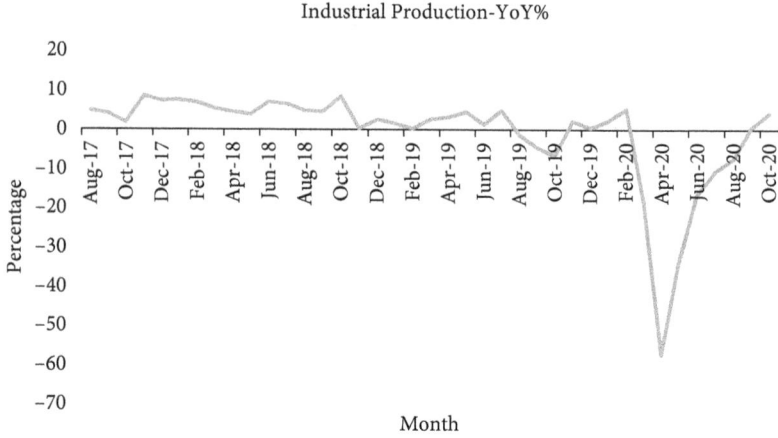

Source: MOSPI, IMA

The IIP, which is representative of manufacturing, mining, and electricity, continued to witness a broad-based contraction, although at a slower pace. Economic activity in India hit a trough in April 2020. The numbers improved from a contraction of 57.6% y-o-y in April to 34.7% y-o-y in May 2020. Data showed that manufacturing activity fared better than the previous month but was still suffering from the after-effects of the extended lockdown and weak demand in the Indian economy and the world over. Amongst the 23 industrial groups within manufacturing, pharmaceuticals scored a positive growth of 2.5% y-o-y. However, in the case of use-based classification of goods, consumer durable and capital goods suffered the largest loss in May, which was reflective of lower capital investments. Stimulus measures announced by the Government of privatization of power distribution in Union Territories, privatization of PSEs, an increase of FDI limit in defence manufacturing from 49% to 74% under the automatic route would yield results with reference to capital investments in the medium to long term. The positive news was that with lockdown restrictions easing, purchasing manager index (PMI) had improved from 30.8 in May 2020 to 47.2 in June 2020. In the short term, IIP was expected to see a temporary uptick due to pent-up demand and sales for small ticket and mid ticket products witnessing a pick-up in June and the first week of July 2020.

To take an example, for sectors such as automobile, retail sales were seen to be higher in May and June against dispatches of vehicles with bookings reaching 85%–90% of pre-COVID levels forcing manufacturers to ramp up output. The manufacturers started meeting the pent-up increased demand by adding factory shifts and hiring more workers. These numbers were forecasted to further improve come festival season with rural demand and traction for SUVs leading the way. Rural India had also been the frontrunner in demand for two-wheelers sales post announcements of Unlock 1.0 and 2.0. Market leaders Hero MotorCorp's June sales were seen to be four times compared to May 2020, thereby being a confidence booster for the manufacturing sector. Also, in view of the shortage of manpower due to migrant labourers going back to villages, efforts by some employers were made to arrange chartered flights and promise accommodation at work sites and even better wages to get them back to work. This was a definitive sign of improved economic activity compelling employers to rush to the labour market.

Not to forget, Central Government schemes such as Mahatma Gandhi National Rural Employment Guarantee scheme (MGNREGs) (additional allocation of Rs. 40,000 crores) and 'Garib Kalyan Rozgar Abhiyaan' worth Rs. 50,000 crores along with a good rabi crop, normal monsoons, and the limited spread of the pandemic in villages was auguring well for Rural India and thereby increasing the demand for FMCG products. As per analysts, the consumption rate of FMCG goods in Rural India had already touched 85% of pre-COVID levels in May as against 70% in urban areas.

What Did the Sensex Show?

With Unlock happening and industry and investor sentiments improving, the BSE Sensex index was found to be the second best-performing equity index across the globe. The downward trend had long since been reversed, and S&P BSE Sensex, bellwether index recovered to the extent of 34% in June 2020 from March 2020 lows that it had touched. There was a sense of heightened optimism in the stock market, which the rising number of COVID cases, India–China border standoff and the grim economic outlook had also not been able to dampen. As of mid-July, the

BSE Sensex touched approximately 36,371.68 as against 25,981.24 on 23 March 2020. The stock market rally was fuelled by an influx of liquidity of USD17–18 trillion stimulus infused worldwide by countries to resuscitate their economies. As per analysts, this was also being driven by a lack of alternate attractive investment opportunities the world over.

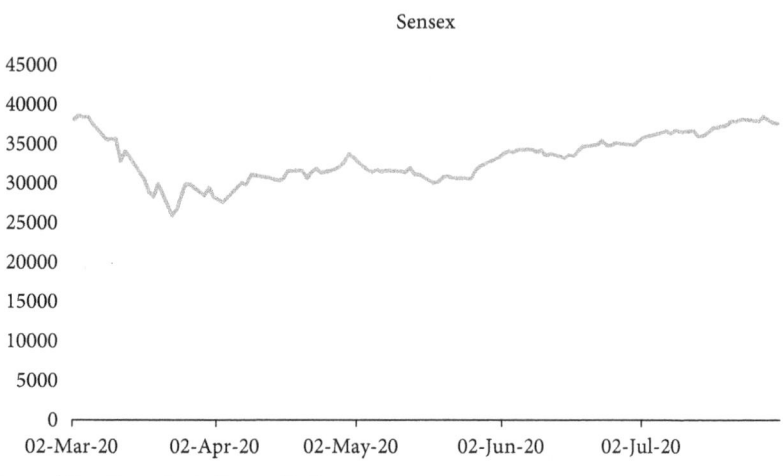

Sensex

Source: https://www.bseindia.com/Indices

Surging Foreign Exchange Reserves

India's foreign exchange reserves increased to USD513 billion in mid-June 2020. Higher Forex reserves generate confidence amongst investors, lead to higher FPIs, support monetary and exchange rate management and limit foreign exchange vulnerability. RBI is thus in a position and ready to buffer the financial market against any contagion. This rise in forex reserves was due to the rise in foreign investments by foreign portfolio investors who had acquired stakes in Indian companies in the past two months resulting in an inflow of USD2.75 billion in the first week of June. Foreign inflows were expected to cross the USD500 billion mark with Jio Platforms garnering Rs. 97,000 crores worth of foreign investments. With crude oil prices falling and foreign travel also declining, demand for dollar outflow had gone down, thereby reducing the oil import bill and saving precious foreign exchange for the country. Also, a cut in corporate tax rates had worked favourably and helped in increasing forex reserves.

Rising foreign exchange reserves help in strengthening the rate of foreign exchange. The forex reserves were adequate to cover one year's import bill for India, thereby demonstrating the backing of domestic currency by external assets and generating confidence for markets and investors.

After a period of 18 years, trade balance for India had turned into a trade surplus with the balance in June 2020 being in the country's favour at USD790 million. Indian exports of 12 out of 30 major items turned positive during the month, but on the whole, exports contracted and shrank 12.41% to USD21.91 billion in June due to lower international demand for petroleum, textiles, engineering goods, and gems and jewellery. Furthermore, imports also contracted for 26 out of the 30 principal items and dropped to USD21.11 billion, ie a fall of 47.59%, portraying a decline in domestic demand. Though the position appeared better, actually fall in imports at a higher rate than fall in exports reflected the adverse impact on industrial production. Declining demand for consumer goods is not so worrisome as against a fall in demand for capital goods/technology or gold which is also export-oriented. Interestingly, import demand for medicinal and pharmaceutical products, vegetable oils, and pulses told a different story. The bright side to the trade story was that exports were back on track and had touched 89% of June 2019 levels. Also, as per Mr. S K Saraf, President, Federation of Indian Export Organisations (FIEO), exporters had been receiving a lot of queries from countries where anti-China sentiments were high. This was perhaps the right time for India to conclude trade agreements with the EU, Australia, and New Zealand and bring the Regional Comprehensive Partnership Agreement (RCEP) back on the discussion table. A trade surplus, rising foreign exchange reserves, and rising foreign investments augured well for the Indian rupee and would help it appreciate against the dollar, thereby recovering a lost ground of 4.6% in 2020 against the American currency.

In its Global Manufacturing Risk Index Report for 2020, Cushman and Wakefield had ranked India third, with China and the United States retaining the top positions. In its annual ranking of 48 countries spread across Europe, the Americas, and the Asia Pacific, India had a competitive advantage from an operating condition and cost competitiveness perspective and was slated to be an upcoming manufacturing hub globally.

While economic indicators were showing a revival of the Indian economy post easing of restrictions, localized lockdowns could very well throw a spanner in the revival growth story. Localized lockdowns and tight social distancing measures had again resulted in disruption of economic activity and cut off supply chains, thus dampening the sentiments of Indians. It would be imperative that the government neutralize the spread of the pandemic and both Centre and State work hand in hand as even short duration lockdowns in industrial pockets could hamper revival.

1.5

Macroeconomic Perspective

In the backdrop of the pandemic and to minimize the negative impact on the health of its citizens, 'India chose to sacrifice its economy and save lives'—'जान है तो जहान है'. The Prime Minister, Mr. Narendra Modi, announced a nationwide lockdown beginning 25 March 2020. The downside of any Lockdown is that economic activity and production come to an abrupt standstill and the economy gets halted in its track of economic growth. Subsequently, in June 2020, the Indian Government with a viewpoint of 'जान भी जहान भी'—'Lives as well as livelihoods' had decided to open the Lockdown in a phased manner and restart the economy.

Economic Analysts had their plates full in revising GDP growth estimates. With the pandemic having struck countries worldwide, IMF in June 2020 revised its global growth estimates to a contraction of 4.9% from an estimated growth of 3.3%. The pandemic had not left any nation untouched and thus, developed nations such as the United States were also expected to face a contraction of 4.3%.

IMF, in its World Economic Outlook, stated that the growth numbers for India in 2021 would be a contraction of 10.3%. As per the estimates of the World Bank in October 2020, the Indian economy was likely to contract by 9.6% in FY2021. The forecast predicted for India by Moody's in its Global Macro Outlook 2021–22 in November 2020 had been revised from an estimated contraction of 9.6% to a contraction of 8.9%. Growth numbers were revised downward, keeping in mind the disruption in demand and supply, resulting in sharp growth deceleration in FY21 (Kaur, 2020).

Key macroeconomic indicators in May 2020, such as GDP y-o-y growth, CPI inflation, CAD/GDP were reflective of the negative impact of the COVID-19 virus (CRISIL, 2020). Consumer Price Index in May 2020 showed a softening of inflation numbers due to increased food grain

Resurgent India. Jagadish Shettigar and Pooja Misra, Oxford University Press. © Oxford University Press 2022.
DOI: 10.1093/oso/9780192866486.003.0005

production. Furthermore, the sharp plunge in oil prices was expected to have a positive impact on CPI and CAD/GDP.

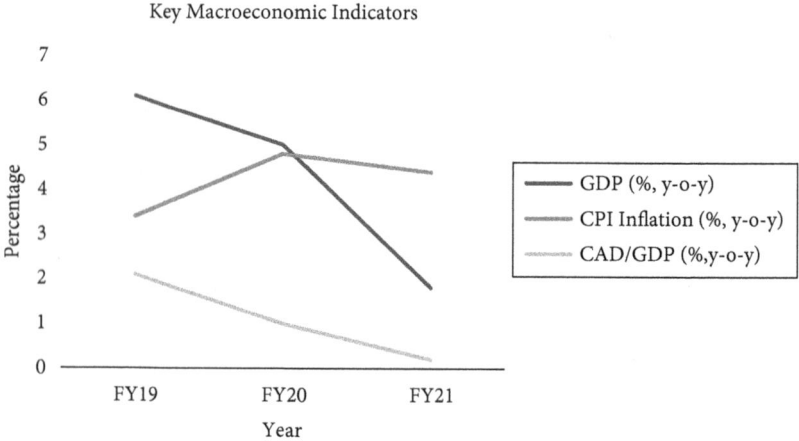

Key Macroeconomic Indicators

Source: National Statistical Office (NSO), Budget documents, Reserve Bank of India (RBI), CRISIL, as of May 2020

With regards to economic recovery, the best case scenario forecasted by researchers and economists in May 2020 was of a 'V' shaped recovery curve to 'U' or 'L'. The 'V' or 'U' shaped curve was highly dependent on the timing and magnitude of government stimulus and how companies and market structures were able to sustain in a scenario of low demand. With Q1 FY 2020–21, ending up as being negatively impacted due to the Lockdown and witnessing a contraction of 23.9%, Q2 and Q3 were expected to be perforated with negative business and declining consumer sentiment resulting in a decline in consumption levels and falling foreign trade adversely impacting the Indian economy.

However, one should not forget the fact that even prior to the pandemic, the Indian economy was already facing a demand slowdown resulting in GDP growth numbers witnessing a deceleration, averaging an 11 year low of 4.2% in 2019–20. The dismal numbers were due to a decline in consumption demand along with investment and exports being in negative territory. The agricultural sector and government expenditure were the saviours in Q4 2019–20.

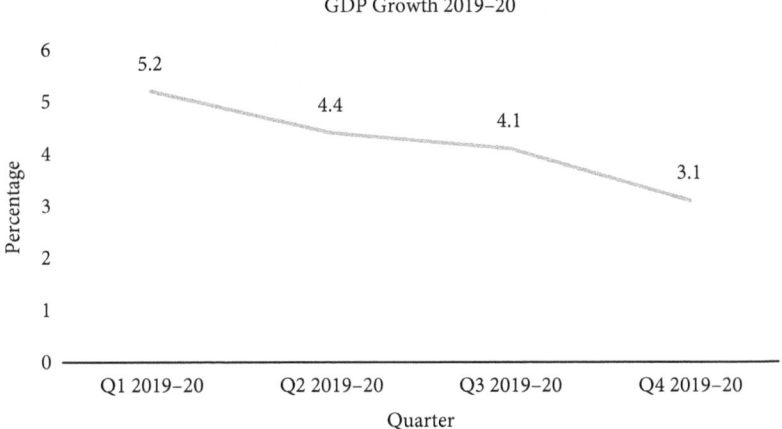

Source: Budget Documents

To add to its woes, with liquidity shortage and issues of credit availability in the pre-COVID-19 times, the already prevalent issues in the financial sector of the economy had only worsened. The bulging of prior NPAs and credit shortage issues in the banking and non-banking financial sector would amplify the effect of a coronavirus-induced shock.

On analysing the demand side, it can be observed that with private consumption declining because of loss of jobs and income in the face of the domestic outbreak, citizens preferred to conserve cash amidst a scenario of increased economic uncertainty. Spending was primarily on essential items such as food and healthcare services. The supply side was indicative of the fact that businesses were cutting back capital expenditure and conserving cash for any unforeseen emergency. Demand and supply chain disruptions along with a liquidity constraint causing a sharp growth deceleration was an outcome of the extended lockdowns.

Countries across the world had been hit by an onslaught of disruption in economic activity and people were seen to be transitioning and adopting to the 'New Normal'. All hopes were pinned on a vaccine being developed or medicines being identified to cure the virus. The picture looked grim at least for the next 12–18 months. Economic indicators such as CPI inflation declining to 5.91 (new base 2012 = 100), compared to 6.58% in February 2020) were a reflection of a fall in demand which was a disturbing sign. Food inflation declined to 7.82% in March 2020 from 9.45% in February 2020.

With reference to the INR exchange rate, the same experienced a depreciation in comparison to the USD and was trading at 1 USD = Rs. 75.33 in June 2020. In terms of the Nominal Effective Exchange Rate (NEER) relative to currencies of 36 trading partner countries the INR had been facing a depreciation, a reflection of the Indian economy's reducing competitiveness since July 2019. Rupee depreciation was likely to have been influenced by the net outflow of FIIs from the Indian stock market in March 2020 due to the pandemic and consequently imposed lockdown.

For emerging markets including India a depreciating rupee poses a worrisome scenario and was reflective of the Sensex/Nifty being adversely impacted due to the uncertainty in the economy. The BSE Sensex had dropped from a high of 38,144 on 2 March 2020 to 25,981 on 23 March 2020 due to the outflow of FII investments from the country. Interestingly, this phenomenon contradicted academic concepts, ie even though the host country offered a higher interest rate relative to the Fed interest rate, FII money preferred to leave the boundaries of the host country.

The announcement of the economy being reopened, ie Unlock 1.0 and relaxation of restrictions taking place, had brought a cheer to the stock markets and with positive sentiments in the stock market being back in the reckoning, the Sensex had rebounded to 34,284 as on 3 June 2020. What was interesting to observe was that in May 2020, driven by large block deals, foreign investors had poured in over Rs 17,000 crores into Indian equities. This could be reflective of the Government's timely and long-term structural reforms.

Not to forget with falling crude oil prices due to lower demand, it had brightened the picture for the Indian government. India imports 80% of its crude oil requirement and with the price of Brent falling to USD19.34 per barrel in April 2020 as against USD32.01 per barrel in March 2020, it helped strengthen India's fiscal position by reducing the import bill. Reduction in import bill would have a positive outcome on the CAD and help curb inflation numbers.

However, one should not forget that the benefit of lower prices had been retained by the Indian Government to strengthen their fiscal position. The Central and State Governments were eyeing increased taxes on petrol and diesel to fill their coffers and help supplement the revenue loss impact due to the Lockdown, thereby helping in compensating for low tax collections. This boosted tax revenue for the Government, which was on the lower side due to production being brought to a halt. Increased tax collections helped build the pool for Government to dip into for their welfare schemes and programmes.

What did the credit rating agencies indicate? Moody's had down-graded India's sovereign (long-term) debt ratings to Baa3 from Baa2 earlier. However, experts and advisors to the Government were of the opinion that the negatives had already been factored in and the country was unlikely to see a short-term impact of this move. The numbers for IIP in February 2020 (prior to COVID-19 having impacted India) showed signs of recovery and increased to 4.5% over last year compared to 2% in January 2020. Manufacturing activity increased by 3.2%, mining output 10%, and electricity generation 8.1%. However, with the pandemic bringing all economic activity to a standstill, countries worldwide were anticipating challenges in terms of production output, employment, de-clining income, and falling demand.

Industrial sectors which had been drastically negatively impacted and felt the major brunt of the pandemic had been aviation, hospitality, tourism, construction, etc. Cancellations were on a war footing for ho-tels and flights as people were largely averse to any travel. Decreasing

Table 1.5.1 Industrial Activity 2020.

	Jan	Mar	Apr	May
Power—Consumption	3%	−9%	−24%	−16%
PMI-Mfg	3%	−2%	−47%	N/A
PMI-Services	6%	−5%	−89%	N/A
	Jan	Mar	Apr	
Imports	−1%	−29%	−59%	
Exports	−2%	−35%	−60%	
Railway Traffic Freight	3%	−14%	−35%	
FASTag (volume)	279%	216%	−61%	

Source: COVID-19: India Perspective5.0, file:///D:/Macroeconomics/Covid19/BCG-India-Perspective-COVID19-25May.pdf

footfalls in marketplaces and closing down of cinema halls were indicative of an adverse influence on discretionary spending, thereby having a rebounding effect on the retail sector. Operating costs of retailers were predicted to experience a rise of 35% due to the implementation of social distancing norms. Restaurants, theatres, and shopping complexes were projected to continue seeing a downslide even after the Unlock of the economy. Due to declining consumption trends, the apparel industry was anticipated to witness a medium to high negative impact. Generation of power coming under the list of essential services was one of the few sectors which had seen a low impact, however with the shutdown, this sector was making an all-out effort to manage the low energy demand.

With production being brought to a standstill and sectors experiencing a negative demand, unemployment numbers were expected to rise. Keeping production facilities closed or alternately operating at minimum levels and with social distancing norms in place, it resulted in reverse migration leading to a shortage of workforce and negatively influencing sectors such as construction and manufacturing. Furthermore, due to dependence on China for the supply of intermediate products, industries such as electronics, chemical products, automobiles, solar power equipment, electrical machinery, leather products, and mobile handsets had been adversely impacted on a mega scale. Agreeably, the negative effect due to the lockdown in China was lessened due to the common practice of Indian firms stockpiling inventory.

Another sector that needed to be closely watched was the FMCG sector. With reverse migration leading to scarcity of labour, it had compelled this industry to operate at scaled-down levels. Labour shortage along with social distancing norms resulted in production levels declining, thus limiting the supply chain. To make matters worse, 37% of the urban regular wage employees of urban India operate in the informal sector and they were impacted by access to indefinite income due to the stalling of economic activity (KPMG, 2020).

To further worsen the situation, the reverse migration of labour to their native villages due to the mental, financial and emotional agony inflicted due to job loss, lack of job, and livelihood opportunities had led to a huge departure of workers from major cities of India to their native villages. Reverse migration was expected to have severe ramifications for labour availability and with social distancing norms in place, the process of production was further hindered. Less supply of labour would lead to an increase in wage rates. The flip side of reverse migration was that states like Bihar and Uttar Pradesh had commenced action steps to tide over this crisis and transform the tragedy into a business prospect. The state governments had begun skill profiling exercises for returning migrants so that the data could be developed to create employment opportunities for the utilization of their skills and development of the State. Data showed that 86% and 68% of the total number of households who worked under MGNREGA in Andhra Pradesh and Uttar Pradesh, respectively had already participated in the job scheme in 40 days in 2020–21. However, it was apparent that for countries worldwide, the adverse influence on growth levels would be higher due to demand-side issues rather than the supply side.

Not all was dark. Sectors such as online education, e-commerce, and business verticals such as food, grocery, health/hygiene, online learning had seen a rise. The 'New Normal' post this crisis was predicted to bring about structural and behavioural changes in the lives of people. Additionally, it was seen that the pandemic had also brought about changes in the geopolitical environment and a shift towards localization of the supply chain. Digitalization had been given a push with 'work from home' being the new model and businesses strategizing towards building agility. The crisis had shaken up the world economic order and in this changing scenario, India's effort was to make the most of the opportunities presented by wooing MNCs that were looking to shift manufacturing activities out of China and concurrently wanting to take benefit of cheap labour to contain their bottom line.

1.6

Farm Crisis

Often farmers from different regions have gone on agitation against the establishment. In fact, the country witnessed much stronger agitations led by more powerful farm leaders in states like Uttar Pradesh, Madhya Pradesh, Maharashtra, and Karnataka. Every time farmers come out with the same demand, that is remunerative prices for their produces. There is nothing wrong with a producer of a product or service demanding a just price. But the fundamental issue is why should only a farmer demand a just price for his product? Why cannot he command a price, especially now that we have adopted market economy in the same way as suppliers of non-agricultural produces?

Unfortunately, neither policy-makers nor so-called farm leaders have tried to address this fundamental question. Instead of pushing the farmers to be at the mercy of the government of the day, an attempt should have been made to strengthen them as an effective supply force in the market. Every time farmers come to the street, political leadership tries to douse the fire as a panic reaction. Maybe, because of the fact that the farm sector constitutes not only a large vote bank but also effectively participates in the democratic process, unlike the comparatively better educated urban sector. No doubt, political leadership devised an easy tool called MSP. It has become a religious ritual that every year central cabinet meets to revise MSP upwards. No government has failed in its duty of revising MSP upwards rather in an attempt to keep the large vote-bank happy. Until 1996 upward revision used to be in the range of around Rs. 10 per quintal, which now has gone up beyond Rs. 100 per quintal since the United Front government in the late nineties. No government, including the Modi government, which appears to have a sound economic approach, has otherwise mustered the courage to re-look at MSP as a tool to rescue farmers. In addition, many state governments also contribute bonus prices.

Resurgent India. Jagadish Shettigar and Pooja Misra, Oxford University Press. © Oxford University Press 2022.
DOI: 10.1093/oso/9780192866486.003.0006

An attempt to resolve the farm crisis is explained in terms of the competitive upward revision of MSP. Still, nobody bothers to understand why farmers continue to commit suicide despite the continuous rise in MSP by practically every successive government. First of all, as the very word 'minimum support price' suggests, it becomes effective in protecting the interests of farmers when the market price crashes. In fact, the very objective of the policy is to ensure a minimum price when market prices crash. This appeared to have worked well until mandis became a competitive market, thanks to the entry of organized retailers. In fact, markets also witnessed a situation when even the government procurement agencies could not compete with private procurers, namely, the organized retail sector, which resulted in MSP falling short of market prices, in other words, ineffective. The market may face a crisis when there is a glut in the supply of agricultural produces like tomato or onion, which may lead to miserably low prices, compelling farmers often to throw away their produces. However, once the principles of the market economy are accepted, fluctuations in price become an integral part of this practice. If one enjoys a price of more than 50 rupees a kg during the period of shortages, he should equally be prepared for a lower price during a glut situation. That is how the market works.

However, often agitation for demanding remunerative price becomes an excuse for a hidden agenda. If the price was the case, farmers should have immediately withdrawn the agitation when the Madhya Pradesh government offered to procure tomatoes at a price eight times higher than the market a few years back. But the agitation continued as the real issue behind was competitive politics among different factions—as the state assembly elections were due in 2018. The purpose of this chapter is to discuss a long-term solution in order to enable the farmers get remunerative prices; not going into the political aspect of the agitation. Basically, two policy-related issues are involved in the context of enabling farmers commanding just prices. First, providing appropriate and adequate infrastructure facilities to farm produces. Second, more importantly, facilitating farmers' direct access to markets. Both would ensure just prices to farm produces. Of course, equally important is getting farmers out of the clutches of private money lenders.

Consumers often have to face the brunt of sky-rocketing prices farm produces—be it tomato or onion or vegetables. At times many farm produces may command prices lower than MSP. For instance, a couple of years back average price for tur dal in Akola market was only Rs. 3500 as compared to MSP of Rs. 5050 a quintal. Similarly, the price of paddy in Cuddalore market was Rs. 1375 as against MSP of Rs. 1470 a quintal. Such a situation was seen in other produces also, such as maize, jowar, groundnut, and soyabean. Going by the market logic, there should not be any scope for farmers complaining about not being able to get remunerative prices. Because, during the competitive market situation as witnessed during mid-2000 with the emergence of the organized retail sector, they were not required to depend on government procurement agencies. Rather, farmers refused to sell to Food Corporation of India (FCI) as they got better prices from the private retailers. However, when market prices crash below MSP, farmers can always look forward towards FCI, which is duty-bound to procure at declared MSP.

But the truth is somewhere else. Whether it is the case of farm produces commanding higher prices than MSP or just MSP during the subdued market prices, poor farmers are nowhere in the picture though successive governments had been taking policy decisions in the name of farmers. The real beneficiaries used to be middlemen, that is, traders. Under the old system, farmers did not have direct access to the market to get the benefit of either high prices or guaranteed MSP. Often, indebted farmers were compelled to sell their produces at much lower prices in advance. To begin with, our banking system should be made more humanistic while dealing with farmers so that they do not depend on money lenders. Unfortunately, credit-risk and KYC principles are applied strictly in the case of farmers, while powerful ones get away with thousands of crores with a guarantee by persons with almost nil bank balance.

With regard to enabling farmers to have direct access to the market, current NDA government under Narendra Modi initiated a historic step by incentivizing the states to amend the Agricultural Produce Market Committee (APMC) act in the last budget. Some states have already initiated steps in this direction. Hopefully, other states will follow soon. Besides, many measures such as preventing diversion of fertilizers to non-agricultural use-through chemical coating, improved crop insurance, or for that matter linking rural employment guarantee schemes to productive agricultural work have been initiated. Perhaps, guaranteeing a price of 50% higher than the cost as suggested by the Swaminathan committee is the one major promise yet to be implemented. The problem with the current government, more so in the ruling party, is the lack of articulating spokespersons capable of effectively reaching out to the general public.

Whenever there is a crisis in the farm sector immediately, political leadership, especially, opposition jumps with a demand for waiving farm loans. This is what the Congress government has practiced over the years as an attempt to douse the fire. Unfortunately, even the BJP promised such a carrot during the Uttar Pradesh elections in 2017. Now other states have also started demanding the same kind of relief. Waiving of farm loans can be considered under an extraordinary crisis situation. But it cannot be the fashion statement among the so-called farm leaders and opposition parties, nor is it a long-term solution.

Apart from enabling farmers' access to the market through amendment of the APMC act and getting them out of money lenders' clutches through the banking sector's attitude, the farm sector should be strengthened as an effective supply force. Farmers should be enabled to decide appropriate timing for selling their produces, that is, only when they can command just price-in the same way as manufactured products. This would mean providing adequate infrastructure facilities, that is, cold storage as well as refrigerated transportation facilities. The Vajpayee government had taken initiatives to encourage the setting up of cold chains. However, the successive government did not take it forward. Similarly, the announcement by Lalu Prasad, the Railway Minister in the first UPA government to provide dedicated railway wagons to transport perishable agricultural products was not implemented. Had there been adequate cold storage facilities supported with refrigerated transportation, there would not be a situation of farmers being compelled to sell tomatoes at one rupee a kg. Whether there is glut or shortage, scientific storage and transportation would act as a balancing factor to the relief of both farmers as well as consumers.

Instead of trying to exploit innocent farmers to achieve a narrow political agenda, it is high time both ruling and opposition treat the farm crisis as a national crisis and attempt to resolve the issue scientifically through a consensual approach.

1.7

Suggestions for 2021–22 Budget

The Indian economy had been facing a slowdown even prior to the outbreak of COVID-19. Indian GDP growth numbers for 2019–20 were at an 11-year low of 4.2% as against 6.1% in 2018–19. With the pandemic having wreaked havoc on not only the Indian economy but countries across the world, the situation of slowdown further worsened. The virus resulted in adversely impacting the economy and leading to negative growth, loss of income, lower consumption demand, and weaker consumer sentiment.

While the pandemic shocker resulted in a contraction of 23.9% in GDP for India (Q1 2020–21), GDP growth numbers for nations such as the United States of America and the United Kingdom were also in the range of (–9.1%) and (–20.4%), respectively. However, with the Indian economy showing signs of recovery in Q2 FY21, the country witnessed a contraction of 7.5%. In early December 2020, Reserve Bank of India (RBI) revised growth projections for the country's real GDP for 2020-21 to (–7.5%) from its assessment of (–9.5%) in October 2020.

In December 2020, of the 48 high-frequency indicators tracked by RBI, 18 were below pre-COVID levels, while the rest were above February levels. Economic trackers pointed towards recovery, gaining traction with double-digit growth in the sale of passenger vehicles and motorcycles, railway freight traffic, and electricity consumption. The Purchasing Managers Index for December 2020 was at 56.4, indicating economic expansion. GST collection for December 2020 stood at Rs. 1.15 lakh crores (y-o-y growth of 11.6%), power consumption demand grew by 6.1% to 107.3 billion units. The easing of COVID-19 restrictions coupled with improved market conditions and a revival in demand due to the festive season supported increased production levels. Thus, it was seen that with Unlock happening, recovery was faster than expected and visible greenshoots were pointing towards an uptick in economic numbers.

Resurgent India. Jagadish Shettigar and Pooja Misra, Oxford University Press. © Oxford University Press 2022.
DOI: 10.1093/oso/9780192866486.003.0007

Factors such as localized lockdowns did act as spoilers, however with the close of the festive season in December 2020, the key point that needed renewed focus was ensuring that recovery levels did not lose steam. Thus, with the budget 2021–22 being formalized and announced on 1 February 2021, the Government made an all-out effort to win the confidence of people and be cognizant of the fact that the Finance Minister could not afford to ignore major issues posing challenges for the Indian economy. Keeping apart policy reforms here, the focus required to be on the state of the economy, looking for a response through budget proposals.

The need of the hour was to kickstart consumption demand which could be dealt with through fiscal policy measures such as personal income tax, GST, welfare measures, hike in overall government expenditure. Measures such as putting more money in the hands of lower bracket income taxpayers by exempting upto Rs 10 lakh; removing the confusion created through half-hearted measures like the option between old and new slabs; removal of tax on perks provided by companies-especially, education allowance, leave travel allowance, accommodation provided by employers required a re-look. On similar lines, the Government should explore the rationalization of GST though the final decision has to be taken at the GST council. There is a need to minimize GST rates to two if not a single rate and bring petroleum products, liquor, and tobacco into the GST net. The proposed redevelopment project of the Central Vista— the nation's power corridor fits the bill for increased government expenditure and would help generate direct and indirect employment and thereby boost economic revival.

India's factory sector had seen a rough 2020. PMI numbers for December 2020 did show that business activity was slowly and steadily improving, however, the eight-core industries, which constitute 40% of the IIP witnessed a contraction of 2.5% in October 2020. The continued current account surplus substantiated the trend. The current account surplus (USD19.8 billion or 3.9% of GDP in Q1 2020–21) was due to a fall in imports which was a clear indication of poor manufacturing activity within. An efficient supply management in the background of subdued industrial production was thus needed.

India has historically been known for its large agricultural sector. In the backdrop of the pandemic, this sector had exhibited strong resilience and experienced growth levels of 3.4% in FY 20. Factors such as favourable monsoons, record production of foodgrains, increased sale of fertilizers and tractors had shown an uptick in the rural economy. To top it further, with the Government announcing policy measures such as setting up of a Rs. 1 lakh crores Agriculture Infrastructure Fund, increasing fund allocation for the MGNREGA scheme and the Ministry of Rural Development securing the fourth highest allocation across Ministries in Union Budget 2020–21 of Rs 1,22,398 crores, etc. had further strengthened the rural economy. In view of the fact that the rural economy had been a cushioning force to the rest of the country, especially the FMCG sector, the budget could have substantiated its commitments in terms of increased budgetary allocations for the agricultural sector including rural infrastructure. Not to miss the key fact that a horizontal expansion of welfare measures was still required and crucial to win over the goodwill of the poor if tough reform measures were to be carried forward.

With the Government announcing game-changing land and labour reforms, giving a clarion call for Vocal for Local, and evolving from Make in India to Make for World (with the perspective of generating employment opportunities and increased income), there was a need to retain confidence amongst the youth who will be the pillars of development of the country in the coming years. India spends 4.6% of its total GDP on education and ranks 62nd in total public expenditure per student. To be able to provide quality education in India and successfully implement the New Education Policy (NEP) 2020, analysts and experts along with Niti Aayog had called for increasing the education expenditure to at least 6% of GDP. NEP 2020, which aims to universalize education and bring quality into higher education by helping students build a scientific temperament from a young age, seeks to be the building block for a new India. The budget should, therefore, have ensured, that there was an adequate allocation for education to give opportunities for innovative education programmes for students and there was provision for effective implementation of the NEP.

The pandemic had brought to light that India's healthcare industry still needed to be strengthened manifold. On an average, India's public health expenditure had remained at approximately 1.2%–1.6% of GDP between 2008–09 and 2019–20 as against other countries such as China (3.2%), the United States (8.5%), Germany (9.5%). As per WHO, India is 184th amongst 191 countries in terms of GDP% spent on healthcare and the Prime Minister's promise to double the spending on public health needed to be borne in mind.

Gender budgeting is a powerful tool to ensure the integration of a gender equality perspective at all stages of policies, programmes, and projects. The Finance Minister also needed to keep an eye on the allocation of resources to the gender budget so that the benefits of development reach the women as well as men; poor, minority, or educated. Fiscal measures such as an increase in income tax exemption limit, interest subvention on housing loans, interest subvention on educational loans for women should be contemplated and looked at. Not to forget that female voters have been the major support base for the Government, especially since the last Uttar Pradesh assembly election, followed by the 2019 parliament election. It is thus crucial to consolidate this base through budgetary provisions.

Without further ado, surely all would agree that the need was to speed up infrastructure programmes. Building infrastructure and connecting supply chains would have numerous advantages for the economy, such as efficient movement of products and services, connecting households across urban and rural areas to higher quality opportunities for employment, healthcare, education. The union budgetary allocation for 2020–21 of Rs. 103 trillion for infra projects under the National Infrastructure Pipeline (NIP) and Rs. 1.7 trillion for transport infrastructure and accelerating highways construction should be increased to facilitate efficient implementation of building of infrastructure for ease of living for citizens. Better infrastructure would, in turn, attract investment, generate employment and thereby give the much-needed boost to consumer demand.

Agreeably, the major challenge before the government was a deteriorating fiscal balance and an increasing fiscal deficit. The Union Budget of 2020–21 did commit to a fiscal deficit target of 3.5% of GDP, however in light of the pandemic, the economic scenario of the country had gone haywire and with fiscal deficit touching 135.1% of FY21 target in November 2020 (as was with other countries struck hard by the pandemic), the government's fiscal commitment had been given up.

With the trail of wreckage left by the outbreak of the virus, leading to a fall in revenue collections and an increased expenditure in terms of conventional and unconventional fiscal and monetary stimulus, there was a clear need to spend money and not worry about fiscal deficit numbers. Under this situation, it would look odd to talk about fiscal discipline and Fiscal Responsibility and Budget Management (FBRM) Act. However, one cannot ignore the cost to the economy. Increased government borrowing due to widening fiscal deficit would mean inflicting pressure on interest rates which in turn would give rise to cost-push inflation. On the flip side, that is a price worth paying as the focus should be on strengthening purchasing power among people and thereby giving a kickstart to the economy. With a recovery being underway, the need was to press full-throttle on the accelerator of development and move the Indian economy back onto the trajectory of economic growth.

1.8

Time for Big-Ticket Reforms

India's real GDP was estimated to contract by (–7.7%) in 2020–21, compared to a growth rate of 4.04% in 2019–20.

However, despite faster than expected economic recovery making experts revise their forecasts for 2020–21 and 2021–22, there were few signals such as falling wholesale price index (WPI), current account surplus, which did not gel well with the recovery mode. Fall in exports by 15.8% to USD200.55 billion during April–December, 2020 from USD364.18 billion during April–December, 2019 was a challenge though it reflected a negative external market. More disturbing was the continued fall in imports though it had improved in Dec2020. Imports which stood at USD258.29 billion during April–December, 2020 saw a 29.08% fall as compared to April–December, 2019, which clearly indicated that the manufacturing sector had still not regained its normalcy point. In December 2020, the trade deficit widened to USD15.71 billion with imports growing by 7.6% and exports contracting for the third month in a row. The fall in exports had been attributed to declining demand in sectors such as petroleum, leather, marine products. IIP contracted 1.9% in November 2020 slowing the trend in increasing factory output seen in the previous two months. Mining and manufacturing witnessed a contraction of 7.3% and 1.7%, respectively. Similarly, WPI at 1.22% might appear music to consumers; but certainly, it did not reflect a positive investment environment.

Thus, keeping the previously mentioned economic scenario in mind and in view of the ambitious target set by the Prime Minister for transforming the country into an Atmanirbhar Bharat, the Union Budget to be announced on 1 February 2021, was the occasion to unfold the road-map in terms of increased government expenditure, increasing purchasing power of the common man who is expected to play a proactive role in demand boosting and building of a robust policy environment.

Resurgent India. Jagadish Shettigar and Pooja Misra, Oxford University Press. © Oxford University Press 2022.
DOI: 10.1093/oso/9780192866486.003.0008

With the general election being three years away, in any normal circumstance, the government could have easily opted for tough measures. However, under the prevailing situation and with the virus resulting in the economic scenario being thrown out of gear, the government might not have been able to enjoy the mid-term luxury of opting for path-breaking economic policy reforms and fiscal measures. The government had to carefully walk through political nuances coupled with a deteriorating fiscal balance, an outcome of the pandemic on one side and economic compulsions on the other, and get back on the trajectory of economic growth. Thus, a well-designed and carefully laid out roadmap to usher economic growth back on track at the cost of short-term political gains would make the budget a historical one.

In fact, the pandemic hit economic crisis was an opportune time and an apt moment for the government to reiterate its commitment to big-ticket reform measures required to give the required boost to the economy. In this direction, fine-tuning of GST in terms of slabs and also intent to bring petroleum products within its ambit would have helped bring down the cost of production, thereby boosting consumption demand.

With the RBI stating in its Financial Stability Report, December 2020 that the banks' gross NPAs were estimated to rise sharply to 13.5% by September 2021, it was time that banks brace themselves for a rollback of the regulatory forbearance announced in light of the pandemic. Similarly, returning to the implementation of the bankruptcy code that too at a time when there is no liquidity crunch in the economy would have given a positive signal, though at the cost of annoying vested interests in the industry.

With the Make in India programme being envisioned to evolve into Make for the World and the call being given for Vocal for Local, thereby laying the building blocks for India to be the manufacturing hub for the world, the government could also unfold its reform intentions revolving around labour and land if a big-push was to be given to infrastructure projects as stated by the PM. Today's youth constitute tomorrow's working population. NEP 2020, which aims for universalization of education and bringing quality into higher education by helping students build a scientific temperament from a young age, seeks to build a base for a vibrant India. The budget should ensure that there is an adequate provision for the effective implementation of the NEP.

Not to miss the fact that it is equally important to consolidate the good-will amongst the poor, educated middle class and marginal farmers. This was all the more the need of the hour when an attempt was going on to mislead the public and build a perception of the Government being anti-farmers. This notion could have been disproved in terms of a big jump in rural budget allocation and kisan-related measures such as substantial allocation on agri-infrastructure like cold chains, ripening chambers, refrigerated transportation along with the promotion of food processing units.

Last but not the least, the middle-class population segment certainly was looking for higher disposable income resulting from a cut in tax burden. With a higher marginal propensity to consume, the middle class can effectively contribute to the revival of demand. A confidence booster from the Union budget could have led to an increase in discretionary spending, which had taken a backseat during the pandemic. Higher spending would lead to increased production, an increase in employment numbers, and higher income levels which would set the ball rolling on the economic growth track. Until and unless the February 2021 budget was a 1991-like budget, if not better than that, the nation was bound to feel disappointed to miss a historic opportunity.

1.9

Economic Impact of the Second Wave

With the second wave of the Coronavirus pushing India into a humanitarian and economic crisis, analysts and rating agencies had been forced to revise the forecasted GDP growth numbers downwards for FY 2021–22. GDP growth for FY 2021–22 was slashed by Goldman Sachs from 11.7% to 11.1%, by Nomura from 12.6% to 10.8%, by S&P Global from 11% to 9.8%, by JP Morgan from 11% to 9%, by Moody's from 13.7% to 9.3%.

The unprecedented rise in COVID-19 cases led to the country facing a severe shortage of medical oxygen, life-saving medicines and drugs. Citizens were forced to run from pillar to post looking for hospital beds, cardiac care units, and healthcare professionals. As against WHO's norms for doctors being 1:1000 and nurses being 3:1000, India had only 1.4 beds per 1000 people, 1 doctor per 1445 people, and 1.7 nurses per 1000 people. To worsen the situation, inequity amongst States in terms of healthcare facilities only added fuel to the fire. With urban India's healthcare facilities collapsing under the sheer weight of increasing virus numbers, rural India's threadbare healthcare system stood stressed.

While India was being battered by the second wave of the virus, most advanced and emerging economies had been on a recovery path. The rise in people falling prey to the virus had forced state governments to announce regional and localized lockdowns, thereby minimizing mobility. High-frequency indicators such as the Google mobility report, decreasing auto sales, rising unemployment levels were seen to be in red. Google mobility trends showed that compared to baseline between March and May, frequency of visits to workplaces, parks, transit stations, retail, recreation, grocery and pharmacy, and residential areas was (−)51%, (−)43%, (−)53%, (−)64%, (−) 28%, and 26% respectively. The Nomura India Business Resumption index declined to 64.5 for the week ending 11 May 2021, down from 69.7 during the prior week. The rural economy had shown signs of strain, unlike past

Resurgent India. Jagadish Shettigar and Pooja Misra, Oxford University Press. © Oxford University Press 2022.
DOI: 10.1093/oso/9780192866486.003.0009

instances including the first wave. This had a bearing on the demand for the essential goods sector, ie FMCG. Tractor and passenger vehicle sales saw a decline of 25.4% and 10.07%, respectively in April 2021 as against March 2021. February–May 2021 witnessed a loss of 7.5 million jobs across sectors such as travel and tourism, hospitality, retail which rely on people's mobility to sustain businesses. April and May 2021 had a double-digit unemployment rate with unemployment levels touching 17.88% at the end of May. A rising trend in the number of persons and households registering under the MGNREG scheme was witnessed in April 2021, ie the number of persons registering for jobs under this scheme increased to 402.71 lakhs in April 2021 as against 359.1 lakhs in March 2021. This significant rise could be attributed to the surge in the second wave of the virus resulting in reverse migration to villages.

However, as stated by the RBI, the impact of the second wave on the economy had not been as gloomy as that of the first wave but enveloping uncertainties had proved to be a hindrance in the short term. Data released by IHS Markit showed purchasing manager's index for April 2021 to be at 55.5 after declining to a seven-month low in March at 55.4. Rail freight grew at 5% compared to pre-pandemic levels, thus suggesting that supply-side disruptions had been less severe. Timely normal monsoons were a good omen and bode well for the rural economy. The silver lining on the wall had been external trade, ie the new export orders, which increased for the eighth consecutive month in April and rose in imports. Merchandise exports remained robust, reflecting increased external demand for Indian products and furthering manufacturing activities. Exports grew at 197% to USD30.21 billion in April 2021. An increase in export orders also came from labour-intensive sectors such as gems and jewellery, leather products. Imports too increased to USD45.72 billion in April 2021 as against 17.12 billion in April 2020.

The RBI, in its monthly bulletin of May 2021, observed that the economic toll of the second wave was more in terms of a demand shock rather than supply. Factors such as decline in mobility levels, reduced discretionary spending, increasing unemployment had dented the economy. Weak consumer sentiments amongst the affluent class and the spread of infection in rural India were some of the economic costs of the second wave of the virus.

In view of the previously mentioned macroeconomic scenario existing in the Indian economy, all eyes and hopes were pinned on universal vaccination happening at an accelerated pace. As of 29 May 2021, the dashboard showed a total of 206.38 million vaccination doses being administered, of which 163.51 million were for the first dose while 42.8 million were for the second dose. For India to achieve universal vaccination, the country required 1878 million doses at the rate of two doses per person for adults (approximately 939 million adults). Not to miss the vaccine still to be developed and administered to approximately four hundred seventy-two million children in the age group of 0–18 years was also to be worked on. Thus, the challenge knocking at the doorstep of the government was to vaccinate 100% of its adult and children population. With the government targeting to cover the adult population by the end of the calendar year 2021, all efforts were to be keyed towards ensuring a seamless supply vaccine pipeline as against the demand for it. Other than the two manufacturers in India, one domestically developed and another with a license, the government was in active negotiations with other foreign developed vaccine companies.

Thus the foremost short-term measure to revive the economy that was explored by the government was expediting universal vaccination. A major demand hindrance had been weak consumer sentiments and reduced discretionary spending, which could be largely minimized by vaccinating the entire population at the earliest. With RBI also maintaining full focus on revival of economic growth as against inflation (CPI for April 2021—4.3% and WPI at 10.49%) and continuing with its accommodative outlook in the monetary policy, fiscal measures such as direct cash transfer, increased allocation of jobs under the rural job guarantee scheme could have been a demand booster by putting more money in the hands of this section of society.

However, it was important that the country in this hour of crisis did not close its eyes towards long term measures that the budget 2021–22 had planned for such as increased capital expenditure, building of a national asset monetization pipeline, setting up of a Development Financial Institution which would be key to generating significant revenue resources, increasing employment opportunities and facilitating regional economic development. Also, reduced revenue collections due to regional lockdowns might have resulted in putting further pressure on the fiscal deficit of the government. Not to forget, if the increasing trend in WPI due to increased commodity prices was extended to CPI, RBI would have been under pressure to relook and prioritize inflationary targeting as against economic growth. Last but the most important point being that the pandemic had brought to light the dismal state of healthcare facilities available in the country and successive governments should look towards building an environment of healthcare management in the country as against disease management. Ultimately, progress in vaccination was the key as demand constraints were due to a behavioural reaction of human psychology and beyond the reach of traditional economic policy measures.

1.10

Surge in GDP Growth in Q1 2022: Real Picture?

With the Indian economy growing at a record pace of 20.1% in Q1 FY22 as against a contraction of 24.4% in the same quarter of FY21, economists and analysts were largely of the view that the low base effect of the previous year's record contraction had contributed to the same. It is important to note that while GDP numbers appeared to look good, it was nobody's guess that India's GDP in Q1FY22 of Rs. 32.38 lakh crores was below the Q1FY20 level of Rs. 35.67 lakh crores, ie approximately 9% lower, and was also below Q4FY21 of Rs. 38.96 lakh crores. However, keeping in mind that during Q1FY22, the country had faced a humanitarian and economic crisis due to the second virus wave, macroeconomic indicators were reflective of the fact that due to less stringent regional and localized lockdowns, the economy relatively was not that adversely affected, ie Q1FY22 GDP was Rs.32.38 lakh crores as against Rs.26.95 lakh crores in Q1FY21.

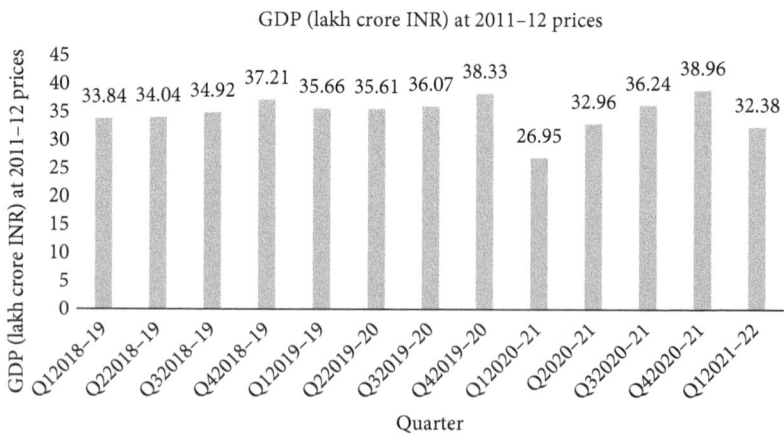

GDP (lakh crore INR) at 2011–12 prices

Source: Ministry of Statistics and Programme Implementation

Resurgent India. Jagadish Shettigar and Pooja Misra, Oxford University Press. © Oxford University Press 2022.
DOI: 10.1093/oso/9780192866486.003.0010

In Q1FY21, while the agricultural sector had shown a growth of 4.52%, there had been a strong rebound in manufacturing and construction. Manufacturing had expanded by 49.63%, while construction had shown a rise by 68.3%. Core sector output grew by 9.4%, ie coal, natural gas, refinery products, fertilizers, cement, steel, and electricity showed a positive growth, while crude oil production declined by 3.2%. With these eight core sectors constituting two-fifths of the IIP and showing an upward tick, IIP numbers for July 2021 were expected to expand at 13%–15%. The silver lining on the wall had been gross fixed capital formation, ie private sector investment, which grew at 55.26% in Q1FY22 and constituted 31.6% of GDP as against 24.4% in Q1FY21, however, it was still lower than 34.6% of pre-COVID Q1FY20. India's Manufacturing Purchasing Managers Index for July 2021 rose to a three-month high of 55.3, thereby denoting an expansion in manufacturing activities.

High-frequency indicators for the Indian economy on an average since June 2021, ie post the second virus wave peak in April–May 2021, had been pointing towards an uptick in economic activity, thereby moving the economy back on the track of economic recovery. GST collection (in August 2021 crossed Rs. 1 lakh crores for the second month in a row), e-way bills, mobility levels, power demand (18.6% increase over last year), auto sales, and exports had been on the rise. Not to miss, work generated under the MGNREGA scheme in August 2021 was 58% lower than July 2021, thereby indicating that rural workers were migrating back to urban industrial areas for work.

On the flip side, while the picture on the canvas of economic recovery was appealing, there were certain watch-outs that the government and RBI needed to look out for and keep on its radar. Of the four demand-side growth engines, ie. private final consumption expenditure, government final consumption expenditure, gross fixed capital formation, and exports, the heavy lifting in Q1FY22 had been done by exports, on the back of the V-shaped recovery being witnessed at a global level. With the second virus wave leaving its mark on nearly all households, q-o-q numbers for consumption showed that private consumption had contracted 8.9% in Q1FY22 as against the previous quarter, while exports not only grew 7.2% q-o-y but also crossed pre-COVID levels. As per the OBICUS survey for Q42021, capacity utilization (CU) numbers showed that while CU had increased to 69.4% as against 66.6% in the previous quarter, it was still not anywhere near 73.6% of Q2, 2019–20. Also, the services sector, especially contact intensive and employment generating sectors, tourism and hospitality, etc., continued to lag. With the pace of vaccinations increasing (as of 1 September 2021, 66.35 crores total doses administered, of which 51.10 crores first dose and 15.25 core second dose) and festival season setting in, the anticipation was that there would be a demand revival but not at a rapid pace provided the anticipated third wave came under control with satisfactory progress in vaccination drive. Improving consumer sentiments especially post the onslaught of the second virus wave would be key to demand recovery and increased discretionary spending.

Agreeably, some more key measures undertaken by the government, such as detailing of the Asset Monetisation scheme and amendment to the Retrospective Tax, had boosted investor sentiments and would help further drive growth. The roadmap laid out by the government for the asset monetization pipeline was a welcome step, and by unlocking the value of unutilized or underutilized public assets and creating new revenue sources only sought to drive employment opportunities along with balanced regional development. Increased employment would lead to increased income and higher demand. However, successful implementation and efficient execution at the ground level is key and the public and private sectors must now collaborate effectively to enable the creation of infrastructure through monetization. Also, with the Government doing away with the retrospective tax, it has perked up the interest and attention of foreign and domestic investors. An unambiguous tax regime with transparency being a key component of its basic framework will help attract foreign direct investments into the country and give the requisite push to building of an Atmanirbhar Bharat.

It would only be fair to state that in these trying times of COVID, the RBI had undertaken conventional and unconventional stimulus measures and stepped up to its role of being the monetary policy administrator. Even though inflation levels were on the rise, RBI in its monetary policy meeting in August 2021, chose to focus on economic growth over inflation. In its Financial Stability Report, July 2021, the monetary authority had stated that the increasing inflation was transitory in nature and with international commodity prices facing a broad-based upswing and global and domestic supply chain facing disruptions, the situation would only improve with COVID restrictions being removed and economic activity reviving. However, with inflation being around the upper tolerance level of 6% for some time now and gross margins of Corporates witnessing a squeeze, it might not be appropriate to consider inflation to be transitory in nature.

With commodity prices being at multi-year all-time high levels in FY21, it had led to increased raw material and input costs for the consumer durable, chemical, and capital goods sector, an attrition-led supply pressure on the availability of labour for the technology sector. Increased input costs of raw materials and labour were only adversely impacting gross profit margins of corporates despite sales levels returning to normalcy. While with current demand constraints, companies were being forced to absorb increased production costs, it was only a matter of time before corporates passed on the increased costs to consumers, especially with demand revival taking place due to the festive season. Thus, the RBI and government probably needed to go back to the drawing board and re-strategize for increased commodity prices, which might not really be resulting in inflation being transitory as was being viewed.

1.11

Q2FY22 GDP: Indian Economy on Recovery Track

With the Indian economy witnessing a real GDP growth rate of 8.4% in Q2FY22 as against a contraction of 7.4% in Q2FY21 and gross value added rising by 8.5%, high-frequency indicators such as GST and e-way bill collections, electricity demand, railway freight traffic, vehicle sales, exports were all pointing towards the economy moving back on the economic recovery track and towards normalization. On the demand side, amongst the four growth engines, private final consumption expenditure, which constitutes 54.5% of total GDP, exhibited a growth rate of 8.6%, gross fixed capital formation, commonly referred to as investments, rose by 11%, while government expenditure increased by 8.7%. On the supply side, agriculture, manufacturing, and mining saw a steady growth of 4.5%, 5.5%, and 15.4%, respectively. Construction activities saw a growth of 7.5%. Contact intensive sectors such as trade, hotels, and transport; and financial, real estate, and professional services witnessed a growth of 8.2% and 7.8%, respectively. In absolute terms, GDP for Q2FY22 at Rs. 35.73 lakh crores was higher than Q2FY20 GDP—pre-COVID levels at Rs. 35.61 lakh crores.

An improved macroeconomic scenario that had set the Indian economy back on the recovery track was an outcome of the abatement of the second virus wave in Q2, resulting in easing state-wise and regional lockdowns coupled with increased vaccination coverage. Q2FY22 witnessed record merchandise exports of USD102.15 billion, the first time ever that the country exceeded USD100 billion mark in the September quarter, as stated by the Ministry of Commerce. The silver lining on the wall was the remarkable growth shown by investments, the second-largest engine of growth constituting 32.0% of total GDP, at Rs. 11.42 lakh crore in Q2FY22 as against pre-COVID levels of Rs. 11.25 lakh crores. With the festival season fast approaching, output, new orders, exports all returned

Resurgent India. Jagadish Shettigar and Pooja Misra, Oxford University Press. © Oxford University Press 2022.
DOI: 10.1093/oso/9780192866486.003.0011

to expansion territory leading to IHS Markit Manufacturing PMI numbers being 55.3, 52.3, and 53.7 (number above 50 signifies expansion) for July, August, and September 2021, respectively. However, while private final consumption expenditure did see a rise, it was still below preCOVID levels, ie Rs. 19.48 lakh cores in Q2FY22 as against Rs. 20.19 lakh crores in Q2FY20. Rural demand backed by a fairly strong kharif output was resilient and had outpaced urban cities. Due to increased mobility levels, Q2FY22 saw a rise in out-of-home consumption and increased sales of discretionary items.

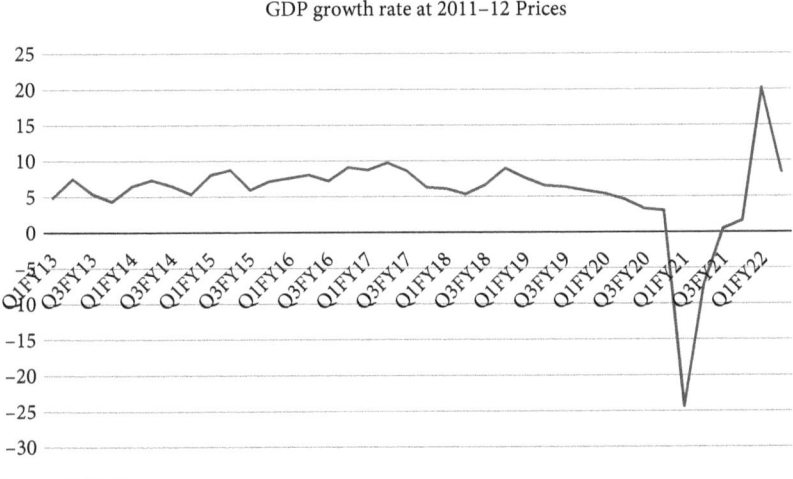

GDP growth rate at 2011–12 Prices

Source: MOSPI

The moot point being: With steady progress in covid vaccinations leading to an improved business scenario and consumer confidence levels slowly and steadily reviving, it had resulted in rating agencies, brokerage, and financial institutions revising their forecast numbers for India's GDP growth rate for FY22. Moody's Investors Service had predicted that economic growth in the country was expected to rebound strongly and had pegged GDP growth for FY22 at 9.3%. Goldman Sachs, SBI Research, and UBS Securities had upped their GDP forecast to 9.1%, 9.3%–9.6%, 9.5%, respectively. RBI had maintained its forecast numbers for the Indian economy at 9.5% GDP growth.

On the flip side, while the country seemed to be fast-moving back on the trajectory of a durable economic recovery, it would only be prudent to keep a keen eye for domestic and global headwinds, the largest looming threat being the virus variant—Omicron. The latest variant posed a renewed risk to global growth levels and India was no exception to the same. Economies across the globe were upping the antennae and renewing curbs and restricting travel for visitors from the impacted regions. This could also further worsen existing global supply chain constraints, which had been on the horizon for over a year now.

To add fuel to the fire, other global cues such as a surge in fresh COVID cases in Europe resulting in Austria announcing a lockdown and countries such as Germany and Belgium renewing focus on precautionary measures had dealt a major blow to investor and business sentiments, especially FPIs. Crude oil prices had been a cause of worry resulting in the United States, India, Japan, Britain, and South Korea announcing release from strategic petroleum reserves.

Not to miss, the elephant in the room being, the US inflation rates spiking to 6.2% (highest in three decades), leading to pressure on the US Federal Reserve to raise interest rates sooner than planned and the Federal Reserve chief, Jerome Powell, being forced to state 'it is probably time to retire the word "transitory" when describing inflation'.

On the domestic front, while the biggest growth engine, ie private final consumption expenditure had shown a rise, it had still not reached pre-COVID levels. Google workplace mobility index showed that as of last week of November 2021, it was 5% above the baseline, while mobility trends for retail and recreation were still 3% below the baseline. Consumption demand under the prevailing circumstances was more related to non-economic factors, ie due to fear of contracting the virus, people were not venturing out to brick and mortar stores resulting in demand being limited to the bare minimum. Offline shopping would have helped induce and motivate people to imitate consumption trends adopted by others, thus setting the demonstration effect of buying behaviour in place. Additionally, increased wholesale price index numbers and their ensuing effect on price levels could result in further adversely impacting consumption demand. The primary cure for the same was effective vaccination, better healthcare management, and appropriate fiscal measures, which would help the economy return back to normalcy.

Additionally, one must not miss the fact that: The government's decision to repeal the farm laws might have been an outcome of its inability to convince a small section of farmers. However, with the farming sector becoming largely un-remunerative due to rising inputs costs and low price realizations resulting in declining income from crop production and lower rural wages, reforms in this sector are much needed. Additionally, this decision has also raised speculation on the shadow that it could cast on the implementation of the labour reforms, which have been waiting in the wings for some time now. With the country aiming to be a USD5 trillion economy and focusing on building an 'Atmanirbhar Bharat', would the much-needed reforms, ie Labour Reforms, Land Acquisition Act, let alone administrative, judicial, and electoral reforms be the victims, prior to the 2024 elections is a key point that must be deliberated on....

PART 2

ANALYSIS OF
POLICY INITIATIVES

With the COVID-19 virus having adversely impacted economies world-wide and being disruptive in terms of economic activity and leading to loss of human lives, Governments and Central authorities had announced numerous stimulus packages to cushion the negative impact. India, being no exception, plummeting domestic and foreign demand had adversely impacted all sectors of the economy. The brunt of the pandemic was largely borne by sectors such as aviation, travel and tourism, retail, realty, etc. Sectors such as textiles, automobile and components, consumer durable, and electronics had experienced a medium-term impact.

Economic analysts had been discussing the probability of economies witnessing V, W, U, K, etc. shaped recoveries depending on the number of people contracting the virus. Governments and Central Banks across the world had been trying to minimize the impact of the virus and had announced a slew of stimulus measures. The Indian Government and RBI to generate employment and provide liquidity support had come up with financial and non-financial stimulus measures under the Atmanirbhar Bharat package 1.0, 2.0, and 3.0 at an overall cost of 15% of GDP.

In Part 2, the authors analyse Policy Initiatives announced by the Indian Government and RBI. It delves into aspects of an Atmanirbhar Bharat, the big push of agricultural reforms with the Government announcing the three agricultural reforms under Atmanirbhar Bharat 2.0 and other measures to revive domestic demand in the economy. This section also discusses the requirement for fine-tuning of GST, looks at negative interest rates, discusses the Government's re-think on retrospective taxes, much needed power sector reforms, and the talked about fiscal deficit, ie should the Government adhere to the target set by the Fiscal Responsibility and Budget Management (FRBM) Act or should the year of the pandemic be treated as an exception?

2.1
Atmanirbhar Bharat

In the backdrop of the pandemic, the main driver of economic growth for any nation is increased Government spending and ensuring credit availability and ample liquidity in the financial system of the economy.

Initially, Rs. 1.7 crore relief package/stimulus had been announced by the Government of India with the objective of helping those individuals and producers who had been hardest hit by the Lockdown. The first stimulus package was primarily focused on cash transfer and food security measures by providing free foodgrains and cereals apart from direct cash transfers to the lesser strata of society. A few of the fiscal measures given by the government initially were: additional 5 kg of wheat or rice and 1 kg of dal monthly for three months which later got extended by every three successive months, Rs. 2000 to be transferred to the bank accounts of 87 million farmers under PM Kisan scheme, free LPG under PM Ujjwala Yojana scheme, Rs. 500 per month to 200 million women for three months under the Jan Dhan Yojana, etc.

With the aim of mitigating losses inflicted by the pandemic and giving the much-needed boost to the Indian economy, the government had, in the second phase of stimulus in May 2020, announced structural reforms to the tune of Rs. 20 lakh crore (close to 10% of the Indian GDP). Critics opined that it was too little, however, should one not be appreciative of the fact that the Government had kept the burden on taxpayers at a minimum. On the one hand, people felt that it was tepid relative to stimulus packages announced by other countries especially emerging economies, while others viewed it as a reformative fiscal package that would have a far-reaching and positive long-term impact on the economy.

A few of the landmark structural changes which had been brought in were in the agricultural sector. With the amendment in the Agricultural Produce Marketing Committees (APMC) Act, the traditional chain of middlemen taking away genuine remunerative prices meant for farmers

Resurgent India. Jagadish Shettigar and Pooja Misra, Oxford University Press. © Oxford University Press 2022.
DOI: 10.1093/oso/9780192866486.003.0012

had been broken, and for farmers henceforth, it was now a scenario of 'my crop, my right'. The amended contract manufacturing act allowed multinational companies to procure directly from farmers with a predetermined agreed price without the intervention of APMCs. This would allow food processing companies and multi-brand outlets to directly procure commodities from the farmers' doorstep. In addition to these long-term measures, the Government had also worked keeping the short-term picture in mind and increased the Minimum Support Price (MSP) by 1.5 times for kharif crops, ie paddy, cotton, oilseeds, pulses, cereals, etc.

With the Prime Minister vying for Indians being 'आत्मनिर्भर', ie self-reliant and 'Vocal for Local', some of the other measures announced by the Indian Government to kickstart economic growth were: Increase in FDI limit in defence manufacturing under the automatic route to 74%; power distribution in UTs to be privatized; Public Sector Enterprises (PSEs) other than those operating in strategic sectors to be privatized and private companies permitted to set up shop in strategic sectors; encouraging of Public Private Partnership (PPP) model in coal and mineral industry; development of world-class airports through the PPP model; fresh initiation for insolvency proceedings to be suspended for one year, the definition of Micro Small and Medium Enterprises (MSME) widened, street hawkers and vendors to be given a collateral-free loan of Rs. 10,000; collateral-free automatic loan to be provided to a tune of Rs. 3 lakh crore to MSMEs, special liquidity scheme of Rs. 30,000 crores for non-banking financial companies/housing finance companies (NBFCs/HFCs); Cash Reserve Ratio (CRR) reduced to 3% leading to additional Rs. 1,37,000 crore liquidity enhancement; additional allocation of Rs. 40,000 crore under Mahatma Gandhi National Rural Employment Guarantee Scheme (MGNREGS) scheme to help boost employment in rural areas and a 10% increase in MGNREGA wage to Rs. 202 per day from Rs. 182 per day.

In conjunction with the above-mentioned measures, there were also some demand boosting measures such as Government bearing Employee Provident Fund (EPF) contribution for those earning upto Rs. 15,000/month for three months, reduction in EPF contribution from 12% to 10% for three months, and direct cash transfers to the people at the bottom of the pyramid.

Monetary measures had also been announced by the Reserve Bank of India (RBI). Repo rate had been slashed by 75 bps to 4.4%, reverse repo by 90 bps to 4%, this was further brought down 25 bps on 17 April 2020. With a view to increasing liquidity in the financial sector, borrowers were permitted a three-month loan moratorium on payment of instalment of term loans (which was subsequently further increased to August 2021), there was auctioning of targeted long-term repo operations (LTRO) of three-year tenor for Rs. 1 lakh crore, CRR was brought down by 100 bps and a special liquidity facility of Rs. 50,000 crore for mutual funds were few of the measures provided under the monetary stimulus.

The stimulus package was largely a mix of monetary and fiscal with ease of doing business processes being worked upon and some fundamental reforms being announced. However, the catch with regards to changing consumer behaviour still remained, resulting in higher demand for essential items, ie food, health and wellness, and lower spending on discretionary and luxury items. Demand for exports and in domestic markets had decreased and access to credit, especially for B2B and B2C customers, had gone down. With businesses still trying to get back to normal and restart the production process, the impact on supply chain disruption had been taking time to recover and settle. This was an important time when businesses could look at re-strategizing, re-imagining operating models, re-defining customer value proposition, and re-building customer confidence.

Interestingly, the Indian Government was alongside seen working on reforming of policies and improving on ease of doing business parameters to emerge as an alternative attractive manufacturing destination and maximizing the opportunity presented by the pandemic. The Government had set up dedicated groups to identify firms that were keen to move their manufacturing facility out of China. Additionally, by trying to come out of the grim situation existing worldwide and supplying hydroxychloroquine to countries, the Indian Government had once again managed to win over both friends and foes.

Thus, it was imperative on the part of policymakers both at the Centre and State to scale up their responses as challenges unfolded. This was mandatory to minimize the damage and shock caused by the pandemic on the formal and informal sectors. This could help pave the way for a V- or U-shaped recovery for the Indian economy at large and help kick-start the journey back on the road to rapid economic growth that India had been treading on for more than over two decades.

Thus, the pertinent questions were: Were these measures adequate to provide the required boost to the economy? Keeping in mind lower GST revenue collection, would it have been wise on the part of the Government to provide tax reliefs to fuel up demand? Should it have given out cash doles, direct income transfer to the lower strata of society, thereby helping them in sustaining their living? This would also have fuelled demand in the economy and given the requisite push to the production process leading to the revival of economic growth. These were some of the questions that the Government and economists needed to ponder upon and act fast.

2.2

Five Trillion Economy

With India striving towards being a USD5 trillion economy and emerge as an economic powerhouse by 2024–25, the moot point now being: Has the pandemic been a spoiler in achieving the aspirational goal set by the Prime Minister, Mr. Narendra Modi? Economists and analysts were forced to rework the GDP growth numbers and as per Moody's forecast (November 2020), India was expected to contract at 8.9% in FY2021. With Q2, FY2021showing signs of recovery, RBI in December 2020 had revised the contraction numbers for India for FY2021 to 7.5%. In these adverse circumstances, the Government and monetary authorities worldwide had announced conventional and unconventional fiscal and monetary stimulus measures. So, what did India's reform story state?

The Make in India programme launched in 2014, an integral constituent of nation-building initiatives and transforming India into a global manufacturing hub was a galvanizing call to Indians and an invitation to potential investors worldwide. This programme is an endeavour of the Government to overhaul outdated policies and processes and move the economy into a region of 'Minimum Government, Maximum Governance'.

In light of this ideology to make India into the world's next manufacturing hub, the Government had been keying in all efforts to improve the country's ranking in the Ease of Doing Business index. From a far 142nd rank in 2014, the country jumped 79 positions to 63rd place (2019) in 'World Bank's Ease of Doing Business Rankings 2020'. Initiatives such as the Insolvency and Bankruptcy Code (2016), the Make in India Programme, and Goods and Services Tax (2017) had come a long way in improving the country's ranking and giving it the much-needed thrust.

However, with India, being a federal structure, it is imperative that State Governments are empowered, and the Central and State Governments work together to make India into an investment destination. States and

Resurgent India. Jagadish Shettigar and Pooja Misra, Oxford University Press. © Oxford University Press 2022.
DOI: 10.1093/oso/9780192866486.003.0013

Union Territories are envisaged to be the key drivers of growth enabling India to grow from a USD2.7 trillion economy (2019) into a USD5 trillion economy. To ensure that focus is maintained on implementing reforms across the country, the Department for Industry and Internal Trade launched the Business Action Reform Plan (BRAP), which concentrates on State Reforms acting as investment enablers.

In order to attract foreign investment and reduce the country's dependence on China for intermediate goods, the Production Linked Incentive (PLI) scheme, 2020, and other schemes under the Atmanirbhar Bharat Abhiyan aiming to give an impetus to businesses were steps in the right direction. The PLI scheme was further expanded in November 2020 to include ten additional sectors such as automobile and auto components, textile, food products, white goods, etc. The sectors under this scheme being largely labour intensive, it would also give the requisite push to employment generation in the country.

However, parameters such as enforcing contracts, registering property, getting credit, and paying taxes in the Ease of Doing Business Index are avenues that the Government still needs to work on. With a viewpoint of being an attractive destination for domestic and foreign investors, land reforms such as digitization of land records and creation of a land record repository, conclusive titling and ownership of property, refining of the Land Acquisition Act, 2013 are some of the areas that need to be rightly addressed.

Important and long overdue structural labour reforms were enacted by the Parliament in September 2020 for reforming the unwieldy and cumbersome labour laws in the country. Successful implementation of these and its efficient execution would help revive the Indian economy and move it back on the path of economic growth. However, refining of the Industrial Disputes Act, 1947 and Contract Labour Act are some of the areas that the Government still needs to attend to.

On enforcing contracts parameter, India ranks 163rd. As per data, in India, it takes approximately four years or 1445 days to enforce a contract and with 3.97 crore cases pending (September 2020), improved management, increase in workings days for the judiciary, and use of technology to improve the efficiency of courts are some of the initiatives that need to be taken for this parameter to improve. It is important that the country draws up a blueprint for judicial reforms and works on it on a war footing.

On paying taxes parameter, it has been seen that in India, it takes 250 hours to pay taxes as against 140 hours in New Zealand and 138 hours in China. While initiatives such as GST and online filing of taxes are steps in the right direction, expanding taxpayer base, fixing loopholes in GST, etc., are some of the areas that need attention. The focus of the Government should be on increasing tax collections instead of repeatedly tinkering with GST rates. A robust, self-sufficient implementation GSTN structure will add to the success story of GST.

In light of the pandemic, it had been seen that even with the RBI, bringing down the repo rate and CRR to ensure adequate liquidity is present in the financial flow of the economy, data showed that deposit growth (10.4% y-o-y, November 2020) clearly outweighed commercial sector credit growth (5.8% y-o-y, November 2020) in the country. Does this point towards the fact that there is a risk aversion by banks and a growing preference for them to park the excess money in safer and less risky instruments against lending it out to businesses and making credit accessibility tougher for corporates?

Yes, the Government had worked on long-term structural reforms in the agricultural sector. The three farm Acts, 2020 were referred to as the dawn of liberalization for the Indian farmer. These farm Acts endeavoured to build a scenario of 'One India, One Agricultural Market' would have gone a long way in giving a thrust to the growth of the agricultural sector, however, efficient implementation of these Acts was needed. With the Government setting aside Rs. 1 lakh crore for the Agriculture Infrastructure Fund (AIF), measures such as refrigerated transportation by rail, providing of an interest subvention of 3% on term loans for the building of warehouses, sorting and grading units, ripening chambers, cold chain warehouses, e-marketing platforms, etc. would give the impetus to the agricultural sector and make it an integral part of the USD5 trillion story. Ensuring that the benefits of contract farming are understood by all and the much needed and overdue step giving freedom to farmers to sell their produce directly to corporations, exporters, processors, wholesalers, restaurants, modern-day retailers, etc. is availed of and rationalization of fertilizer subsidies are some of the avenues that the Government needs to focus on.

Keeping the geopolitical scenario in mind, with the ratio of India's net exports to GDP being 31.4% in 2019, any upheaval in the external economy does have a bearing on the Indian economy. Not to forget the fact that with the coronavirus having unfavourably impacted countries worldwide, it has had an adverse impact on India's net exports too. However, the positive angle is that India has a large domestic market, ie it is a domestic driven emerging economy and its dependence on the external economy relative to other countries is still low. Also, with Mr. Joe Biden coming into power, and both heads of state reiterating their firm commitment to the Indo-US strategic partnership, sectors such as IT/ITeS are expected to be positively impacted. With regards to the eastern countries, India opting out of RCEP is a step in the right direction. Rather, the Government should work towards making the Quad forum into a robust coalition and attempt to reposition itself in the World Economic Order.

Thus, in its effort to being a USD5 trillion economy, India still needs to work on structural reforms such as land, judiciary, labour, taxes, power sector, administrative, etc. but not to forget structural measures already initiated such as Make in India, skill development, the three labour bills, insolvency and bankruptcy code has already put us on the road to being a global economic powerhouse. The target of being a USD5 trillion economy by 2024–25 is certainly a challenging one and the virus might end up postponing the realization of this ambitious goal by a few years, but yes, in light of the several structural and long term reforms initiated by the Government, India is fast moving on the right track.

2.3
Historic Reforms in Agriculture

The Indian Government had brought about sweeping landmark policy changes in the Indian agricultural sector on 5 June 2020. Critics stated that for the Indian industry, the dawn of liberalization happened in 1991, while for the Indian farmer, liberalization had set in with the three farm reform bills which were passed by the Parliament in the third week of September 2020, one of them being The Farmers Produce Trade and Commerce (Promotion and Facilitation) Act 2020. This Act had been brought about with the perspective of promoting barrier-free inter-state and intra-state trade of farmer produce outside the boundaries of markets or deemed markets earmarked under State agricultural market regulations. The Farm Act had endeavoured to bring about transparency in the agricultural sector and make it more efficient by enabling farmers to be able to sell their produce outside the mandis giving them the benefit of 'my crop, my right'.

The Act had been widely proclaimed to be a 'game-changer' for the Indian agricultural sector. It was promulgated with a viewpoint of building a scenario of 'One India, One Agricultural Market' for the benefit of farmers and sought to break the monopoly of Agriculture Produce Marketing Committees (APMC) by enabling farmers to be able to access markets directly and gain benefits of higher prices for their produce.

Rather deliberations for liberalizing the Indian agricultural sector had been on the cards for quite some years, whether it was the NDA Government or the UPA Government in power. In 2003, the Ministry of Agriculture had formulated a Model APMC Act, 2003 provisioning for freedom for farmers to sell their farm produce. The perspective behind the formulation of this Act was to develop an efficient market system, promote agricultural products and agricultural processing units, along with building an effective and resilient infrastructure for marketing agricultural produce and providing the benefit of higher prices to farmers

Resurgent India. Jagadish Shettigar and Pooja Misra, Oxford University Press. © Oxford University Press 2022.
DOI: 10.1093/oso/9780192866486.003.0014

for their crops. Subsequently, with the Government changing hands in the Centre in 2004, the incumbent UPA Government, headed by Dr. Manmohan Singh, had started persuading states to adopt the Model APMC Act, 2003 with a viewpoint of liberalizing the state agricultural marketing laws. Thus, efforts to reform the APMC Act by the Central Governments in power had been under discussion for over two decades now.

The reformative Farm Acts were slated to prevail over the State APMC Acts. A few of the key provisions under the Act were: Encourage and provide for barrier-free trade outside the areas designated as market yards, thereby freeing the farmers from the shackles of the mandis and restricting the power of the mandis; permit electronic trading of farmers produce under e-Nam and permit new electronic trading platforms to be set-up by private individuals, Farmer Producer Organisations (FPOs) and Co-operatives; payment to the farmer for his produce to be done on the same day or within a maximum of three working days of the transaction of exchange of farmers produce; no levying of any market fee, cess, or charge on farmers, traders and electronic trading platforms; provide for a dispute resolution mechanism whereby the aggrieved party might apply to the Sub-Divisional Magistrate for relief through reconciliation.

APMCs were originally set up with the idea of ensuring price discovery through the efficient operation of market forces of demand and supply for the agricultural produce via a competitive process of auctioning. The institutional infrastructure was put in place to ensure that farmers brought across their agricultural produce to designated market areas and traders with licenses were permitted to participate in the auctioning process of the graded produce. However, over the years, it was seen that the APMCs had become a cartelized operation and the objective of transparency and price discovery was sidestepped. The APMCs, which were supposed to be managed by an elected board and were to operate as democratic institutions, were superseded with administrators appointed by State Governments whose main prerogative was revenue collection as against looking after the interests of the farmer community. All efforts to reform APMCs were thwarted by vested interests and the fear of States losing out on means of revenue collection. In a nutshell, most farmers would be in agreement that the functioning of the mandis had been inefficient, non-transparent, politicized, and cartelized.

The Farm Acts sought to free up the farmers from the clutches of traders and moneylenders and permitted them to sell their produce to anyone and anywhere in India. Inability to get the right price for their farm produce had led to many farmers being in a situation of financial distress and being exploited by the middlemen and moneylenders. The financial crisis would force farmers to knock at the doorstep of predatory moneylenders and take loans at preposterously high-interest rates along with committing to sell their harvest at predetermined low prices to them. This Act would have set the needle right and enabled the farmers to sell their produce to the highest bidder/retailer and get the benefit of rightful higher prices for their products.

Keeping the farm-to-fork mark-up price in mind, data showed that the difference between the price that the farmer gets and the price that the retailer sells at was as high as 65% in India as against 25% for a country like Indonesia. Thus, with the Farm Acts being passed by the Parliament, farmers would not be constrained to sell the farm produce only in the designated mandis close to their farms or to predatory moneylenders, rather through FPOs and e-Nam they could look for the highest bidder within the State or alternately outside the confining boundaries of the State too thereby strengthening their bargaining position as sellers. The proposed law permitted farmers to identify and sell to consumers of their choice, be it food processing companies or restaurants or five-star hotels, etc. FPOs could also avail of new profitable avenues and take their rightful place as an aggregator and work to maximize the revenue for the farmers.

Additionally, with the farm Acts approved by the lawmakers, for transactions done outside the market yards or sub-yards, there would be no licensing or fee requirements to be paid by the farmers to the APMCs, thereby enabling farmers to be in a position to avail of higher prices for the produce. Thus, with the compulsion no longer being at the farmer's end of paying a market access fee, the farmer could have availed of higher prices.

However, one must be aware that while the new Act sought to set up an ecosystem of allowing the farmers to sell to anyone, anywhere, it did not do away with the APMC mandis, which are an integral and essential part of the Indian agricultural markets. APMCs would not be dismantled, rather they would continue to co-exist with other agricultural buyers thereby, giving the farmer the opportunity to sell his produce to the highest bidder. The endeavour of the Government via these Farm Acts was to further build on the prevalent agricultural markets a more efficient, transparent, market forces run ecosystem which would prove to be a building block for a sustainable profitable future for the farming community in the long run.

Keeping the observations of the Shanta Kumar high-level committee report, 2015 in mind, one must be cognizant of the fact that only 6% of Indian farmers are able to avail of the advantages of the Minimum Support Prices (MSPs) as only 22 crops are procured under MSP. The balance 94% of the Indian farmer community have already been facing the whims of the open market. Moreover, despite the successive central governments increasing MSPs of crops substantially especially since the United Front government, it has been observed that increased prices have been benefiting the middlemen instead of reaching farmers. In the back-drop of a retail boom a decade back though private sector and multina-tional corporations had stepped forward by offering Rs. 100 per kg higher than the MSP for sourcing the farm produce for their supermarkets and hypermarkets, again it was the turn of the traders to be benefited.

However, on the flip side, we must be cognizant of the fact that the practice of the Government declaring an MSP was not going away any-where and the fear of farmers that this Act would end the MSP regime was completely unfounded. The MSP, which is a safeguard for the farmer to be able to earn a minimum profit for the harvest in case the market price is lesser than the cost of production, was still going to be prevalent, as clarified by Prime Minister Mr. Narendra Modi. Rather, this concept of the Government setting a floor price for agricultural crops to protect the interests of farmers is a practice not only followed by India but also pre-vails in developed countries worldwide.

Thus, the important question now is: Is a Government controlled mechanism required for the Indian agricultural sector or should the agri-cultural sector be rightly liberalized and market forces be allowed to de-termine the right price for the crops? The liberalized agricultural sector and a transparent and efficient agricultural market have been the focused agenda of agricultural experts for more than two decades, and this reform was long overdue. Instead of strengthening the hands of farmers as an effective supply force in the market, many Governments in the past be-lieved in offering lollipops like waiving farm loans. At last, the visionary

Modi government initiated bold steps to take on the vested interests. Along with a liberalized agricultural market, what is needed now is for the Government to invest time, energy, and resources in developing and implementing a robust ecosystem for a liberalized agricultural market to succeed and sustain by itself.

Critics are of the view that States such as Punjab, which has an 8.5% commission rate or cess to be paid up by farmers under the APMC act (whether or not the farmer uses the facility of the market yards) in 2019–20 had collected Rs. 3600 crores as revenue through trade fees which was supposedly used for the development of rural infrastructure. However, with the constitution of the AIF of Rs. 1 lakh crore by the Government in July 2020, this gap of an underdeveloped rural infrastructure can be largely overcome. AIF by creating post-harvest physical infrastructure will build an ecosystem for farmers to be able to successfully directly sell to retailers inter-State and intra-State and thereby get the best price for their products. The focus of AIF is to attract investments and build post-harvest infrastructure, which has been the weak linkage in the agricultural supply chain. Projects such as the building of warehouses, sorting and grading units, ripening chambers, cold chain warehouses, e-marketing platforms, etc., would be able to avail of an interest subvention of 3% on term loans. For loans up to Rs. 2 crores, the guarantee would be provided by the Central Government under the AIF. Thus, with post-harvest infrastructure and other structural measures being undertaken by the Government, such as refrigerated transportation by rail, etc., the farmers will be in a position to command better prices for their produce in the medium to long term.

AIF is another enabling step by the Government towards getting agricultural markets right. Thus, the three reformative Farm Acts, 2020 in conjunction with the AIF were a major step in the right direction of liberalizing agricultural markets and building an efficient and robust ecosystem. These long-term structural reforms would have helped break the monopoly of middlemen and traders and free the farmers from the shackles of illegal moneylenders. It would have built a viable environment for farmers to be able to sell their produce to the highest bidder, ie 'my crop, my right' and move on the path of 'One Nation, One Agricultural Market'. It is really difficult to understand how a few opposition parties had taken a politically suicidal stand by dumping farmers in order to satisfy the vested interests. It is really baffling that the Congress party which made a commitment to amend the APMC act in the 2019 Election Manifesto openly opposed the game-changing proposal. Unfortunately, the government got the three farm Acts repealed in November 2021 as a section of the farmers could not be convinced about the positive impact on agriculture and farmers—as admitted by none other than the Prime Minister. An expert committee would examine the future course of action.

2.4

Steps to Empower Farmers

With the three agricultural Farm Acts promising to be a game-changer by the Government, it was important to take cognizance of the fact that these Acts were meant to empower the farmer community by enabling them to come out of the shackles of the traders, middlemen, and predatory moneylenders. Providing the required legal framework to facilitate contract farming in agriculture and allied activities was the main objective of The Farmers (Empowerment and Protection) Agreement on Price Assurance and Farm Services Act 2020. Contract farming is a well-known concept worldwide and has been prevalent in India for decades now.

The Act aimed to liberalize agricultural trade and to accord considerable benefit to both parties, ie farmers would have a guaranteed purchaser while uncertainty regarding prices would be minimized. In some cases, the buyer would also be willing to give loans in kind to the farmer, ie seeds, fertilizers, supply of farm inputs, land preparation, technical inputs, etc., thereby moving them away from the clutches of traders who would also act as moneylenders. Furthermore, purchasing firms would have a guaranteed supply of agricultural produce that met their specification with regards to quality, quantity, and time of delivery. The reform would have helped improve market linkages, provided access to new technology, led to improved quality of produce, which in turn would lead to a risk-free higher income and better living standards for the farmer community. It would have helped increase farmers' income, especially the small and marginal farmers as they would get access to better quality inputs, better farm practices, and secured buyers.

The disconnect between what the farmer earns and what the consumer pays has always existed and structural reforms such as the framework for contract manufacturing could go a long way in setting the needle right and providing a win–win solution to both parties. The company entering into a direct contract with farmers would ensure better control on the

Resurgent India. Jagadish Shettigar and Pooja Misra, Oxford University Press. © Oxford University Press 2022.
DOI: 10.1093/oso/9780192866486.003.0015

quality of end products with both stakeholders having an equal interest in its success. Directly contracting with buyers would increase competition leading to higher prices of farm produce for farmers and higher income. The legal framework would have set the foundation for the transformation of Indian agriculture leading to a robust supply chain for businesses and higher income for farmers.

The Act provided a national framework and attempted to bring uniformity in the provisions of contract farming. The Act had three main constituents: Farmer can enter into a written agreement specifying terms and conditions of grade, quality, price, time of supply, etc. The agreement can be for a period of anywhere between one and five years' duration (ie one crop season or one production livestock cycle) and importantly for any variation in terms of the price, existing prices in APMC/e-Nam or electronic portal will be the benchmark. It gave a framework for contract farming by an agreement between the buyer and farmer prior to the production or rearing of the agricultural produce. The Act aimed at liberalizing agricultural trade and providing freedom to the farmers to transact with a buyer of their choice and obviously the highest bidder. It made provisions to guide the contracting parties to prematurely agree on a mutually agreeable price and also took care of open market price fluctuations making it a win–win solution for both parties concerned. There was also a provision for an amicable settlement of disputes through a reconciliation board. It stipulated a transparent process for any dispute settlement with a clause categorically stating that no action could be taken against the agricultural land of a farmer for recovery of any dues.

This Act had brought in its wake a lucrative solution for both the farmers and buyers, ie a farmer could finalize the buyer and the price of his agricultural produce even prior to the harvest while the buyer was assured of the produce and price at the time of harvest itself. Until now, a farmer was prohibited from selling his produce to food processing companies or retailers directly, they were forced to go through a licensed trader for the same. Such a set-up left the farmers at the mercy of the intermediary or middlemen whose objective was to increase their own revenue, thereby not letting the farmer get the rightful price for his crop. This Act would have facilitated 'my crop, my right', improved the bargaining position of farmers and would have helped the farmers get benefits of higher prices for their produce.

While the concept of contract farming as of date in India is still not mainstream, there have been successful models that have evolved over the years. To take an example, seed production is primarily done through contract farming between seed corporations and producer farmers. Another widely quoted example is that of PepsiCo. In 1989 when PepsiCo entered India, the pre-condition set by the Indian Government was that to help farmers improve crop yield by adopting the latest technologies, the company would engage in contract farming. This model was tested by the company by identifying tomato processing as a potential activity. The company witnessed wide-scale success resulting in yield improvement of tomatoes by leaps and bounds, leading to increased yield helping farmers increase their income despite lower prices for the product. Survey results were reflective of the fact that contract farming in Punjab helped increase farmers' income, reduce indebtedness, reduce their exposure in case of risk of crop failure, encouraged them to adopt the latest technologies and use modern farm implements. Rather, PepsiCo had launched a special programme 'Awaaz Mitti Ki', where over the years, they had partnered and supported over 24,000 farmers spread across 13 States of India by providing new technologies, new crop varieties, facilitating financial services to de-risk farming, and introducing sustainable farming practices.

One constraining factor in the case of contract farming is that large corporations, food processing companies, processors, modern retailers are hesitant to engage with hundreds of small and marginal farmers and thus prefer to opt for hiring a middleman called an organizer. On the other hand, farmers too are nervous about being exploited by large organizations. This drawback can be overcome with the help of promoting FPOs/Farmer Producing Corporation (FPCs) to mobilize and coordinate small and marginal farmers to benefit and avail of scales of economy in production and post-production activities.

The Indian Government has released guidelines for setting up and enabling 10,000 FPOs in the country. FPOs can group together small landowners into a co-operative and give a shareholding to the farmers in proportion to their land-holdings (giving them a sense of ownership), thereby making them into an integral stakeholder in the company, which can subsequently enter into a contract with modern retailers. The FPOs would be there to deal with commercial activities related to agricultural produce and would be expected to work and strive for the benefit of farmer shareholders. Thus, the farmers' interest would also not be compromised as being part of an FPO, their bargaining capacity will improve and entering into a legal contract will justify investments made by companies on agri-technologies and farms.

Interestingly, companies such as ITC Limited, which is an integrated agri-business enterprise and has considerable backward linkages in the agricultural sector, had also set its eyes on contract farming. The company, which is one of India's leading organizations in the agricultural sector, is based on strong and enduring partnerships with farmers and has led to farmer empowerment through e-*Choupals* and web-enabled the Indian farmer. This initiative of ITC has developed a large family of 35,000 villages serving over 4 million farmers and agriculturists spread over 10 States of India. The company aims to further expand its business on contract farming and involve FPOs which the Government is actively promoting. While some critics are sceptical that the small and marginal farmers might end up being exploited in a contract farming framework, the country does have successful examples of the farmer community reposing their trust in the very same conglomerates too.

Thus, long-term structural agricultural reforms such as the Farmers (Empowerment and Protection) Agreement on Price Assurance and Farm Services Act 2020 would have gone a long way in transforming the Indian agricultural ecosystem. It was a win–win solution for both farmers and large corporations such as food processing companies, modern retailers coming together and working as ONE leading to the implementation of best practices on the usage of modern-day farm implements and high yielding variety seeds, etc. resulting in bringing in efficiencies of scale for small and marginal farmers thereby increasing their income and assuring corporations of quality, quantity and on-time delivery of the produce. Prematurely locked-in prices and buyers for their produce could have mitigated risks faced by farmers while buyers would have been rest assured of supply and prices at harvest time. It was a much needed and overdue step giving freedom to farmers to sell their produce directly to corporations, exporters, processors, wholesalers, restaurants, modern-day retailers, etc. thereby promoting competition on the part of the buyers to prematurely secure the produce and enabling farmers to get the best price for their produce.

2.5

Socio-Economic Cost of MSP

It is time to debate on the socio-economic cost of making the MSP mandatory. The farmers' demand was to repeal the three farm laws.

World-over, the rationale governing the MSP is that the farmer is assured of a minimum price which ensures that they can recover their cost of production and make a reasonable return on their investment. Thus, the MSP is in order to protect farmer interests when the market crashes to the disadvantage of farmers, as the term itself describes. With eyes closed, one would agree that the Government cannot afford to do away with this scheme. Rather, even after bringing in the ordinance on the farm reforms in May 2020, the government continued the practice of revising the MSP upwards and procurement at a higher MSP had taken place. The Cabinet Committee on Economic Affairs (CCEA) in June 2020 had approved an increase in the MSP for Kharif crops to the tune of 50–83% more than the cost of production. The same was ordained with a perspective of ensuring that farmers get a remunerative price for their produce.

On the flip side, it could also be debated that procuring farm produce at the MSP has become more of an appeasement strategy to cultivate the vote bank. Data is reflective of the fact that procurement of foodgrains by the Food Corporation of India (FCI) in January 2021 had overshot the buffer stock limit and the country had reserves of foodgrains of more than 2.7 times of what was required. This was higher than the country's demand for food security and other welfare schemes, such as the distribution of free wheat and rice under the PM Garib Kalyan Ann Yojna. As of July 1, 2020, FCI had an excess stock of grain piled up with them of at least 50 million metric tonnes. Analysis had shown that even at a conservative estimated cost combined economic cost of excess rice and wheat with the FCI beyond the buffer norm was to the extent of Rs. 1,50,000 crore. Not to forget losses borne by FCI due to mountains of wheat and

Resurgent India. Jagadish Shettigar and Pooja Misra, Oxford University Press. © Oxford University Press 2022.
DOI: 10.1093/oso/9780192866486.003.0016

rice being stocked with them exceeding the total capacity for protected and scientific coverage, amounted to 15% of post-harvest foodgrains.

Interestingly, it was seen that procurement of wheat from Punjab at the MSP amounted to 99.5% of the total stocks offered by farmers for sale. In Madhya Pradesh and Haryana, the Government had sourced nearly 99% and 95% of the market arrivals. So, what will be the consequence of making the floor price into a bill as suggested by agitating farmers and leftist thinkers?

Keeping in mind that as it is farmers from Punjab, Haryana, and Western UP are used to producing wheat and paddy irrespective of the farm produce that the market actually demands with successive governments continuously revising MSP and procuring many times of what is required, it will be a waste of the taxpayers' money. This can be said to be in no way different than the United States resorting to dumping the excess foodgrains supply into the sea in order to balance market forces to the advantage of their farmers. Also, not to forget the fact that apart from increased procurement and enhanced MSP, farmers who felt hurt [naturally] by the reforms also get power and water-free, unlike fellow farmers from other states.

For the sake of argument, in the 2006 procurement season, it was seen that the private sector was offering a minimum of Rs. 100 higher than the existent MSP and FCI had to struggle to procure foodgrains. Thus, in case MSP is made floor price to the market, would the government agency, ie FCI be able to procure foodgrains at least for the welfare schemes? In fact, the government had to resort to muscle power [though unofficially] to be able to procure the required minimum to run the public distribution system (PDS). Failure to do so would mean putting the PDS into jeopardy and consequently adversely impacting the fate of the poor.

If the government agency fails to procure a sufficient amount, how can consumers' interests be protected during the period of market havoc? For instance, if traders resort to hoarding during the period of supply constraints, how would the government come to the rescue of consumers if their buffer stocks are left empty?

Moreover, agriculture would never become a 'buyers market'. It would continue to be a 'sellers market' unlike the industry, which got transformed as a result of the liberalization reforms introduced in 1991. Agricultural productivity will fail to be competitive as compared to international norms. Being the devil's advocate, India is the largest producer of pulses but ranks 138 in the world in terms of productivity levels. Not to forget the environmental cost borne especially due to depleting water belt and stubble burning. Analysts have stated that Punjab's current cropping patterns of growing paddy, which happens to be a water-guzzling crop, is economically unsustainable and groundwater depletion is a serious concern (groundwater level on 92% of Punjab farms has depleted by over 0.60 metres annually, one kilogram of rice requires 2500–5500 litres of water).

Last but not the least, data shows that hardly 6% of farmers are able to access the benefit of MSP. Thus making it a bill will keep a substantial section of small and marginal farmers outside this privilege and lead to socio-economic inequality apart from geographical imbalance. To top it further, rich farmers who are privy to free water and electricity, guaranteed procurement, and dynamic MSP still enjoy a tax-free income, thus further worsening the socio-economic inequality balance between the rich and small and marginal farmers.

2.6
Agricultural Reform: Need for Effective Communication

As and when an attempt had been made to reform the agricultural sector, the government faced strong resistance by vested interests in the guise of farm leaders. Tracing back history, often the incumbent governments were made to roll back the proposal and seldom showed courage to touch this sensitive sector. Prior to Mr. Narendra Modi, Dr. Manmohan Singh in 1991, Mr. Yashwant Sinha in 1999, and Mr. Jaswant Singh in 2003 made an attempt to reform the fertilizer subsidy which was in tandem with the opinion of scientists. But each and every time, the effort was scuttled due to vested interests operating under the mask of so-called Farm Leadership. This proved to be the primary reason why the political wisdom of all Governments in the past cleverly avoided seeing the economic wisdom of introducing the three crucial farm Acts despite experts strongly advocating the same.

Fortunately, the Narendra Modi-led government showed courage in biting the bullet and advocating and introducing the three farm reform bills in Parliament in September 2020. Reasons ascribed to this move by the Government had been varied, ie the incumbent Prime Minister's strong commitment to economic reforms or being a stable government having majority support after three long decades.

One must bear in mind that the Farmers Produce Trade and Commerce (Promotion and Facilitation) Act 2020 did not encroach upon the APMC act, it only promoted free movement of farm produce, inter-state and intra-state trade and allowed them to trade outside the boundaries of deemed markets earmarked under State agricultural market regulations. It encouraged the development of new mandi farm infrastructure, thereby improving market access and reducing logistic costs for farmers. A higher level of competition would have brought a better price, higher income, and revenue for farmers.

Resurgent India. Jagadish Shettigar and Pooja Misra, Oxford University Press. © Oxford University Press 2022.
DOI: 10.1093/oso/9780192866486.003.0017

Looking at the Act proposing contract farming, it is important to consider that many States in the past several decades have passed separate contract farming acts. Rather, large farm holders have seen success in signing up for contract farming with MNCs such as ITC, PepsiCo, etc. Taking a cue from the same, the Farmers (Empowerment and Protection) Agreement on Price Assurance and Farm Services Act 2020 set the ground and encouraged small farmers to come together by forming of FPOs (thereby increasing their bargaining capacity) and availing of economies of scale in production and post-production activities. With the support and guidance of the contract farming MNC, it would have helped small and marginal farmers reap benefits of higher price, higher income, low interest rates on loans, improving crop yield by adopting the latest technologies, and use of modern farm implements.

Looking at the ironical situation: Two major political parties have gone to the voters in the 2019 elections with a commitment to amend the APMC act. However, the major opposition party was seen subsequently opposing the move. Not to forget the fact that critics had stated that the liberalization era for the farmers had just dawned with these three farm reformative Acts. Thus, one cannot fathom how enabling farmers to have direct access to markets and breaking the monopoly of mandis was against the well-being of farmers? How would bringing of transparency in the agricultural sector, opening up market access, and giving them the benefit of 'my crop, my right' be against the interests of farmers?

Does it mean that the so-called farm leaders are keen to depend on middlemen to sell their produce for them? In reality, whose cause were these people fighting for? Farmers or middlemen?

Surprisingly, even left parties were actively backing the ongoing agitation. Was this agitation, in reality, to protect the domain of middlemen and political leaders relying on commission is a question that all need to ponder on?

With regards to demand for clubbing the MSP in the laws, throughout the world, it has been a practice by the governments to come to the aid of farmers in case of market failure through procurement at MSP. Rather, the Prime Minister had repeatedly reinforced the fact that even with these Acts, the practice of procuring farm produce at MSP would not be done away with. On the flip side, if including MSP is a sensible commitment, why had the Congress government in Rajasthan and Chhattisgarh not gone ahead despite the public commitment by the central leadership?

It is equally true that the ruling party had also not done enough to reach out and communicate with the farmers. Apart from the Prime Minister, the party cadre should also have moved into the forefront and discussed the pros and cons of the Acts at the ground level. In fact, the party should have used this golden opportunity to widen its support base. Being the devil's advocate, was the not so enthusiastic approach due to the ruling party's DNA being traditionally a trader's party?

Farmers who had reached the capital might have been misguided by vested interests with a narrow political motive. Without standing on prestige or protocol, the government should have directly engaged the agitating farmers and convinced them how the three farm laws were in their interests.

If needed, the government should have also resorted to engaging through experts and social leaders. This was a historic moment to defeat the design of the vested interests who had been thriving for decades and wrongly reaping the benefits owed to innocent farmers.

2.7

Power Sector Reforms

With the Indian economy having set its eyes on and aspiring to be a USD5 trillion economy by 2024–25, there are short-term and long-term structural reforms that the Government has been initiating and working towards. One such key reform on which there is still work pending is that related to electricity and power. An energetic and sustainable power sector is needed to stimulate an economy badgered with the woes and adverse impact of COVID-19. Having an uninterrupted power supply is a key requirement for all sectors of the economy to function smoothly, be it industry, agriculture, or services. The Electricity Act, 2003 and the Amendment Act, 2020 sought to resuscitate investments and promote growth in tandem with the vision of the Prime Minister, Mr. Narendra Modi.

The Electricity Act, 2003 covered generation, transmission, and distribution in power and delicensed power generation. Statistics for FY2019–20 was indicative of the fact that India still suffers from a power supply deficit. Though the deficit has considerably narrowed in the past decade, the country still has some way to go to achieve the status of an economy with 'power for all'.

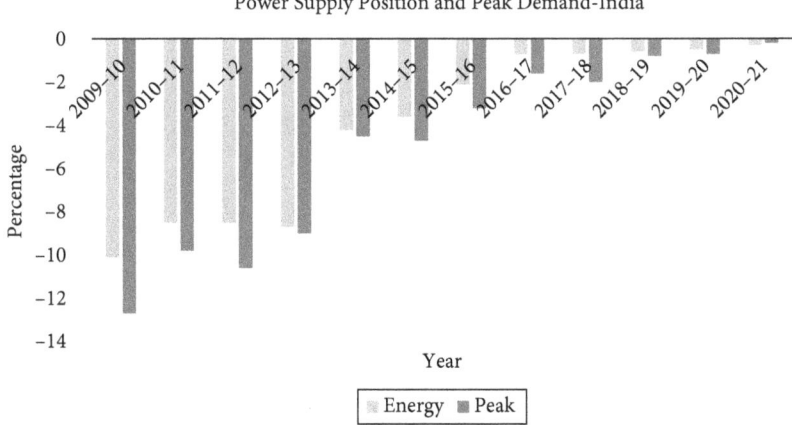

Power Supply Position and Peak Demand-India

*Upto September 2020 (Provisional). *Source*: CEA.

Resurgent India. Jagadish Shettigar and Pooja Misra, Oxford University Press. © Oxford University Press 2022.
DOI: 10.1093/oso/9780192866486.003.0018

The objective of the Electricity Act, 2003 was to make the electricity sector competitive, ensure consumer centricity and promote ease of doing business. The Act provided for electrification of rural areas, licence-free generation and distribution, compulsory metering, and rigorous penalties for theft of electricity. It sought to privatize discoms as they were perceived to be the weakest link in the value chain. Discoms are known to be riddled with low revenue collections, high cost of buying from power generating companies, inadequate hike in tariffs, and mounting dues from government departments. This has resulted in mounting aggregate technical and commercial losses (AT & C losses), which have plagued the power sector. Data given by the Power Finance Corporation in 2018–19 showed that power distribution utilities recorded AT & C losses of 22% during 2018–19. AT & C losses comprise a combination of technical loss, theft, billing inefficiency, payment default, and collection inefficiency. Thus, the need of the hour is to help power distribution companies pare their losses and effectively monitor electricity consumption.

India's electricity distribution reforms scheme aims to cut electricity losses below 12%. The scheme aims to ensure an uninterrupted power supply and negate tariff gaps. This can be effectively done by moving ahead on the path spelt out by the Government even in the May 2020 stimulus measures announced by the Finance Minister, Ms. Nirmala Sitharaman, of privatization of power distribution in Union Territories. Not to forget to move fast on the trajectory of loss reduction, privatization of discoms in States should also be undertaken. The Central Government should work hand in hand with State Governments and approach them for a public–private partnership model on the lines of states like Odisha and Delhi.

Trends in AT & C Losses

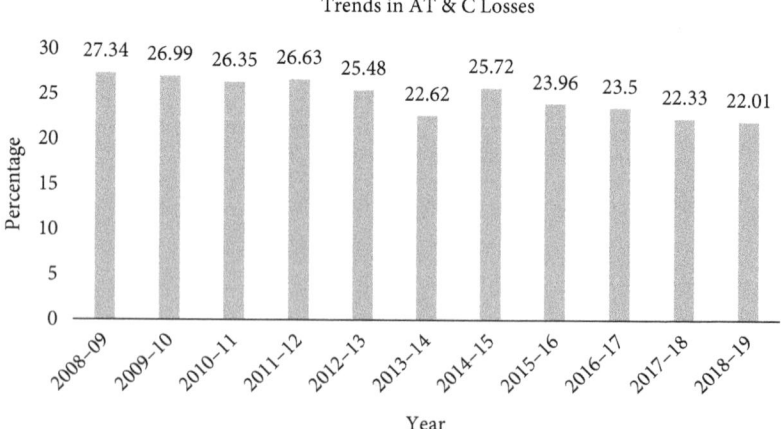

Source: PFC's Report on Performance of State Power Utilities 2018–19

Private utilities are serving 10% of Indian consumers, largely restricted to urban areas. To take a case in point: Delhi privatized three of its discoms in 2002; however, in 2016, Central Government-owned NTPC, which generates power, threatened to cut off the power supply to two units of the private discoms of Delhi due to delay in payments. This pointed to financial distress gripping private discoms. Data showed that the three discoms, ie BSEL YPL, BSES RPL, and Tata Power Delhi Distribution Ltd. were saddled with over Rs. 36,000 crore of power purchase cost yet to be recovered. This was due to the fact that the power sector being a regulated sector and supplying an essential item to consumers, does not enjoy the freedom of fixing the selling price based on the current cost. Though the State Electricity Regulatory Authority is semi-judicial in terms of power vested, it has not been allowed to function with full autonomy. Earlier it was alleged to have tilted in favour of the private distributors and now it seems tariff decisions are being taken without taking into account the cost of power purchase from the power generating companies.

However, one should not forget that the function of any regulator is to maintain a balance between the service provider and consumers and the balance certainly cannot be titled towards the consumer alone. While the Electricity Act mandates recovery of the incurred cost of supply of power, this does not happen on the ground. Delays and deferments have become a way of life. The focal point of concern is that rationalization of tariffs is required. The Electricity Regulatory Authority should function as a semi-judicial authority and power tariff should be decided by striking a balance between interests of both distributors and users.

Focus also has to be brought on electricity losses due to technical inefficiency. Technical losses happen due to the resistance of wires and equipment as electricity passes through them. Some loss is inevitable, but old and worn-out transmission wires add to the problem. Thus, the authorities should take it upon themselves and replace the wires to minimize losses which are an outcome of technical inefficiency. The Government should focus on modernizing the aging distribution infrastructure. Another point that needs to be addressed is that of untimely receipt of subsidy reimbursement from the authorities, which has further weighed down on the losses faced by the distribution companies.

Losses incurred by discoms due to theft of electricity is another worrisome point which needs to be addressed. Ways and means adopted by consumers such as bypassing the meter, tampering the meter, bribing of utility officials, resisting installations of smart meters is unethical in nature, and the consumer should be penalized for the same. A societal change has to be brought about, which discourages any such unethical means adopted by consumers and makes them conscious of their moral responsibility to pay up for products and services consumed by them.

The financial bailout of discoms is not the solution or a cure-all for losses incurred by them. Discoms have been a strain on the Indian power sector and the Government has time and again bailed out beleaguered state electricity distribution companies with the latest being that of set-ting aside Rs. 90,000 crore liquidity injection to help discoms get back on their feet amidst the adverse impact of the coronavirus crisis. The Government needs to increase competition in this sector by encouraging private participation and penalizing discoms for an unnecessary power cut and thereby formulate a long-term plan to address the long-ranging issues. Private power companies generating power should be allowed to sell directly to industrial consumers as they might be in an advantageous position of being able to generate power economically. Giving out mul-tiple licences for the distribution of power for a single area will encourage competition and reduce the deadweight loss faced by this sector due to its close to monopoly market structure. Introduction of common distribu-tion cables facilitating the supply of power by more than one distributor can facilitate providing of choice to the consumer. An idea worth giving a thought to is: Can consumers be allowed to port their power supplier?

2.8

Fiscal Measures to Revive Demand

The Indian economy was seen fast settling to a 'New Normal' with Unlock 2.0 effective 1 July 2020, relaxing the night curfew timings, provision of additional domestic flights and trains and more activities being permitted in a calibrated manner outside of containment zones. The Government had progressively moved from—'जान है तो जहान है' (Jaan hai to Jahaan hai ie India can achieve heights only when its citizens are healthy) to 'जान भी जहान भी' (Jaan bhi Jahaan bhi ie Lives as well as livelihoods). With the pandemic having negatively impacted countries globally, the International Monetary Fund (IMF), in its revised projections of June 2020, had predicted that the Indian economy would contract 4.5% in FY21 as against the optimistic forecast announced of 1.9% growth in April 2020. The reason cited for the revised downward forecast had been the pandemic led severe nationwide extended lockdown which had led to supply chain disruptions, massive job losses with unemployment numbers in India rising to 27.1% (as per CMIE) in May 2020, resulting in loss of income, lower consumption demand and weaker consumer sentiment. Interestingly, CMIE data showed that with Unlock 1.0 happening, unemployment numbers ending 7 July 2020 were at 9.19%, nearer to pre-COVID levels. Also, a better than normal monsoon had resulted in a positive impact on the agricultural sector, which was forecasted to improve by 3.0% approximately and the services sector was expected to increase by 4.4%. These two sectors contributed more than 70% to the overall GDP of the country. The demand in the FMCG sector was returning to pre-COVID levels and the rural market was almost intact as per the Nielsen survey reports.

In response to the economy being halted abruptly in its track of economic growth with the lockdown announced on 25 March 2020 and with a viewpoint of being able to provide a kickstart to the economy on 8 June 2020 with Unlock1.0 happening, the call by the Prime Minister, Mr. Narendra Modi was for the citizens to aim for being 'आत्मनिर्भर', ie

Resurgent India. Jagadish Shettigar and Pooja Misra, Oxford University Press. © Oxford University Press 2022.
DOI: 10.1093/oso/9780192866486.003.0019

self-reliant and 'Vocal for Local'. Some of the policy announcements to provide the much-needed boost to the Indian economy were:

The Government of India had already announced a stimulus package to the tune of Rs. 20 lakh crores (equivalent to 10% of the country's GDP). Some termed the stimulus provided by the Government as being tepid compared to other emerging economies and far lesser than those announced by advanced economies, while others viewed it as a reformative fiscal package. We would agree with the latter, ie the stimulus package was a reformative one that would have a far-reaching impact in the medium to long term.

The first stimulus was announced by the Union Finance Minister, Ms. Nirmala Sitharaman, on 26 March 2020, which included free foodgrains for three months for 80 crore of India's poorest section (extended in the second stimulus for another three months), one-time transfer of Rs. 2000 to 7 crore farmers, Rs. 500 transferred to 20.05 crore women Jan Dhan account holders for three months to be able to deal with the COVID pandemic. So while on the one hand, it was a case of free foodgrains/money transferred to the poorer section of society, on the other hand, one needs to bear in mind that the Government had sourced the foodgrains and thereby started the demand cycle of growth. This was followed by measures being announced by the RBI to infuse liquidity in the financial circular flow. Subsequently, the Finance Minister announced a five-part stimulus package between 13 May and 17 May 2020 and pronounced other far-reaching policy reforms for the economy such as amount to be paid under MGNREGA being increased to Rs. 202 per day from Rs. 182; an additional allocation of Rs. 40,000 crore for this scheme (this was in addition to the Budgetary provision). This would again enable extra income in the hands of people from the lower strata of society, thereby fuelling up consumption levels in the economy.

For the Indian farmers, there had been sweeping policy changes made, leading to critics stating that liberalization for the Indian Industry happened in 1991, but for the Indian farmers, liberalization had just set in via three ordinances, ie amendment to the APMC Act, which was to enable farmers to be able to sell their produce outside the mandis giving them the benefit of 'my crop, my right', Essential Commodities Act, 1955 focusing on lifting the restrictions on commodities such as cereals, pulses, onions, etc. Farmers (Empowerment and Protection) Agreement on

Price Assurance and Farm Services Ordinance, which provided a charter for farmers to engage in contract farming with large food multinational companies leading to a scenario of 'One India, One Agricultural Market'. The advantage for farmers being able to access markets directly (without the intervention of the middlemen and thereby breaking the monopoly of APMCs) would help them gain the benefits of higher prices for their produce. This would lead to increased income in the hands of these farmers, which in turn would result in increased demand for products and services. Also, with the infrastructure of cold chain and refrigerated transportation being encouraged to be built by the Government, the farmers would be in a position to command better prices in the medium to long term.

To top it further, on 30 June 2020, the Prime Minister, Mr. Narendra Modi, had announced that under the Pradhan Mantri Garib Kalyan Ann Yojna, 80 crore people would be receiving 5 kg free ration and 1 kg dal per month till November end 2020. Under the aegis of 'One Nation, One Ration Card', the benefits of this scheme would be derived by the lower economic strata, including the migrant workers and their families.

With economic activities grinding to a halt due to the pandemic, COVID-19 had dealt a double whammy to a large section of the Indian population. It had resulted in the loss of cash and income, especially for people at the bottom of the pyramid, and to further worsen the situation, migrant workers had also lost access to food and shelter. Critics stated that the policy measures announced by the Government were largely supply-side measures (such as FDI limit in defence manufacturing increased to 74%; Rs. 3 lakh crore to be given as collateral-free automatic loan to MSMEs, etc.) and were inadequate.

As per critics, it was demand-side measures that were needed to be able to provide the requisite boost and reverse the contractionary momentum of the Indian economy. As stated earlier, the Government had worked on this front too, by allocating Rs. 50,000 crore for implementation of public infrastructure works across six States and 116 districts being earmarked for the migrant workers returning home; Government bearing the EPF contribution for three months for those earning upto Rs.15,000 per month, reducing EPF contribution from 12% to 10% for three months for those in a higher income bracket thus leading to more cash available in the hands of the individual to spend, etc. Thus, once the economy got a kickstart due to the above demand increasing measures, it would have a multiplier effect on the entire economy. It should also be contemplated that prior to the COVID-19 pandemic, the Indian economy was already facing a demand constraint.

Thus, in such a scenario, giving out cash handouts to the poorest section of society was not the answer to the revival of consumption demand. Proponents of demand-side measures claimed that providing more cash handouts would increase private consumption demand in the economy. This would restart the circular flow of goods and services and consumption and production would gain momentum. However, in place of giving hard cash and thereby starting the demand cycle, by providing foodgrains, the Government was boosting demand on behalf of this section of society which in turn would kickstart the revival of the economy.

Cash doleout would lead to additional Government expenditure and with revenue collections plummeting due to lower tax collections during the Lockdown, it would have exerted pressure on an already rising fiscal deficit number of the Indian economy. The Government would have had little option but to ask RBI to monetize a part of the fiscal deficit. Was monetizing of fiscal deficit the need of the hour?

The concept of monetization of fiscal deficit had been abandoned two decades ago with big-ticket reforms enabling the citizens to partake of single-digit inflation since then. With the FRBM Act 2003 in place, the focus of this Act was to bar RBI from participating in primary issuance of Government Securities since 1 April 2006. There is an escape clause which states that RBI can subscribe to the primary issue of Central Government securities in case the fiscal deficit target is exceeded on 'grounds of national security, act of war, national calamity, collapse of agriculture severely affecting farm output and incomes, structural reforms in the economy with unanticipated fiscal implications, decline in real output growth of a quarter by at least three per cent points below its average of the previous four quarters'. The permissible deviation in the Act is to an extent of 0.5%. However, this escape clause had already been invoked by the Government on 1 February 2020 prior to the COVID-19 pandemic. To further add to the already existing woes in the economy, monetization of fiscal deficit would also lead to increased money supply resulting in inflationary pressures.

A contrarian view was that increased Government expenditure can be netted out by increased direct taxes. But, one should bear in mind that increased taxes would lead to lesser income in the hands of taxpayers, thereby once again negatively impacting consumption levels. It would lead to a situation of the trade-off between consumption levels increasing for essential items if cash doleouts were given as against increased discretionary spending by the taxpayers. The Government, in this case, needed to choose between which of the two was the lesser devil?

Another fact that needed to be looked at and considered was that the full-blown impact of the pandemic had not been experienced by the economy. With Unlock happening in phases, people contracting the virus were increasing by leaps and bounds. With the increased fiscal deficit already having put the Government in a corner, was this the right time for the cash handout to be given, or should the Government have waited and watched for some time. Rather, as the stimulus package had already permitted delayed tax payments, if the economy did not revive fast enough, one would have also needed to consider if the Government would need to cut tax rates, including GST and put more money in the hands of people.

So, were cash handouts needed or would it not have been wiser for the Government to use the limited fiscal space to be able to facilitate schemes such as Garib Kalyan Rozgaar Abhiyan and expedite implementation of public infrastructure works and those related to augmentation of livelihood opportunities. In our perspective, in lieu of cash doelout, giving of free ration coupled with the Ayushman Bharat Scheme (free health coverage) and the Pradhan Mantri Awas Yojna (housing for all) was an adequate measure to help this section of the population sustain and survive. Moreover, by providing foodgrains, the Government was boosting demand on behalf of this section of society which in turn would kickstart the revival of the economy. This would also ensure that the limited fiscal space was available for the Government to invest in infrastructure projects which in turn would generate employment for the lower-income strata and enable them to sustain their livelihood. Concomitantly, shouldn't one appreciate the fact that the Government had kept the burden on taxpayers at a minimum?

The million-dollar questions thus were: Keeping the available limited fiscal space in mind, should the Government have given out cash doleouts to people at the bottom of the pyramid or used it for implementation of public infrastructure works and those related to augmentation of livelihood opportunities was a better solution?

If the economy was not able to reverse the contractionary trend fast enough, shouldn't the Government have cut tax rates and increased money in the hands of people leading to increased consumption of essentials and propelling discretionary spending, thereby giving the necessary boost to consumer durables and electronics, automobiles, apparel, luxury products, etc.

In the post-COVID-19 scenario with productive activity in the economy coming to a standstill both demand and supply-side measures implemented hand in hand were the need of the hour. Thus, the Government had rightly strategized for a mixed bag of stimulus to stabilize and refuel India's economic growth track and also adequately provided for the lesser strata of society, ie free foodgrains, free healthcare facilities, housing for all, and employment generation through public infrastructure works.

2.9

Credit Disbursal versus Green Shoots

The coronavirus pandemic had sent financial markets worldwide into a tailspin. In order to provide relief from its adverse impact, an amalgamation of monetary, fiscal, and regulatory interventions were announced by the Indian Government along with the RBI. A slew of measures were initiated in the backdrop of increasing geopolitical tensions, an overleveraged non-financial sector and economic losses —an anticipated fallout of the virus. The corrective measures were initiated to mitigate the negative impact of the novel coronavirus on demand as well as the supply side of the economy and to ensure close to normal functioning of the financial markets.

The RBI had in no way failed to respond to the unprecedented economic crisis due to the pandemic. A series of monetary measures were announced to strike a balance between financial stability, preserving the economic value of businesses and protecting depositors. It was done to shield the macroeconomic and financial environment from the negative influence of the virus and mitigate its bearing on credit demand and asset quality of scheduled commercial banks. The easing of financial conditions was done to boost system-level liquidity and sector-specific funding. However, it needs to be investigated if the deployment of conventional and unconventional tools that the RBI had resorted to, for restoring financial stability had yielded the desired results?

Analysis of credit and deposit growth numbers showed that deposit growth had been on the rise and clearly outweighed credit growth numbers in the Indian economy. Rather credit growth numbers in March 2020 were at 5.9% as against deposit growth numbers at 8.6%. This brings to light that against the backdrop of a weak macroeconomic environment, there could be a risk aversion by banks and a growing preference for them to park the excess money in safer and less risky instruments or alternately demand for credit by businesses and corporates as planned by RBI had really not taken off.

Resurgent India. Jagadish Shettigar and Pooja Misra, Oxford University Press. © Oxford University Press 2022.
DOI: 10.1093/oso/9780192866486.003.0020

As per data under the reverse repo window, there had been a dramatic increase in deposits by banks with RBI from Rs. 41,214 crores as of 1 January 2020 to over Rs. 6.3 lakhs crore on 28 May 2020. Was this reflective of the fact that businesses that had been facing the onslaught of liquidity stress and tightening of financial conditions amidst disruptions of cash flows and working cycles were still not borrowing?

On further investigation of the credit and deposit growth numbers, it can be seen that deposit growth (8.6% and 10.3% in March 2020 and on 25 September 2020, respectively) clearly outweighed credit growth (5.9% and 5.3% in March 2020 and as on 25 September 2020) in the Indian banking system. The inability to lend had become so dominant that banks had huge amounts of cash lying unutilized. This clearly outlined a lack of credit-offtake in the Indian financial system.

A micro-level analysis of bank credit growth, time deposit growth and demand deposit growth numbers showed that bank credit which was already on a decline in Q3 and Q4 of 2019–20 had witnessed a further downswing. Rather, the difference between deposit and credit growth numbers for India had widened even more during the pandemic. Contrary to RBI infusing liquidity in the financial system, bank credit growth which on 27 March 2020 was at 6.3%, saw a fall to 5.3% as of 25 September 2020. It only witnessed a temporary increase to approximately 7% in April 2020. So, the pertinent question was: Were businesses and corporates not engaging in borrowing from Banks?

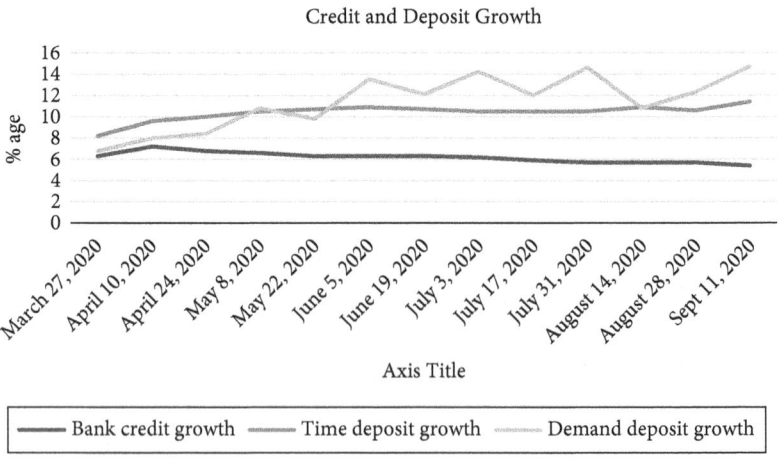

Credit and Deposit Growth

Axis Title

——— Bank credit growth ——— Time deposit growth ——— Demand deposit growth

Source: Reserve Bank of India

On the flip side, deposit growth numbers y-o-y on account of private commercial banks had shown a steady upswing during the pandemic. Growth in time deposits had increased from 8.2% y-o-y as of 27 March 2020 to 10.3% y-o-y as of 25 September 2020. Additionally, demand deposits had also shown growth from 6.8% y-o-y as of 27 March 2020 to 11.3% y-o-y as of 25 September 2020. One must be cognizant that this growth in time and demand deposits had happened despite the lowering of interest rates by the lenders on term deposits and savings bank accounts. In the backdrop of the pandemic, was this reflective of the fact that the precautionary savings motive was being highly dominant as against the transaction and speculative motives of money?

On further investigation of the deployment of gross bank credit by major sectors, it was observed that non-food bank credit growth was on a downswing. In July 2020, non-food bank credit growth stood at 6.7% (same as in June 2020) lower than the growth of 11.4% in July 2019. August data indicated no different results. On a y-o-y basis, in August 2020, non-food bank credit growth decelerated to 6.0% from 9.8% in August 2019. Credit growth to industry decelerated to 0.5% in August 2020 from 3.9% in August 2019 and to 0.8% in July 2020 as against 6.1% growth in July 2019.

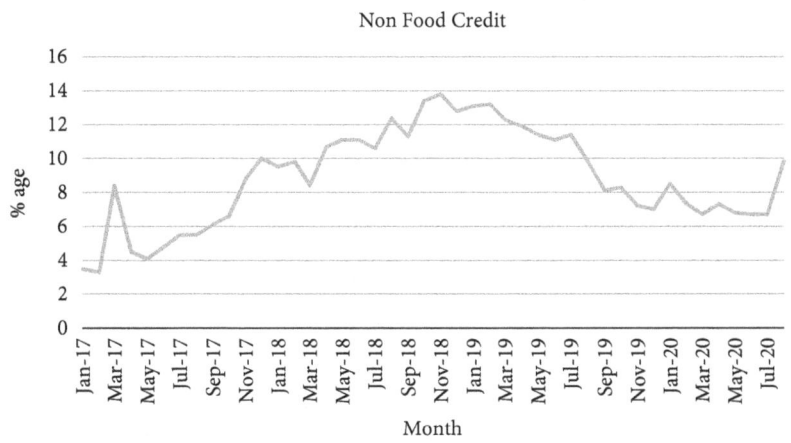

Non Food Credit

Source: Reserve Bank of India

The decline in demand for non-food bank credit growth reflected a decelerating demand by industry and coincided with declining demand in the economy and falling capacity utilizations. On the flip side, thrusting money into banks and financial institutions without boosting demand could have resulted in an increase in bad loans and non-performing assets (NPAs). The excess liquidity in the financial system could have resulted in a huge social cost and led the country into a liquidity trap with a large increase in money supply and not much use of it by corporates, businesses, and households.

Thus, the pertinent question that one needed to ask was: Was credit growth declining due to a lagged effect of a weakened demand being faced by corporates? Had supply-side interventions been able to clear supply-side bottlenecks in the Indian economy and generate demand? Signs of green-shoots observed in the month of September did indicate a revival of the economy. Purchasing Managers' Index (PMI) at 56.8 was the highest in eight and half years; GST collections at Rs. 95,480 crores were the post-pandemic record collections and also 4.0% higher than the corresponding month of the last year; E-way bills at 57.4 million set a record; power demand at 169,000 MU showed a 4.8% increase. Importantly, the number of persons seeking support from MGNREGS at 29 million was the lowest since May, which was a definite sign of improvement in employment opportunities. The FPIs would not have become net buyers of Indian debt instruments after 11 months without seeing a positive signal in the Indian economy.

Pick-up in consumer demand was likely to get further intensified during Q3 and Q4 of FY21. In this highly uncertain economic environment, retailers had pinned their hopes on Q3 festive demand, ie from Diwali to the onset of the New Year 2021, to revive flagging sales. The festive season typically accounted for 20–30% of the annual sales and businesses were waiting with bated breath for the season to yield positive results for them. Attractive offers were being lined up to influence consumer demand and the pedal had been pressed on aggressive promotions and advertising campaigns. To be able to bring cheer and respite from the pandemic-linked slumber, it was time for companies to woo back customers through behavioural nudges.

However, the baffling question here was the mismatch between RBI's noble intentions in facilitating the availability of liquidity vis-à-vis the corporate sector's unenthusiastic response in availing the offer. Did it mean that the corporate sector was flush with cash and hence did not need to rely too much on the banking system? In a way, it was a good sign now that the government borrowings had begun to expand horizontally as well as vertically.

2.10

Viability of Banking Institutions

With the COVID-19 pandemic having negatively impacted countries both in terms of healthcare and economic activity, banking regulators worldwide had announced monetary measures to increase liquidity in the economy. One such monetary measure announced by the RBI was that of the availability of moratorium on repayment of debt for businesses and individuals. This loan moratorium facility would help businesses sustain in times of financial stress caused by a disruption in economic activity due to the coronavirus pandemic.

Initially, the moratorium facility was applicable from 1 March 2020 for a period of three months. Subsequently, keeping in mind the grave situation existing still, the same was extended for another three months upto 31 August 2020. However, in its Monetary Policy Committee (MPC) meeting on 4–6 August 2020, RBI had announced that the moratorium facility would not be extended beyond 31 August 2020 and banks would be allowed for a one-time restructuring of loans of corporates and MSMEs. While appreciating the monetary measures announced by the regulatory authority in the light of the pandemic, it was also imperative that RBI kept the best interest of depositors in mind and came up with an appropriate policy response. On the flip side, the million-dollar question is: Had RBI studied the implications that these measures could have on the financial health and well-being of depositors?

The pandemic had forced countries worldwide to re-think, re-strategize, and thereby ease the financial burden on businesses and livelihoods. The objective of the moratorium was to offer temporary respite to the borrowers. With a viewpoint of not impacting credit scores, along with the moratorium facility, a freeze in customer ratings of people

Resurgent India. Jagadish Shettigar and Pooja Misra, Oxford University Press. © Oxford University Press 2022.
DOI: 10.1093/oso/9780192866486.003.0021

benefitting from the loan had also been proposed. Interestingly, people of reckoning from the financial world such as Rajnish Kumar (SBI Chairman) and Deepak Parekh (HDFC Chairman) were of the view that RBI should not extend the interest moratorium beyond August 2020 and that banks be permitted for a one-time restructuring on loans. It was important to bear in mind that any extension in the moratorium beyond the period of six months could have negatively impacted the credit behaviour of the borrowers and resulted in rising delinquency situations.

With economic activity gathering pace, post announcement of Unlocks temporary measures would not have been a viable solution to address the cashflow problem of borrowers. A more durable solution was required to take care of the financial stress of viable borrowers who were unduly impacted by the 'Black Swan event'. One-time restructuring of loans would allow banks to provide respite to the debtors by giving them tailor-made solutions which would take cognizance of specific issues based on their needs—An any day more viable and durable solution in comparison to a broad-brush approach in dealing with the issue.

The Financial Stability Report (FSR) of RBI, released in July 2020, stated that the implications of monetary relief measures on the financial health of commercial banks were yet to be ascertained. The aim of the report was to gauge the degree and nature of financial risk and its implications which could have a bearing on financial institutions, financial markets, and the macroeconomic environment of the country. The report based on stress tests assessed the resilience of the financial sector. As per the FSR, the pandemic had led to a deterioration in the macroeconomic and financial environment of the country and negatively impacted asset quality, demand for credit, capital adequacy, and profitability of banks.

The FSR had presented a grim picture of the status of NPAs in India. The challenging situation posed by COVID-19 as per RBI could have resulted in the Gross Non-Performing Assets (GNPAs) increasing to 12.5% by March 2021 as against 8.5% in March 2020. There was apprehension that GNPAs could even worsen to 14.7% by March 2021 if proper checks and balances were not put in place.

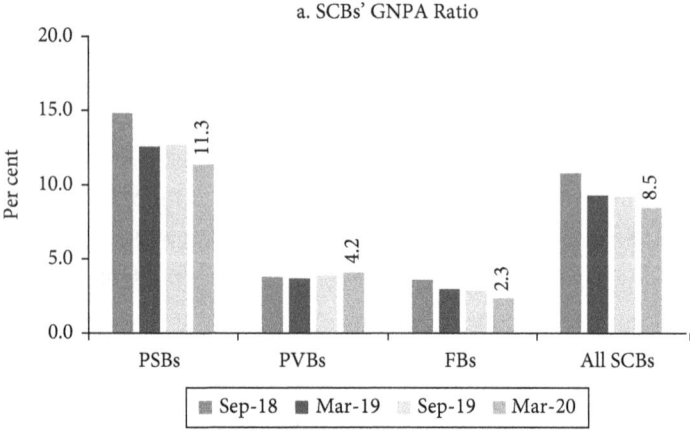

a. SCBs' GNPA Ratio

Source: RBI's Financial Stability Report, 2020

To add to the already prevalent worrisome scenario of GNPAs, the picture painted by credit and deposit growth numbers in the financial sector of the Indian economy was also not bright. The weakened credit growth prior to the pandemic due to the demand slowdown in the Indian economy had dropped to 5.9% in March 2020 and had remained muted upto June 2020. Decline in credit growth numbers reflected that borrowings by individuals and corporates were on the decline even prior to the pandemic and the situation had not improved even with a decline in lending rates and a fall in the cost of borrowings from banks. This showed the absence of financial deepening and normal cyclical upturns.

Also, on further investigating the credit and deposit growth numbers, it could be seen that deposit growth (8.6% in March 2020) clearly outweighed credit growth (5.9% in March 2020) in the Indian economy. This brings to light that against the backdrop of a weak macroeconomic environment, there was a risk aversion by banks and a growing preference for them to park the excess money in safer and less risky instruments. The inability to lend had become so dominant that banks had huge amounts of cash parked with them. Data showed that there was a dramatic rise in deposits with RBI by banks under the reverse repo route from a few thousand crores in January and February (Rs. 41,214 crores as of 1 January 2020) to over Rs. 6.3 lakhs crore on 28 May 2020. This situation was highly detrimental to the bank's profitability. Would the lack of credit-offtake have resulted in banks easing lending rules? In such a scenario, wouldn't banks have been less stringent in terms of evaluation of project viabilities of loans applied for resulting in weak loans being sanctioned at the outset itself was a thought worth contemplating?

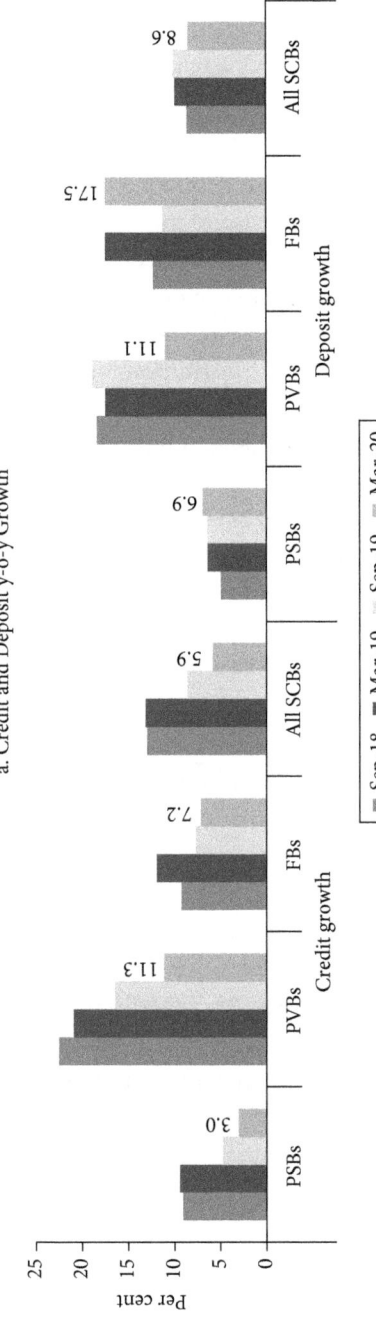

a. Credit and Deposit y-o-y Growth

Source: RBI's Financial Stability Report, 2020

On the flip side, deposit growth numbers y-o-y on account of private commercial banks showed a moderated growth in 2019–20, which subsequently improved slightly in the first few months of 2020. The same was reflective of a weakened savings capacity on account of the pandemic as many had lost their means of living due to the lockdown while a large number of people were forced to accept pay cuts by employers. The situation had not improved still despite unlocking on account of the pandemic. Thus, it was worth considering that in a continuous scenario of declining interest rates and increasing GNPAs, would banks have been able to attract depositors? Rather, would depositors want to keep their hard-earned money in financial institutions which they knew were not able to give them an adequate return in terms of interest? For the majority of investors, declining interest rates on deposits had made them an unattractive investment option. To worsen it, would these depositors want to invest their money with banks that were reporting higher NPAs? Understandably any unprecedented situation requires out-of-the-box thinking and out-of-line strategies, but it was worth rationalizing if the fall-out of loan moratorium and increasing NPAs was just to depositors?

In light of loan moratorium and one-time loan restructuring, NPA risks of banks were sky-high, and to further add to the woes, monetary measures such as collateral-free credit availability schemes for MSMEs continued to exert pressure. Thus, would it not be right to say that while RBI was providing monetary stimulus and ease of borrowing facilities to borrowers, they also needed to focus on the impact that this would have had on depositors and existing lending rules and regulations. In fact, attracting deposits was crucial for the very sustenance of the banking business. It is worth recollecting, here, how modern banks had learnt the practice of banking from goldsmiths. Initially, people used to deposit surplus money with goldsmiths at a fee due to safety provided by the latter, however, once the goldsmiths saw a business opportunity and started lending to the needy, they felt the importance of attracting deposits by paying interest rates to the latter.

2.11

Are Negative Interest Rates on the Horizon?

The pandemic had brought in its wake a new norm of lowered consumption levels and deepened cash conservation. It had resulted in an increasing trend in unemployment levels, massive job layoffs, and demand disruption. The virus had brought economies to a halt abruptly in its trajectory of economic growth, leading to a contractionary performance in Q1 FY2020–21 for all countries worldwide. With the Unlock, the Indian economy did initially witness signs of green shoots but localized lockdowns had proved to be the dampener. The grim picture being painted on the wall had ensured that people were refraining from discretionary spending and indulging only in the purchase of essentials. The foremost thought in the minds of one and all was to engage in the precautionary motive of money and conserve cash.

To provide relief from the onslaught of the pandemic, the Central Government and RBI did announce a slew of fiscal and monetary measures. The continuous effort on the part of the regulatory authorities was to strike a balance between financial stability, preserve the financial and economic value of businesses and protect depositors simultaneously. However, a micro-level investigation of bank deposit and credit growth numbers showed that the difference between deposit and credit growth numbers for India had widened even more during the pandemic. Even with RBI infusing ample liquidity in the financial system of the economy through its monetary policy stimulus, bank credit growth which on 27 March 2020 was at 6.3%, saw a declining trend to 5.4% as of 11 September 2020. Furthermore, deposit growth numbers y-o-y had shown a steady upswing. Growth in time deposits had seen an increasing trend from 8.2% y-o-y as of 27 March 2020 to 11.4% y-o-y as of 11 September 2020.

Resurgent India. Jagadish Shettigar and Pooja Misra, Oxford University Press. © Oxford University Press 2022.
DOI: 10.1093/oso/9780192866486.003.0022

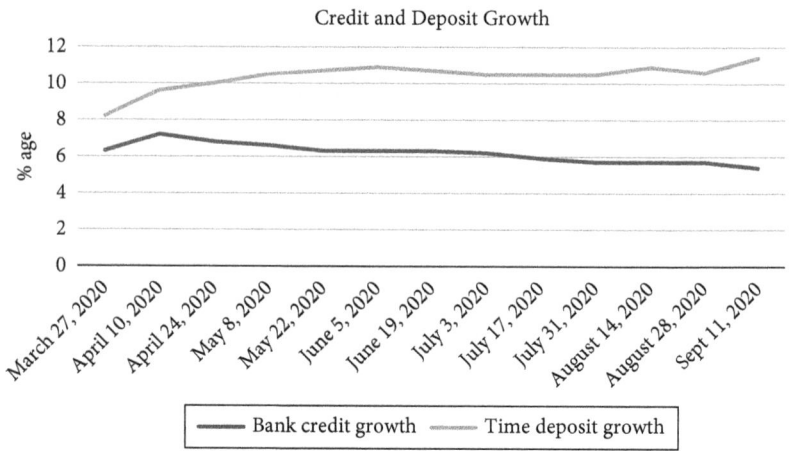

Credit and Deposit Growth

Source: Reserve Bank of India

Taking into account the fixed deposit interest rate in India and inflation numbers, even with real interest rates close to zero, were depositors in these unprecedented times more keen to focus on the precautionary motive of money? With SBI interest rates ranging from 3.30% to 6.50% for 7 days to 10 year period and Consumer Price Index (CPI) inflation well above the 4–6% bracket at 7.34% in September 2020, real interest rates were close to zero and bordering around the negative territory. The relevant point was that positive interest rates are generally the enabler for depositors to gravitate towards banks and engage in higher savings. However, the virus had resulted in a paradoxical situation of depositors saving more money even in the face of negative real interest rates.

Additionally, one must be conscious of the fact that as of 11 September 2020, the credit deposit ratio of banks in India had fallen to a low of 71.8% from 76.4% as of 27 March 2020. Given the fact that CRR and SLR rates as of 11 September 2020 were 4% and 18%, respectively, funds available with banks to lend were to the extent of 79% of the net demand and time deposits (as per the current monetary policy). Thus, with 7.2% of loanable funds still available with the banks, the relevant question was: Why were these funds lying as unutilized money with banks? Was this indicative of the fact that the Corporates were flush with funds and had adequate surplus liquidity available with them and thus were not dependent on the banking system? Or, were they misusing the facility of loan moratorium extended by RBI as a stimulus measure from April to August 2020? This also raised the question: Was there undue pressure on the monetary authority to facilitate more liquidity in view of the so-called liquidity crunch in the financial flow?

Banking stalwarts such as Rajnish Kumar (SBI Chairman) and Deepak Parekh (HDFC Chairman) at the end of July 2020 had opined that the RBI should not extend the loan moratorium beyond August 2020. This could be attributed to the fact that even corporate units with comfortable loan servicing capacity were perhaps avoiding fresh loan demands now that moratorium facilities could be availed. Alternatively, the declining trend in borrowings could also be an outcome of inter-corporate or inter-unit fund support, which is a case for an in-depth study.

Rather, the subsequent monetary measure of one-time loan restructuring under the K V Kamath-led Committee report clearly identified only 26 specific sectors based on financial ratios for resolution plans for borrowers under loan restructuring and did not recommend that banks be allowed for loan restructuring for all Corporates. It identified sectors such as power, steel, real estate, cement, construction, travel and tourism, retail and wholesale trade, roads, textiles, etc., which had been hardest hit due to the pandemic for loan restructuring and did not recommend the measure for all sectors, ie one size fits all. Thus, the question here is: Did undue misuse of loan moratorium facility have a negative influence on the financial health of Banks as also acknowledged in the July 2020 FSR of RBI?

With deposits witnessing an increasing trend and rising to Rs. 142.5 trillion, and the total amount of loans being disbursed shrinking to Rs. 102.3 trillion in September 2020 and thereby seeing a declining trend, the important question in the minds of economists and analysts should be: Was India heading towards a realm of negative interest rates? Was India, an emerging economy moving in the direction of a borrower being paid with interest for borrowing money and depositors paying the bank a parking fee for safekeeping of their money?

The business of banking is to earn profits by accepting deposits at lower interest rates and thereafter lending the same money at a higher interest rate. They make money and earn margins on interest charged on corporate borrowings, mortgages, personal loans, etc. Given a supportive monetary policy environment, both deposit and credit disbursal play a crucial role in that direction. The global financial crisis of 2008 had resulted in expansionary monetary policies and quantitative easing being espoused by Central Banks worldwide. This led to low and negative interest rates being adopted in advanced economies. The European Central Bank had implemented the unconventional negative interest rate policy, ie banks were required to pay interest for depositing their surplus funds with it—an effort to penalize them and rather lend more to kickstart the economy. Was India too moving in the direction of savings and deposits losing value and borrowers being paid to take a loan?

Negative interest rates could have an adverse effect on depositors not being ready and willing to deposit their money with financial institutions. Rather, many financial institutions worldwide are hesitant to charge for deposits and thus strategize for lowering borrowing costs, ie squeeze the margins or spread between what they pay for deposits and what they earn by lending money to borrowers. The downside of this could result in the policy backfiring and banks becoming less hesitant to lend. This would not have been ideal for capital scarce economies like India. It would amount to the underutilization of capital which was scarce in supply compared to demand. If at all the situation moved in that direction, it would be detrimental in terms of deepening capital scarcity too at a stage when we are still an emerging economy.

Considering that India is an emerging economy and is capital scarce, is this advisable? It is pertinent to bear in mind that financial institutions play a role in creating credit, which in turn leads to increased production, higher employment levels, and increased consumer spending, thereby fuelling the economic growth.

Thus, in these unprecedented times, it was prudent that India be cautious. Different economies' dependence on their interest rate structure varies. In a scenario of negative interest rates, would India be in a position to attract foreign investments? Would negative interest rates not create an unstable financial environment? Banks could find it difficult to attract money for further lending. Depositors would be more keen to hold on to cash and start scouting for alternative safe non-bank deposits. While in India, negative interest rates seemed to be implausible, the negative real interest rate was certainly not unthinkable and the RBI and policymakers needed to sit up, take notice, and plan accordingly.

2.12

Inflation Targeting

In the backdrop of rising inflationary numbers and a grim economic per-spective, the RBI, in its MPC meeting on 4–6 August 2020, had decided to leave the repo rate and reverse repo rate unchanged at 4% and 3.35%, respectively. The RBI maintained that its stance on the monetary policy was 'accommodative' as had been the case even prior to the pandemic. With the COVID-19 resulting in demand and supply chain disruptions and brusquely bringing the Indian economy to a halt, the regulatory body's response had been of reducing repo rate by 115 basis points since February with a viewpoint of enhancing liquidity to the tune of approx. Rs. 1,37,000 crore. The decision to keep repo and reverse repo rates un-changed had been in light of retail inflation showing an upward trajectory and touching a high of 6.93% in July 2020. On the flip side, with experts predicting a contraction for the Indian economy of anywhere between 14% and 21% in Q1 of 2020, should RBI have focussed on inflation or ec-onomic growth?

In March 2016, RBI had formally adopted the mandate of a flexible inflation targeting framework and agreed to maintain inflation numbers around 4% with a band of (+/−)2%. The first MPC had been judiciously achieving its target for a considerably large part of its tenure in office. The six-member committee had managed to maintain inflation within the target band of 2–6% for most of the time; however, the record had been tarnished by consumer price growth being well above the range towards the end of its tenure with CPI numbers at 6.93% in July 2020. At this point of time, due to the 'Black Swan' event created by the pandemic, should the RBI have additionally analysed and assimilated information on indices such as consumer food price inflation, core inflation, wholesale price index (WPI), and GDP numbers and thereafter strategized for the well-being of the economy?

Resurgent India. Jagadish Shettigar and Pooja Misra, Oxford University Press. © Oxford University Press 2022.
DOI: 10.1093/oso/9780192866486.003.0023

Consumer Price Inflation—India

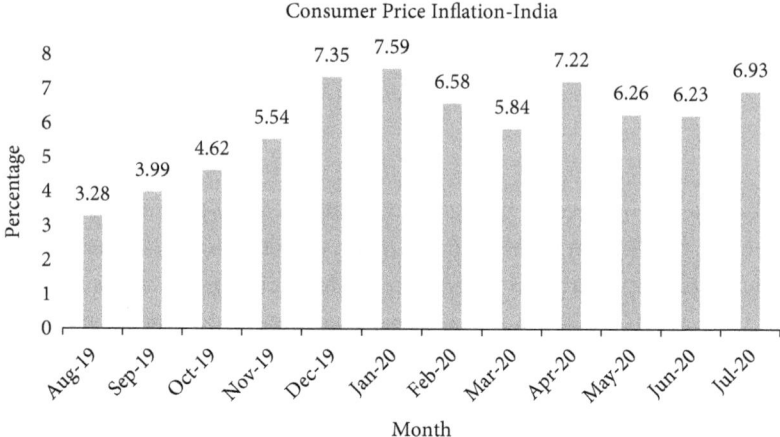

Source: tradingeconomics.com, Ministry of Statistics and Programme Implementation, MOSPI

Economic Outlook Based on Other Indices ...

An in-depth analysis of the upward trend in the Consumer Price index portrayed that higher prices of food articles had contributed to the increased elevation. The Consumer Price Index y-o-y for June 2020 was at 6.09%, while Consumer Food Price India y-o-y June 2020 was at 7.9% (as shown in Figure 2.12.1). Rather, the Consumer Food Price Index in July 2020 had surged to a high of 9.62%.

Data released by the Ministry of Statistics & Programme Implementation portrayed that this spike in CPI was on account of higher food prices, ie rise in the price of pulses and products, meat and fish, oil and fats, spices, and vegetables. But, the other side of the coin showed that the benefit of increased food prices had not actually reached the farmers. We still read stories of farmers dumping their products as they were not able to recover their cost of production. It would only be right to state that increased food prices were on account of supply chain disruptions caused by localized and regional lockdowns. Better monsoon, easing of lockdown and the three ordinances approved in June 2020 under the APMC Act, Essential Commodities Act 1955 and Farmers (Empowerment and Protection) Agreement on Price Assurance and

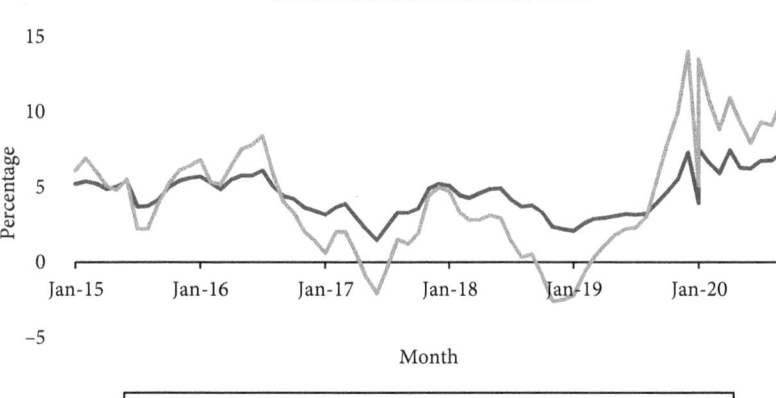

Figure 2.12.1 CPI and Consumer Food Price Index
Source: MOSPI (CSO), IMA

Farm Services Ordinance, would have helped reduce food inflation and thereby brought CPI within RBI's target of 2–6%. Unfortunately, the farm reform measures stand repealed with effect from November 2021. At this juncture, it was needed that the Central and State Governments worked towards improving and stabilizing the supply chain and ensuring a quick and efficient flow of food, vegetables, pulses, fruits, etc., from the farms to the mandis to the retailers. The panacea required for the increase in food prices was not an intervention by the RBI but the Government ensuring a smooth and efficient supply chain solution for farmers, retailers, and consumers.

Another index that showed that the status quo strategy of RBI could be further deliberated upon were the Core CPI numbers. On deep diving into CPI and Core CPI numbers, data showed that while CPI y-o-y for Q1 2020 was at 6.6%, core CPI y-o-y for Q1 2020 was at 4%. Core CPI is an inflation index that excludes temporary price volatility in terms of food and fuel. Core inflation is estimated to arrive at the actual inflation, excluding the effects of temporary shocks and volatility. Thus, as seen in Figure 2.12.2, while CPI was above the 2-6% band, core inflation for Q1 2020 was still very much within limits and was at approximately 4%.

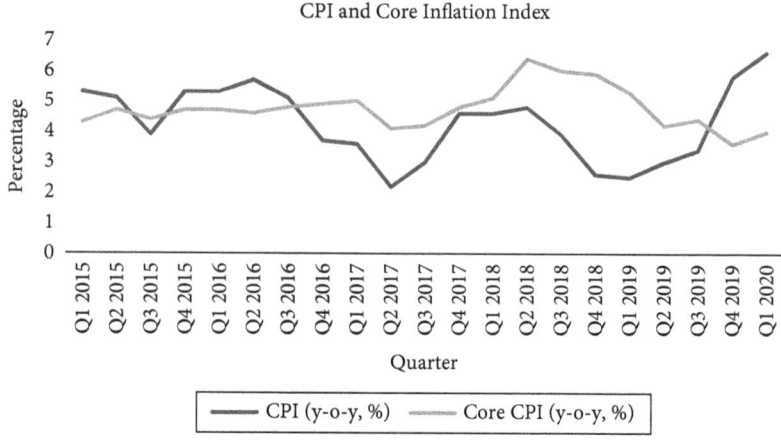

Figure 2.12.2 CPI and Core Inflation Index
Source: MOSPI (CSO), IMA

Last but not the least, importantly, RBI should have also looked at the story that was being told by the WPI. WPI is the index measuring the prices of a basket of goods at the point of sale of wholesalers. It measures the price changes of goods sold and traded by wholesale businesses, ie at the factory gate prior to the retail level. This helps track the supply and demand in industry, manufacturing, and construction primarily. The picture painted by WPI showed that inflation at the wholesalers' point stood at (−)0.58% (as shown in Figure 2.12.3) even as Consumer Food Price index surged upward. This was largely on account of a reduction in global crude oil prices and demand for non-essential items sharply declining. The WPI deflation was reflective of a decrease in discretionary spending by consumers and an indicator to producers of a slowdown or recessionary trend in the economy.

With the lockdown resulting in demand and supply chain disruptions, there was a considerable decline in consumption. Manufactured products constitute 64% in WPI and with the lockdown bringing the economy to a halt, it had significantly contributed to the overall deflation in WPI. Weak demand for non-essential items was reflective of a fall in the production of industrial goods. WPI inflation was indicative of a steep decline in consumer demand and there was an early warning of recessionary trends appearing in the Indian economy.

Wholesale Price Inflation

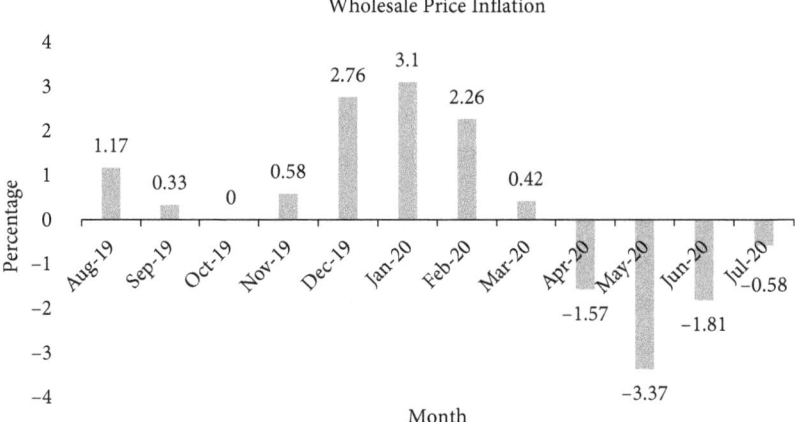

Figure 2.12.3 Wholesale Price Inflation—India
Source: tradingeconomies.com, Office of the Economic Advisor, India

Economists had opined that recovery of the Indian economy might take some time while coronavirus cases were on the rise and the pandemic had spread to the rural areas and other interiors of the country. National Council of Applied Economic Research (NCAER) had pegged Q1 at (−)25.7% contraction while Nomura had estimated a contraction of (−)15.2% in Q1 2020. This was indicative of declining business confidence, people losing jobs, less income available to spend, and negative consumer sentiments. At this juncture, it was important that the country gained control over the outbreak of the pandemic and ensured that economic recovery and growth were back on track. Manufacturing and services had borne the brunt of the pandemic and industrial production, manufacturing and services had shrunk, ie (−)35.9%, (−)40.7%, and (−)35% in Q1. A comprehensive fiscal and monetary policy was needed, which could further restore and reinforce the business confidence of producers.

Yes, with Unlock1.0, pent-up demand resulted in buoyed consumer sentiments initially and showed green shoots of economic recovery but it was imperative that in an unprecedented situation, both the Government and RBI primarily focus on and work consistently towards reviving economic growth. Economic growth/recovery would fuel production, leading to increased jobs resulting in increased income and purchasing power in the hands of the people. Only with increased income and purchasing power and control of the pandemic would there be a revival of demand for non-essential items and a rise in discretionary spending. Thus, at this point of time, RBI had rightly been focusing on the revival of economic growth and economic recovery and not on inflation alone as its primary focus.

As an exception, RBI should have taken monetary policy decisions based on WPI numbers also as against CPI numbers alone and rightly have aimed for economic recovery at the earliest. Further rate cuts would increase business confidence and support consumer sentiments fuelling up demand in the economy. However, one should not forget that this could have happened only when the jobs of people were intact and they had income in their hands. Yes, we agree that an eye should be kept on food inflation, but the same was rightly controlled by ensuring that supply chain disruptions were minimized and efficient and quick flow of fruits, vegetables, pulses, etc., was maintained from the farm to the fork.

Thus, in our perspective with the prediction of the contraction for the Indian economy being anywhere between 14% and 21% in Q1 of 2020, the RBI should have also looked at WPI along with economic recovery/growth as its main objective while deciding on policy recommendations and not at CPI numbers alone. After all, an unprecedented situation calls for out-of-the-box thinking and out-of-line strategies. While respecting the autonomy of the monetary authority, it was expected from RBI that it stood up to the extraordinary economic crisis in terms of policy response.

2.13
Fine-Tuning of GST

Goods and Services Tax (GST) implemented in 2017, one of the biggest tax structure reforms of the country, proved to be a game-changer and aimed at moving India into the next phase of economic growth. A value-added tax levied at the point of consumption, it enabled the doing away with double taxation or tax on tax structure which was previously in vogue in India. 'One nation one tax', ie unification of indirect taxes under one umbrella, it has facilitated Indian businesses to be competitive globally and has led to an efficient tax collection system, minimizing revenue leakage, and enabling easy inter-state movement of products.

While the 1991 reforms are perceived as being crisis-driven, the second phase of reforms under the Atal Bihari Vajpayee government as being consensus-driven, the third generation reforms of GST in 2017, labour reforms 2020, etc. currently underway under the able leadership of Prime Minister, Mr. Narendra Modi would help the country in emerging as an economic power. In the backdrop of the pandemic, post the lockdown announced in March 2020, October 2020 was the first month that witnessed GST surpassing Rs. 1.05 lakh crore, the highest recorded since February 2020.

Trend in GST collection (in Rs. Crore)

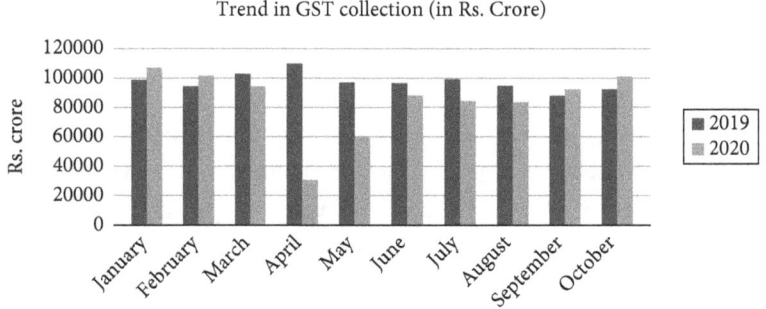

Month

Source: http://gstcouncil.gov.in/gst-revenue

Resurgent India. Jagadish Shettigar and Pooja Misra, Oxford University Press. © Oxford University Press 2022.
DOI: 10.1093/oso/9780192866486.003.0024

However, the key point that needed to be addressed now was: Any new reformative measure comes with its bag of teething issues. In case of the revolutionary GST reform has India overcome the initial problems or is fine-tuning still required?

The Kelkar Task Force had made several important and landmark recommendations for reforming the indirect tax system of the Central and State Governments in 2004. With a rationale of replacing the existing tax regime and removing of inefficient and distortionary taxes, it had recommended withdrawal of all cascading taxes. GST enacted on 1 July 2017 had subsumed a multiple tax structure of service tax, central excise, luxury tax, sales tax, etc., under one roof and simplified the tax calculation and collection process. A single tax structure was expected to help bring down the price of goods due to the eradication of economic distortions and bring about transparency in calculations. It had improved the economic efficiency of industry and made it easier for Corporates to operate. The backbone of the GST, the GSTN network, had enabled an integrated platform ensuring the smooth functioning of GST activities. However, like all other newly initiated reforms, the enacted GST structure does have its loopholes, and it is time that the Government focused on them and bridged the gaps.

A scan of the international arena showed that most of the 160 countries that have incorporated GST tax structure have a single unified GST system. Countries such as Canada and Brazil have a dual GST structure in place, a model which India chose to adopt. France was the first country to adopt GST in 1954. While India has a four slab GST structure in place, a multi-rate GST system, international best practices show that maximum countries have a single slab and 28 countries worldwide have a dual slab. India, along with five other countries, is an outlier with four slabs in effect.

The primary objective of GST was to bring transparency and simplify the process, thereby making it easier for businesses to operate. The current practice of four GST slabs provides ample scope for vested interests to lobby their case with political bosses and bureaucrats, thus undoing the very objective. Were these changes permitted due to, and are they an outcome of the compromise that the Central Government had to make as they had to take State Governments on board is a question that we need to answer. The rationale behind four tax rate slabs largely is that products of necessity and luxury cannot be bucketed together as it would have an adverse impact on the welfare of the common man. On the flip side, do we need four tax rate slabs or as the NITI Aayog in 2019 has recommended two tax rate slabs under GST would work well. Former Finance Minister, Late Mr. Arun Jaitley, who had spearheaded the GST negotiations with the States, was also of the view that two tax rate slabs would ensure that common man's products are not taxed exorbitantly while the products easily afforded by the affluent class could be taxed at a higher rate.

Another interesting point of debate has been that products such as alcohol, petrol, diesel, etc., have been kept outside the ambit of GST. The reasoning being given for the same was that neither the Central nor the State Governments were in favour of a heavy revenue loss in terms of taxes collected on petrol and diesel. This is reflective of the fact that Centre and States are reluctant to give up a revenue tool in their hands to meet any contingency situation. This, again, is a narrow view.

In the backdrop of the coronavirus pandemic due to declining demand and with the price war happening amongst the key oil-producing countries, ie Saudi Arabia, Russia, and the United States, prices of crude oil had weakened, with Brent price declining to USD19.34 per barrel, April 2020 as against USD32.01 per barrel, March 2020. However, in spite of declining prices of crude oil, the benefit had not been passed on to the consumer, rather it had been retained by the Government to strengthen their fiscal position.

In this scenario, the total tax incidence on petrol was on an average 45–50% and on diesel 35–40%. Being the devil's advocate, if petrol and diesel were to be brought within the purview of the GST structure, prices of these two products would drastically decline leading to higher demand and fuelling up consumption of the same. This would lead to increased tax collections from the very same two products and higher profit margins for the oil marketing companies. Also, the negative impact of lower taxes on petrol and diesel could be further netted out by increased corporate tax collections from the two goods and increased dividends being paid out by the PSUs to the Government. A win–win solution for both consumers and the Government with scope for substantial political dividend. Is this a thought worth contemplating, is something that the Government needs to brainstorm on and the RBI Governor has been pointing towards.

It is worth mentioning here that the GST council has been closely observing the implementation of GST on a regular basis, and has been consistently taking inputs from the industry and business sectors on issues faced by them. However, on the contrary, with three years being completed since GST saw the light of the day, are regular meetings of the GST council still needed? With 43 meetings having been already conducted since the first one on 22–23 September 2016, isn't it time that Government ensures that the structure is robust and lets it function on its own? Instead of deliberating on transitionary issues relating to the implementation of GST, the Council focuses on the reshuffling of products under different slabs, which puts a question mark on the transparency aspect.

Frequent requests for reduction in the rates and the tendency of all sectors to petition for lower rates add to the political drama around it. The focus should now be on increase in the collection of GST rather than repeatedly tinkering with rates. Apart from providing scope to confusions due to repeated changes, regular interventions by the Government raises the scope of lobbyists and influencers having their say and impressing their thoughts upon the Government, thereby defeating the purpose of the tax reform of bringing in transparency, reducing the scope for manipulation and minimizing corruption in the system.

2.14

Doing Away with Retrospective Tax

Retrospective tax is a tax levied on a deal or transaction which was conducted in the past. The amendment introduced in 2012 in the Finance Act enabled the Government to impose retrospective taxes on transactions conducted after 1962 involving shares transfer in a foreign equity that owned assets in India. This was introduced to fix existing loopholes in the then existing tax regime and was triggered by the Vodafone Hutchinson deal in 2007 when Vodafone purchased a 67% stake in Hutchinson. The tax demand raised by the authorities was to the tune of Rs. 7990 crores in capital gains and withholding tax.

In the case of Cairn Energy in 2014, tax reassessment proceedings for the 2006 internal corporate restructuring transaction was initiated. A tax demand of Rs. 10,247 crores on capital gains made by it during the corporate restructuring undertaken in 2006 prior to the listing of the local entity was issued. Cairn Energy did appeal before the Income Tax Tribunal in India for which in March 2017, the Income Tax Apellate tribunal (ITAT) upheld the capital gains demand on the company post which, the company approached the High Court in Delhi.

In the interim, Cairn Energy in March 2015 also initiated an international arbitration under the 1994 Bilateral Investment Treaty (BIT) between India and UK. On 21 December 2020, the international arbitration tribunal constituted in the case of Cairn Energy Pls and Cairn UK Holding Ltd. in Hague ruled in favour of Cairn Energy and declared that India should pay damages worth USD1.2 billion to Cairn Energy. The ruling stated that India had failed to comply with its obligations under the purview of the 1994 India-UK BIT. Post the ruling in its favour, with the Indian Government refusing to comply with the order and filing for an appeal, Cairn started identifying overseas assets owned by the Indian Government which could be seized in the absence of a settlement. It also initiated proceedings in the court of law of countries such as the United

Resurgent India. Jagadish Shettigar and Pooja Misra, Oxford University Press. © Oxford University Press 2022.
DOI: 10.1093/oso/9780192866486.003.0025

States, the United Kingdom, France, the Netherlands, Quebec, and Singapore in an effort to enforce the ruling in countries where the Indian Government had assets.

In light of the above-sketched details, the government had acted pragmatically and laid to rest the ghost of the retrospective tax, though initially, there was thinking within to challenge the verdict by the Arbitration Council. The entire focus was mainly on long-term interests of the economy for which attracting investment is a prerequisite instead of standing on false prestige.

This long-drawn battle between the company and the Indian State is a fine example of a dilemma between sovereign authority and the need to attract investment. The Indian Constitution gives the Government the right to tax individuals and organizations. However, the tax being levied is required to be supported by a law passed by the legislature or Parliament. Importantly, the canons of taxation, ie the characteristics or qualities that a good and efficient tax system should possess, should be borne in mind while deciding on tax laws: (1) Equity, (2) Certainty, (3) Economy, and (4) Convenience. Interestingly, while the first is debatable on the ground of doubtful interpretation or a case of ego move by the then government, the concept of introducing a retrospective tax certainly side-lines the other three principles, especially in terms of long-term damage to the economy.

Not to miss, follow-up developments with Cairn Energy dragging the government to International Arbitration Council, more so move to get assets owned by PSUs are certainly against the principle of sovereign rights broadly accepted by the comity of nations and legally debatable. No country can surrender sovereign rights against an individual corporate entity.

On the flip side, from the viewpoint of showcasing India into an attractive destination for foreign and domestic investors and making India into a manufacturing hub, certainty and not being arbitrary about its tax regime and ensuring that the tax laws are transparent is a key requisite. A stable and unambiguous tax regime is necessary to promote domestic and foreign investments. While, the move by the Government on 5 August 2021 to scrap and do away with the retrospective tax law has certainly been a welcome move and should be well applauded, keeping in view the overall Ease of Doing Business and need to attract foreign investment, the matter should have been handled with maturity, especially when the new government took over in 2014. There were similar other sixteen such cases which had resulted in a lot of ambiguity for investors. Though the then Finance Minister, late Arun Jaitley, had made a statement that there would be no more retrospective tax measure, at the same time, the government had retained the right to impose retrospective tax. Moreover, pending cases were left untouched for the 17 litigations. With the recent move by Cairn Energy, other companies may have also gotten emboldened.

Application of the amended tax provision to the ongoing cases is conditional that cases against the government should be withdrawn. There should not be any problem as sensible corporate entities would not like to take on the government and find themselves on the other side of the discussion table. However, the government should have also engaged with the companies using negotiating skills in the overall interests of the economy without providing scope for the narrow ego to squeeze in.

The move by the government to scrap the retrospective tax was a step in the right direction and the need of the hour. It is certainly a laudable step from the point of Ease of Doing Business in India, especially at a time when foreign investors have started withdrawing from China and are exploring other attractive destinations to set up their manufacturing units and operate their businesses. This bold move by the Indian Government would act as a booster at a time when the economy has just started reviving from the COVID-19 induced economic crisis.

2.15
Tweaking Fiscal Deficit

The COVID-19 pandemic had resulted in an unprecedented situation for countries across the world, and India was no exception. With a negative growth rate of $(-)4.5\%$ predicted for the Indian economy by the IMF in June 2020, declining tax revenue collections due to demand disruption, and higher healthcare expenditure were pointing towards fiscal deficit numbers being higher than the budgeted estimate. Rather, India's fiscal deficit had already touched a record high of 83.2% of the target for the whole of the financial year in the April–June 2020quarter. This was indicative of the impact of the pandemic on tax collections and front-loading of the Government's spending. Doubts were being raised on India being able to achieve its fiscal deficit target of 3.5% of GDP for FY2021 as specified by the FRBM Act of 2003 and predictions were that fiscal deficit would touch 8% of GDP for 2020–21.

The stimulus package announced by the Government of India to the tune of Rs. 20 lakh crore (equivalent to 10% of GDP) had raised many an eyebrow. Contrarian thinkers were of the viewpoint that this package amounted to anywhere between 0.8% and 1.5% of GDP. However, the million-dollar question was two-fold: Did India have the fiscal space to announce a bigger package?; With uncertainty around the second wave of virus hitting many countries and localized lockdowns being announced in India, would it have been prudent for the Government to announce a demand stimulus package at that point of time or would it have been judicious to announce the same closer to the vaccine coming into the market? The announcement of any bigger stimulus would come hand in hand with an increased fiscal deficit.

In the Budget Speech on 1 February 2020, the Finance Minister, Ms. Nirmala Sitharaman had announced that due to lower revenue collections and higher government expenditure, the fiscal deficit for 2019–20 was at 3.8% as against 3.3% and would be 3.5% for 2020–21 as against the

Resurgent India. Jagadish Shettigar and Pooja Misra, Oxford University Press. © Oxford University Press 2022.
DOI: 10.1093/oso/9780192866486.003.0026

FRBM target of 3% (aided by disinvestment). Rather, the Government had already adopted a fiscal expansion path and invoked the 0.5% escape clause of Section 4(3) of the FRBM Act. Section 4(2) of FRBM provides for a trigger option for a deviation from the estimated deficit numbers due to introduced structural reforms. However, the Centre's fiscal deficit for 2019–20 came at 4.6% (a seven-year high) against the revised estimate of 3.8% due to lower-than-predicted GDP growth and low revenue collections across the board. Thus, with limited fiscal space available, contrarian thinkers were vying for a deteriorating deficit and were of the view that in an unprecedented situation, a worsening deficit should be permissible.

Let us trace back history a little. It was seen that in 1991–92, the combined fiscal deficit of the Centre and States was as high as 9.3%, which came down to 6.3% in 1995–96 and then again rose to over 9.0% approximately from 1998 to 2003. Deficit monetization (RBI monetized the deficit by the issuance of ad-hoc treasury bills) was in vogue in India to manage the high fiscal deficit scenario. With the FRBM Act, whose aim was to bring about fiscal discipline, subscribing to primary issues by RBI was barred from 1 April 2006. The downside of a widening deficit is that it triggers inflation.

To address the slowing down of the economy, the RBI had already been forced to bring down repo rates and pump in money into the financial system by buying bonds leading to increased liquidity. Numbers showed that excess liquidity as of 1 June 2020 was to the tune of Rs.4.02 lakh crore. With the economy on the recovery path and consumer demand on the rise, increased liquidity would lead to higher inflation rates. Rather, CPI inflation for India in July 2020 (with reduced demand) was already at 6.3%, which had forced RBI as of August 2020 to keep policy rates unchanged. In such a scenario, a deteriorating deficit would have only further worsened inflation numbers. Excess money supply would have also resulted in further depreciation of the Indian currency worsening the situation for exporters.

Looking at it from the supply side, a worsening deficit would lead to increased market borrowings by RBI on behalf of the Government, which could negatively impact businesses. Increased borrowings by the Government would lead to an increase in interest rates and less space available to Corporates and industrialists to borrow from the market, thereby demotivating businesses to make capital investments. Increased interest rates would result in a rise in the cost of production, leading to higher product prices for consumers. Index of Industrial Production (IIP) numbers showed contraction by 16.6% in June 2020, an improvement from 33.8% in May 2020. The eight-core sector industries, which constitutes 40% of IIP, contracted by 17.1% in June 2020 as against 38.4% in May 2020. In such a situation, increased inflation would result in lower demand for products and services, thereby again negatively disrupting the flow of goods and services in the Indian economy.

Another option available in the hands of the Government to cover the increasing fiscal deficit was an increase in taxes, which could be a direct or indirect tax. With approximately 6.0% of the population paying income tax, would it have been fair on the part of the Government to increase direct taxes and make these 6% bear the extra burden? Tax base has been gradually getting widened from hardly 1% a couple of decades back to 6% of the population now, thanks to tax reforms. One cannot think of reversing the process under the pressure of a fall in revenue collection. The Laffars Curve proved long back that the lower the rate higher is the revenue collection. Moreover, under the current demand constraint situation confronting the Indian economy for the last couple of years, raising the tax rate would have had an adverse impact. On the flip side, assuming that income tax was raised by the Government to increase tax collection and reduce the fiscal deficit, higher taxes would result in lesser disposable income in the hands of this section of society, leading to a further reduction in demand. This again would have had a negative impact on economic growth and would have worsened the anticipated contraction in 2020–21 for the Indian economy. Rather, a further cut in tax rates might have been the viable option.

If the Government had decided to increase indirect taxes, ie the GST, it would have resulted in increased prices of products. The increased price of products would have impacted all sections of the economy alike, thereby making the situation worse for the lower-income section of society. Thus, an additional stimulus package would have resulted in an increased burden on fiscal spending, only worsening the deficit numbers.

Rising fiscal deficit numbers were one of the three main causes for the downgrading of India's sovereign credit ratings by international agencies such as Moody's, Standard and Poor and Fitch Ratings. Agreeably, this was not the time for the Government to worry about the ratings, but one must not forget that sovereign credit ratings by international agencies influence the flow of foreign portfolio investments into the country and influence the inflow of foreign direct investments. In addition to the announcement of structural reforms under the Atmanirbhar Bharat scheme in May 2020, the Government was also working on introducing more structural measures in terms of land and labour reforms as announced by the Prime Minister. These land and labour reforms were from the viewpoint of improving the ease of doing business in India and wooing foreign investors into the country, thus making it important for the Government to also keep an eye on the sovereign credit ratings of the country.

A higher fiscal deficit has also had other repercussions such as the Central Government deciding not to pay the increased dearness allowance to its employees. This clearly meant lesser spending by Government employees resulting in lower demand. Last but not the least, it is important to bear in mind that gross market borrowings had increased by 54% from Rs. 7.8 lakh crore to Rs. 12 lakh crore already and this is debt that our future generations will have to pay in the coming years. Thus, was it advisable that we spend beyond our means and leave the burden for our future generations to bear? Agreed, a demand stimulus was needed to give the one big push to the Indian economy, but would it not have been wiser that it happened closer to the vaccine being launched into the market, thereby once and for all propelling the Indian economy back into the trajectory of economic recovery?

Importantly, the fiscal crisis should have been treated as an exception under the extraordinary condition created by the pandemic as no country had been left unscathed. Earlier, the government's fiscal health is brought back on track; better for the economy. Otherwise, it would mean leaving a scope for an irresponsible political set-up to go for populist measures without a caring economy.

Interestingly, the Government in its Union Budget Announcement 2021–22, did peg the fiscal deficit for 2020–21 at 9.5% of GDP and for 2021–22 at 6.8% of GDP with a five-year glide path to rein it in at 4.5% by 2025–26.

2.16

Corporate Banks

In the background of RBI's Internal Working Group recommending permission for business houses setting up of banks and eliciting public opinion, two former central bankers strongly condemned the proposal while another economist termed it the promotion of crony capitalism. Though the three are reputed to be habitual critics of the present regime, their opinion on this particular issue should not be brushed aside lightly.

Banking institutions are supposed to ensure safety with maximum possible returns to the depositors while providing easy liquidity support at an economical cost to the investors. It is a well-known practice amongst industrialists to avail of easy fund support from wherever possible—be it diverting from one's own business to another or promoting ones' venture at the cost of stakeholders in another. In this context, how can a business unit be expected not to use or misuse the fund controlled by a bank promoted by none other than itself? Having an in-house bank will give easy access to funds with no questions asked. What is the guarantee that such loans do not get written off, as in the case of Yes Bank or Gitanjali Jewellers? On the flip side, it is also worth contemplating that, will competitors have the same access to funds as the promoter of the Bank? Can it be said with conviction that the ensuing banks will ensure that it would be indiscriminately a level playing field for all borrowers?

Keeping in mind that in the recent past, RBI rejected banking licence applications by leading business houses while some of them were permitted to set up payment banks, the relevant question is: What major changes have taken place within a couple of years, that too at a time when there is no liquidity crunch? Rather, non-food credit growth has been decelerating and of late, banks have started approaching prospective borrowers through phone calls and SMS with liberal loan offers.

In the arena of private sector banking, though there have been success stories such as Kotak Mahindra Bank, at the same time, it is also

Resurgent India. Jagadish Shettigar and Pooja Misra, Oxford University Press. © Oxford University Press 2022.
DOI: 10.1093/oso/9780192866486.003.0027

worth recollecting the modus operandi of businessmen ransacking public money through cases like Nirav Modi. Yes Bank, another classic example, where the promoter was himself involved in siphoning off the money of trusting depositors to help business friends in lieu of a consideration amount. This warrants the fact that the lines between business and banking should not be blurred. To further add to this worrisome picture of the financial landscape being blotted by failures, one must also not turn a blind eye towards umpteen instances of wilful defaults, which ultimately compelled the banks to write off these loans or classify them under NPAs.

Moreover, one must concede that NBFCs belonging to industrial houses and conglomerates have performed well and have not been found guilty of any wrongdoings. However, cases such as IL&FS do point towards the fact that strengthening of monitoring of NBFC's is also needed. Also, are we sure that RBI will be able to rigorously supervise the lending done by the banks to their group companies? Once again, the past track record of Yes Bank, Lakshmi Vilas Bank, and the never-ending list of wilful defaulters of existing banks comes surging to the forefront. The arduous weight of a failed bank/wilful NPAs ultimately rests on the shoulders of the taxpayer's money.

In view of the dynamic macroeconomic and fast-changing financial scenario existing in the country, even if one considers that there might be merit in this idea, it would be only right to state that RBI and Finance Ministry, as a first step, should put additional checks and balances in place. Prior to venturing into an amendment of the Banking Regulations Act, 1949 the central bank should be well advised to strengthen the existing financial framework so that the lax seen in case of IL&FS or any such case of fraudulent siphoning of the depositor's money does not recur.

Additionally, if one were to closely examine the recommendations of the IWG, the criterion for entry into the banking business should have been in terms of a certain amount of equity, asset, or number of years of experience in related areas. What is the logic behind 3 years in case of payment banks while 10 years in case of NBFCs? For the record, the working group appears to be cautious by suggesting raising promoters' equity from 15% now to 26% in 15 years.

Here is a catch. If the group was seriously concerned about taking care of all stakeholders, it would not have recommended raising equity holding beyond 25%. The moment it reaches 26%, the promoter is capable of promoting his own business interests. Besides, promoters should be barred from getting into the Boards of Directors panel and refrained from playing any role in the recruitment of personnel. Also, in the eventuality of the bank going bust due to direct or indirect connected lending, the interests of depositors should be protected by attaching the assets of the parent business units. This may require necessary amendments to the Company Law.

Last but not the least, if the central bank still thinks that the proposal is worth experimenting with, why cannot it suggest to the government to divest equity holding in PSBs in favour of corporate promoters, with the condition that the corporate sector's individual or collective equity holding does not cross 25% nor should they be allowed to get into the Boards directly or indirectly.

The central bank is supposed to play the role of a regulator protecting the interests of depositors and savers while ensuring adequate liquidity support is available for investors. It is for the government to provide a healthy business environment to different sectors. Let the RBI continue to be the banking regulator and watchdog of the economy by keeping a safe arm's length and healthy distance from interested parties.

2.17

Union Budget for 2021–22

With BSE Sensex skyrocketing 2050 points and investors' wealth seeing a jump post the announcement of the Union budget 2021–22, it is only fair to state that the bulls were back in action and market sentiments were positively high. The Government had clearly focused on growth revival and it aimed to leave no stone unturned to achieve the same. The strong emphasis on infrastructure and healthcare would give the required boost to the economy and drive it back on the trajectory of economic growth.

In light of the pandemic and Pillar 1, as mentioned by the FM being Health & Wellbeing, the Government's proposal of increasing its spending on healthcare by 135% was a step in the right direction. Keeping in mind the fact that world over countries were in the throes of the virus, the Government had spelt out that the attention was still on 'Jaan Bhi, Jahaan Bhi'. Increasing the FDI cap from 49% to 74% for the insurance industry would help revive the economy, mobilize resources for infrastructure development, encourage competition in the insurance sector, leading to advantage consumers and improve quality of human capital.

Interestingly, analysts and economists have been mooting the point of making power distribution networks into a competitive one. However, previous Governments have not been able to bite the bullet, citing reasons such as technical difficulty, etc., previous Governments have not been able to bite the bullet. It is heartening to see that the Government was willing to create a competitive environment and provide consumers the choice to choose the discom that it wants to source the power from, thereby making it beneficial for the consumer.

Pillar 2 was dedicated to the big infrastructure push that focuses on capital expenditure and asset monetization. With a proposed outlay of Rs. 5.54 lakh crore on capital expenditure it aims to drive projects under the National Infrastructure Pipeline and spend on PLI schemes along with making Indian textiles competitive globally. Increased allocation

Resurgent India. Jagadish Shettigar and Pooja Misra, Oxford University Press. © Oxford University Press 2022.
DOI: 10.1093/oso/9780192866486.003.0028

to rural infrastructure development will give the necessary thrust to the rural areas and drive employment opportunities. Higher spending on the building of roads, highways, expressways, etc., will have a propelling effect on other sectors such as cement, steel, etc. Not to forget the advantage being given to affordable housing for all will also have a multiplier effect on all other related sectors and give a boost to the real estate industry.

With out-of-the-box thinking of asset monetization, it will not only give the Government access to financial resources but will also lead to the regional development of areas around, thus serving a two-pronged strategy. Asset monetization will unlock the value of unutilized or underutilized public assets, which can be justly used for commercial purposes and will also drive employment opportunities along with balanced regional development. Monetization of assets as an overall strategy of mobilizing revenue through non-tax means will also lead to development along with employment generation. Increased employment will lead to increased income and higher demand. Thus, with the Government aiming to unlock the optimal value of public sector assets that have not yet yielded their potential return is a welcome step.

Under the Atmanirbhar package in May 2020, with the Government having already announced its policy on disinvestment and that there would be a maximum of four PSU in strategic sectors while all state-owned firms in non-strategic sectors would be privatized, the announcement of disinvesting in two public sector banks and one insurance company was a step forward. Asset monetization, disinvestment, and privatization will only help garner resources for infrastructure development, creating value, and bridging the fiscal deficit gap.

As anticipated, the extraordinary economic situation due to the pandemic had led to a complete shift in priority from the economy to healthcare and resulted in a fall in revenue collection and rise in Government expenditure, increased unemployment, and an economic contraction. With the fiscal deficit for 2020–21 being summarized to be 9.5% of GDP, it is only fair to state that in the background of the pandemic, the effort should be to drive growth through increased Government expenditure and not focus on trying to achieve the FRBM target. It is well accepted by countries across the world that the pandemic has necessitated deviation from the fiscal deficit target. However, one would want to mention that a path spelling out well-contemplated steps for achieving fiscal consolidation by FY26 of 4.5% of GDP as stated by FM would have been welcome. Not to miss bringing off budget liabilities back into the fiscal deficit numbers only lends transparency to the process. The flip side is that a higher fiscal deficit could likely impact interest rates and external commercial borrowings and ratings. However, this is the price that the economy should be prepared to pay, keeping long-term interest in mind.

With reference to the agricultural sector, a higher allocation was expected. However, one should not forget that game-changing policies in this sector had been initiated in 2020, along with the allocation of more than Rs. 100,000 crores to the Agricultural Infrastructure Fund. In the Union Budget announcement, the focus of the Government on showcasing procurement of record foodgrains might have been in the background of the ongoing agitation.

The announcement of setting out of policy measures for easy and time-bound access to deposits of stressed banks will help many aggrieved depositors heave a sigh of relief. Also, by reducing the reopening of the assessment period from six years to three years except in cases of serious tax evasion and further driving faceless income tax assessment and pre-filing of returns will only lead to ease of filing and bringing down tax evasion and corruption levels along with increasing transparency. This will also trigger a widening of the tax base.

The budget indicated that the government was back in business focusing on the economy and there were signals on emerging positive business environments both through supply side as well as demand boost. It had proposed innovative ideas, especially in terms of revenue generation, research, human capital, etc. Last but not the least, with the Union Budget 2021–22 primarily focusing on the supply side aiming to kickstart growth in the economy, it would create an environment of increased employment, leading to increased income in the hands of people and thereby giving the requisite boost to the demand cycle.

2.18

Asset Monetization with Transparency

The Finance Minister in the Union Budget 2021–22 announced on 1 February that a National Monetization Pipeline would be launched and a dashboard would be set up to ensure transparency and track progress. The proposal was to monetize public infrastructure assets that are under-utilized or unutilized with the Government and PSUs. These unutilized assets can prove to be a major financing option for purposes of infra-structure construction and strengthening the capital base of the con-cerned PSU owning them. To take an example, Indian Railways owns approximately 47,000 acres of underutilized land, which can be put to commercial use.

Asset monetization will create new revenue options by unlocking the value of unutilized assets owned by the Public sector units. The budget announcement also proclaimed that the plan of the Government is to transfer five operational roads worth Rs. 5000 crores to the Infrastructure Investment Trust (InvIT) of NHAI and transfer transmission assets of Rs.7000 crore to PowerGrid's Investment Trust, respectively. There are talks on the anvil for Indian Railways to monetize its Dedicated Freight Corridor assets, oil and gas pipeline of Indian OIL, Gail and Hindustan Petroleum, warehousing assets of CPSEs, etc. In many cases, it has been seen that these assets are occupied by unauthorized persons, especially, with regards to railway lines, sea ports, airports, and gas/oil pipelines. Thus, it is high time that these national assets are converted and utilized for productive purposes and income generation. Monetization will serve a two-fold advantage, ie generate appropriate returns for the concerned PSU owning them, for which until now, these unutilized assets or land was more of a dead investment giving no returns. The second is that with the private sector stepping in and bidding for them, these assets will sub-sequently be utilized for productive purposes and factory establishments, etc. will be set up, thereby generating employment opportunities and leading to the economic development of the area concerned.

Resurgent India. Jagadish Shettigar and Pooja Misra, Oxford University Press. © Oxford University Press 2022.
DOI: 10.1093/oso/9780192866486.003.0029

However, one needs to be cognizant of the fact that it is equally important for the Government to move forward on the out-of-box idea of asset monetization with utmost caution. The Government is bound to face resistance on ideological grounds or it may be used as a mere excuse in the name of 'selling family silver', however, the Government, in its announcement in August 2021, has specifically stated that these assets would not be sold but would be leased for a specific period of time.

There could also be resistance by vested interests who are illegally occupying unutilized Government/PSU-owned land, often with political backing. The best course of action would be constituting a Commission for identifying assets for monetization, modus operandi of monetization, and use of funds. The commission may be headed by a retired supreme court judge and may consist of eminent persons from the public, thereby creating a transparent mechanism open to viewpoints from all concerned stakeholders and minimizing the scope for resistance and opposition. On successful identification of the assets lying idle, they can be handed over to a national trust that would act as the caretaker, including the monetization process and use of funds. This well-laid out process might require the setting up of a National Trust for Surplus Public Assets.

Another point that needs to be borne in mind and made amply clear is the use of funds generated through monetization. It is essential to clarify that these assets belong to the concerned public sector undertakings or authorities concerned. Hence, revenue raised through monetization should not be utilized for benefiting the government in terms of short-term budgetary support, thereby strictly adhering to company law norms. On the flip side, if the funds help minimize borrowing of the concerned PSU and thereby interest payment burden, the central government will also indirectly benefit from higher dividend receipts. Not to forget that it may also reduce the burden of budgetary support required to strengthen the capital base of the public sector unit. However, wherever it is essential to modernize or upgradation of technology is the requirement, for instance, Indian Railways, then the funds sourced through asset monetization should be used in lieu of budgetary support from the government.

Another point worth deliberating on is the modus operandi that could be adopted for ensuring successful implementation. In certain cases, the assets may be transferred on a long-term lease, while in other cases, the public assets may be developed by private investors on a Build-Operate-Transfer basis. This would depend on the nature of the asset as well as how these assets are utilized. The details of the modalities can be worked out by the suggested National Commission.

With the Government focusing on the initiative of affordable housing for all, some assets can be earmarked for affordable housing projects where preference may be given to sections such as armed forces and national security personnel, migrant workers, etc. Efforts may also be made to accommodate unauthorized occupants. Not to miss depending on location of the asset, private initiatives in social infrastructure may also be encouraged in sectors such as healthcare, education, etc., thereby helping in making the existing social infrastructure more robust. It is only right to state that certain tracts of land such as the ones adjacent to railway stations or airports cannot be used for housing or social infrastructure. Thus, these properties will be fit primarily for commercial use.

The Government in August 2021 has laid a tentative framework and a roadmap spelling out the sector-wise monetization pipeline for FY2022–25. The framework has three key imperatives:

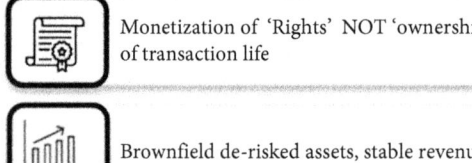

Monetization of 'Rights' NOT 'ownership', Assets handed back at the end of transaction life

Brownfield de-risked assets, stable revenue streams

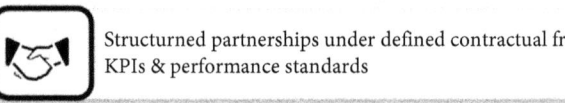

Structurned partnerships under defined contractual frameworks with strict KPIs & performance standards

Source: https://pib.gov.in/PressReleseDetail.aspx?PRID=1748297

The asset pipeline under NMP for the period FY22–25 is valued at Rs. 6 trillion and includes more than 12 ministries and 20 asset classes and would involve brownfield assets where investments have already been made and are lying unutilized or underutilized.

Sector-wise NMP (FY22–25)	
Sector	Rs. billion
Road	1602.0
Railways	1525.0
Power transmission	452.0
Power generation	398.3
Telecom	351.0
Warehousing	289.0
Mining	287.5
Natural gas pipeline	244.6
Product pipeline/others	225.0
Aviation	207.8
Urban real estate	128.3
Ports	150.0
Stadiums	114.5

Source: https://pib.gov.in/PressReleseDetail.aspx?PRID=1748297

Like the Government has stated, the objective of this initiative is to enable 'Infrastructure Creation through Monetization'. Thus, while the proposal is an out-of-the-box idea and high time translates into action, it is important for the Government to be focused, adhere to set timelines, and take the general public into confidence with regards to the modus operandi and ultimate beneficiaries. This would make the process highly transparent and help the Government gain the confidence and buy-in of not only all concerned stakeholders but also the citizens of India, thereby making the process of asset monetization a successful and historical one.

2.19

Disinvestment of Air India

With the Tatas being declared as the successful bidder for the ailing Air India, the national carrier has finally made its way back home to its original address. Interestingly, on tracing back history, it is seen that this disinvestment proposal was, in fact, started by the Vajpayee government in 2000–01, when attempts were drawn to re-privatize the Maharaja. The airline which was founded by Shri J.R.D. Tata, way back in the 1930s, flew its first domestic flight from Mumbai to Trivandrum. In 1953, the Government of India passed the Air Corporations Act and took over the reins of the airline, much to the anguish of the pioneers in the aviation industry. The efforts of the Vajpayee Government to re-privatize the airline have finally seen the light of the day with the Government ceding control and announcing the landmark deal in October 2021, and declaring Tata Sons Pvt. Ltd. as the new official owner of the Maharaja.

With the Vajpayee Government long back, largely believing that there should be a gradual withdrawal of the government from non-strategic areas and it should give up its pro-active role in economic development and rather be a facilitator by providing an investor-friendly business environment, the airline has been able to find a new although original address for itself. At this juncture, it is important to recall the recommendations of the Ramakrishna Committee in 1998, which had suggested disinvestment of Air India during the previous NDA government. Somehow, the so-called national pride delayed the process, resulting in amassing a colossal debt for the airline, a fine example of 'A stitch in time would have saved nine'. With the current Government in power also believing that 'Government has no business to be in business except in strategic areas' it is key that the nation now focuses on disinvestment in certain sectors such as hospitality, etc. where the human touch is crucial and can be better managed by the private sector.

Resurgent India. Jagadish Shettigar and Pooja Misra, Oxford University Press. © Oxford University Press 2022.
DOI: 10.1093/oso/9780192866486.003.0030

Not to miss the fact that this ground-breaking deal has had its fair share of criticisms levied on the pretext that: Is it right to sell the family silver or the so-called national symbol of the country? However, it is important to bear in mind that irrespective of who owns the airlines, it would continue to be the national pride—maybe better-shaped in terms of service and efficiency, an outcome of the managerial efficiency of the Tatas with its proven track record of successfully managing Vistara and AirAsia. Most importantly, with the borrowing burden of the Government to fund the colossal debt of Air India getting largely reduced, it would not be a burden on the taxpayers' money. To put things in perspective, as of 31 August 2021, the airline was under a mountain of debt of Rs. 61,652 crores, of which Tata Sons holding company, Talace Private Ltd. is to assume Rs. 15,300 crore, while the balance Rs. 46,262 crore will be taken over by the Government's Air India Asset Holding Ltd. (AIAHL). Additionally, the Tata group will also pay Rs. 2700 crore in cash to the Government.

On the flip side, it would also be key to state that with the nation suffering from the onslaught of the pandemic, there could not have been a more ideal time for Air India's disinvestment. From the point of view of the Government, it would have been too much to bear the burgeoning financial loss that too in the background of pandemic-hit public revenue. Routing the taxpayers' money towards Air India's losses and denying funding support to welfare measures as well as infrastructure projects for a country that is at the juncture of economic revival would have been criminal injustice to the general public.

Another point worth noting is that through this much-awaited big-ticket disinvestment process, the government has been able to give a clear-cut signal about its intention of moving ahead with its economic reforms agenda. With already a couple of PSUs lined up for the disinvestment process to kick-off, on the back of the Air India sale, the Government should now go all out and focus on its disinvestment strategy and work on the mega push to privatization that it had given in its Budget 2021–22 announcement.

The landmark deal has again brought the spotlight on the Modi government's aggressive reforms agenda and helped in instilling confidence amongst domestic and foreign investors. With macroeconomic indicators already pointing towards economic revival, concluding the disinvestment of Air India has provided an impetus to the whole economy and will only further boost the country's business and economic prospects. Moreover, Tatas being the successful bidder has provided a positive vibe both on the economy and the government front.

Also, last but not least, now that the government is back on the reform track, it may get foreign portfolio investors to re-think about the potential of Indian capital and domestic market, especially in the wake of the Federal Reserve going ahead with a policy rate hike in a year or so. With a renewed confidence being instilled in the Government's economic policies and agenda and investors being all-out positive about the Indian economy, it might help in minimizing the downside of the tapering effect. Proportionately, damage to the domestic economy, be it expected capital market crash or depreciation of the rupee and consequent current account deficit or crude oil price hike, may get lessened.

Most importantly, at the end, would like to state that at the same time, the government should go full force and move ahead with concrete economic measures in all directions and rapidly work towards achieving its dream of India being a USD5 trillion economy.

PART 3

POLICY SUGGESTIONS

The intense lockdown has proved to be a winning strategy to save lives and livelihoods and set India on a V-shaped economic recovery path as stated by the Economic Survey 2020–21. The lockdown was able to successfully flatten the virus curve and push the peak to September 2020, post which declining cases were seen even with increased mobility. The V-shaped recovery resulted in a GDP contraction of 23.9% in Q1 FY2020–21, 7.5% in Q2, and an expansion of 0.4% and 1.6% in Q3 and Q4, respectively.

Agriculture, services, and construction sectors witnessed a good performance in Q3, resulting in Asia's third largest economy exiting an unprecedented recession. Sectors such as the trade and hotel industry, which had largely been adversely impacted and suffered the brunt of the pandemic, registered a contraction of 7.7% in Q3 FY21. In Q3 2020–21, farming sector saw a 3.9% growth while manufacturing registered a growth of 1.6%, construction of 6.2%, and electricity, gas, water supply, etc., witnessed a growth of 7.3%.

Q3, 2020–21 was the first quarter since December 2019 in which investment levels recorded growth, an outcome of increased levels of capex spending. Furthermore, private consumption continued to show a contraction. However, consequent upon vaccination programme having started in January 2021(frontline workers to start with), Q4 of 2020–21 showed a better growth rate of 1.6% as expected.

In response to the pandemic hit recession, India was the only country to have announced structural reforms on the supply side, which would have a positive impact in the medium to long term for the economy. The demand side witnessed calibrated measures so that the requisite push could be given when brakes on economic activities are removed and post the vaccination, when people are more upbeat and confident about the economic and health scenario. The four-pillar strategy adopted by the Indian Government of containment, fiscal and financial sector reforms had yielded positive results with GDP being forecasted to contract by 7.7% in FY2020–21 and grow by 11% in FY2021–22. Interestingly, hard numbers showed the GDP of the Indian economy contracting at 7.3% in FY21 and the Indian economy growing at a record pace of 20.1% in Q1 FY22. A declining number of cases of the virus, a buoyant stock market, current account witnessing a surplus of 2% of GDP in FY21, the agricultural sector being the silver lining as against manufacturing and construction sector being hard hit and India remaining a preferred investment destination have been the building blocks for the K-shaped recovery. With regards to the fiscal deficit, the projection was that 2020–21 would see a deficit figure of 9.5% of GDP while 2021–22 will witness fiscal deficit of 6.8% of GDP. 2025–26 will be the year when India will come close to the FRBM target with the fiscal deficit being projected to be 4.5% of GDP.

Thus, the picture being painted on the canvas for the Indian economy was becoming brighter by the day, an outcome of the conventional and unconventional measures adopted by the Government and RBI. However, keeping in mind the Prime Minister's goal of India becoming a USD5 trillion economy and a global manufacturing destination, the country still has miles to travel. In light of the same, the authors in Part 3 have recommended reforms that the Government needs to work upon to be able to achieve the goal of making India into an Atmanirbhar Bharat— a self-reliant nation.

Taxation, Land Acquisition, Banking, Labour, Judicial, Petroleum, Administrative reforms, along with building a culture of citizens giving back to society, are much needed to enable the country to move back in the trajectory of economic growth and fast traverse the path towards making India into an Atmanirbhar Bharat. Also, for the country to position itself on the world map as a major manufacturing destination and the factory for the world, upgradation of technology is key, and it is important that India 'innovates its way' into the future.

Keeping in mind that universal vaccination was the need of the hour, relaxing IPR provisions for vaccines for COVID-19 or, for that matter, all crucial medicines has been looked at. Not to miss, with India having a federal system of governance, Cooperative Federalism is very important and for any reforms to succeed, it is required that the Centre and State Governments work hand in hand. Last but not the least, the challenges before the Government in building an Atmanirbhar Bharat have been discussed.

3.1

Agenda for Atmanirbhar Bharat

'Make for the World' was an appeal by the Prime Minister from the ramparts of the Red Fort in his 74th Independence Day speech. The graduation from 'Make in India' to 'Make for World' despite yet to recover to the pre-lockdown stage reflected his confidence in achieving the set target. The COVID-19 pandemic has not left unscathed any country across the world. The International Monetary Fund (IMF) in June 2020 had predicted that the global economy would contract at (−)4.9% and the Indian economy at (−)4.5%. In response to the negative impact of the coronavirus on the healthcare of citizens and the economic impact on the Indian economy, the Government, under the leadership of the Prime Minister, Mr. Narendra Modi, gave a clarion call for an 'Atmanirbhar Bharat', ie a 'self reliant' India. He also propounded the term 'Vocal for Local'.

Atmanirbhar Bharat or a self-reliant India is an endeavour towards making the country into an economic powerhouse that is self-generating and self-sustaining. The vision of the Prime Minister entails making India into a competitive, self-sufficient, resilient, and competitive nation embedded in the World economy as a nation actively engaging with the rest of the World in terms of trade, a manufacturing hub, and a knowledge exchange nation.

Tracing back history, prior to the 1990s, ie in the pre liberalization era, India was a closed economy with industrialization happening under close supervision of the State. License Raj was prevalent, businesses were regulated, high tariffs were levied on trade with the rest of the world and import licensing was in place. Import substitution was given predominance and restrictions were existing on foreign investments entering Indian shores. The principal mindset was that the country should rely on domestic markets for development and not look towards international trade.

Resurgent India. Jagadish Shettigar and Pooja Misra, Oxford University Press. © Oxford University Press 2022.
DOI: 10.1093/oso/9780192866486.003.0031

In 1991, with the onset of the LPG, ie liberalization, privatization, and globalization, liberalization policies had made economic activity less constraining and reduced the prevailing high tariff and non-tariff barriers. Privatization opened doors and encouraged private sector entities to set shop and partake in the returns that a large domestic market offers. Last but not the least, globalization gave the impetus to the expansion of economic activities globally and increased private sector participation in all sectors.

However, the painting on the canvas was still not complete. Reforms and progress is ongoing. Thus, keeping the same in mind, the Prime Minister's vision of making the country into an Atmanirbhar Bharat is more about developing the country into being a manufacturing hub and a sourcing destination wherein domestic manufacturers are confident about selling their wares and products globally. Does an Atmanirbhar Bharat mean being protectionist and anti-trade? If yes, considering that we are in a globalized world, this would contradict the 'Law of Comparative Advantage' advocated by David Ricardo in 1817. The law simply means that if countries have a comparative advantage in producing a good in terms of efficiency and price over others, then they should utilize their resources in the production of this commodity and subsequently trade with others. The net effect will be that countries across the world would stand to be gainers from international trade. Thus, in our perspective too, even with the existing geo-political tensions, the call by the Prime Minister was not for contradicting the law of comparative advantage and being protectionist or anti-trade. But by being Atmanirbhar, the endeavour is to build a self-reliant India. While emphasizing export promotion focusing on indigenous strengths as per the comparative cost advantage, the PM showed his interest in acquiring state-of-the-art technology as modern international trade suggests. Advances in nuclear, space technology, IT are just a few cases of pride. After all, security was monitored by indigenous drones while the PM was addressing the nation. Being Atmanirbhar is not about looking inwards, not about protectionism, not about import substitution. It is more about making the country into a self-reliant nation by building an eco-system that allows Indian businesses to be competitive on the global platform.

A self-reliant India would mean an India reducing its over-dependence on imports by focusing on 'Make in India'. Self-reliance means strengthening the country's competitive power in the long run, unlike the import substitution of the seventies. The natural evolution of any economy has been from an agricultural state to an industrialized nation to a services-dominated nation. Industrialization generates employment opportunities, encourages better utilization of resources, provides a variety of goods and services at cheaper prices and of better quality to its citizens. However, as is widely known, India largely moved from being an agricultural state till late 1980s–early 1990s to being a services-dominated nation post-1990s. Thus, India jumped the industrialization phase and lost out on its benefits.

In today's date, an Atmanirbhar Bharat will help the country regain the lost ground of industrialization. A self-reliant India would be an India that is built on the pillar of ease of doing business (EODB) and availability of better infrastructure facilities for industrialists to invest in manufacturing. This would help generate jobs and employment, taking advantage of the demographic dividend and leading to more income in the hands of individuals resulting in higher demand for products and services. Higher demand will incentivize producers to further expand and diversify, once again propelling India into the growth trajectory path.

An 'Atmanirbhar Bharat' is envisioned as one where trade imbalances are reduced by identifying industries where it has the comparative advantage and the potential and capability to scale up and be globally competitive. The endeavour of the Government by way of structural measures should be to identify certain industries for special treatment in terms of technological upgradation, taxation, clearances, etc., and evolve and engineer a shift from low-end manufacturing to a high-end producer of goods. The Government should create an environment to reduce dependence on global suppliers and encourage domestic industries to develop so that they are able to withstand global competition instead of operating in a protectionist environment.

A self-reliant India will be a country building on its existing skillsets and being 'Vocal for Local' in areas where it has a comparative advantage such as handicrafts and other labour intensive industries, ie apparel, leather, food processing, etc. To take an example, the Khadi brand, which used to be the politicians' attire, has converted its brand image to a fashion item and promoted itself through an appropriate marketing strategy. It is necessary to ensure that India ensures balanced regional development by encouraging local products and being 'Vocal for Local' on the one hand, while on the other, it should work towards industrializing itself and moving up the value chain. 'An India should not be one which keeps exporting raw material and importing finished products' as said by the Prime Minister. Rather, it should also be a technology-driven country encouraging innovation resulting in value addition and moving up the manufacturing value chain to capital intensive manufacturing. This will ensure that the country is able to move towards a better standard of living and improve on per capita income. To put the same in perspective, India's per capita income (nominal) is approximately USD2388 while that of China and USA is USD10,872 and USD67,000, respectively. So does India have considerable catching up to do? Yes, it does. Policies and structural reforms such as the New Education Policy, building its infrastructure by integrating key modes of transportation, ie air, road, rail, waterways, etc., will go a long way.

This is an opportune time for the Government and fellow Indians to reboot, redraw and reinvent the wheel of progress and paint a new standing in the World Economic Order. A few structural measures which would help the country move on this path would be:

1) **Land and labour reforms** are on the anvil as has been indicated by the Prime Minister. With regards to ease of doing business, land, and labour are still the two existing challenges for any industrialist. Structural reforms in land and labour around transparency and acquisition of ownership, over 200 state labour laws and 40 central labour laws making it cumbersome for industrialists to operate, etc., are needed. Encashing on his tremendous goodwill, the PM should go ahead with big-ticket reforms, especially land and labour. In order to attract investment foreign and domestic investors, it is crucial to reform the Industrial Disputes Act 1947 and Contracts Labour Act. Similarly, Insolvency and Bankruptcy Code should be operational.

2) **Reforming of the judiciary:** The next area for the Government to focus on should be the judiciary. Even under the ease of doing business rankings, India ranks 163rd on the parameter of Enforcing Contracts. This is a reflection of the state of the judiciary in India and is a major negative for investors. In the Economic Survey of

2017–18, it was stated that India required to address 'pendency, delays and backlogs in the appellate and judicial arenas'. Should dispute resolution like out-of-court settlement, mediation, and arbitration be permitted as is in other nations across the World?

3) **Research and Development:** India spends 0.7% of GDP on research and development which is far lower than other BRIC nations, Israel (4.6%), USA (2.8%), Japan (3.2%), UK (1.7%), Canada (1.6%), Brazil (1.3%), China (2.1%), etc. This is abysmally low when compared to the developed and developing nations. Thus, if India wants to reposition itself in the global economic order and ensure that it is able to produce products of a global standard, it needs to put in more money in research and development.

4) **Federal State:** While the roadmap for a federal state, ie Centre and States working together, has already been put in place, the pandemic has shown that for an effective outcome on the ground level and for the country to be able to defeat the virus both the Centre and States needed to work hand in hand. With regards to economic growth also, it should be kept in mind that GDP is not only a Centre subject. The States should bear equal responsibility and create a conducive environment for wooing industries into its geography, thereby creating livelihood for its people and decongesting cities and metros. The same will be a panacea for the overall economic development of the country.

5) **Skillset Mapping:** What the country needs now is to map the skill set of its citizens and attract entrepreneurs and foreign investors accordingly. Skill sets should be mapped region wise and industries should be set up there itself, which will take care of a three-point agenda: the first being providing livelihood to its people and generating income, the second being the production of goods and services, and the third being balanced regional development.

6) **Quality Education:** Yes, the focus of the New Education Policy moving away from rote learning to more meaningful learning is certainly going to be a positive for the country. With universal primary education being compulsory (schemes such as midday meal, have worked positively in ensuring that students attend school), India still needs to ensure that quality education is provided for in the Government and public schools. Centres of excellence should be

built by identifying brilliant students from families irrespective of caste and creed. The Government should aim for special grooming of talented kids right from an elementary stage. With vocational training being provided in the initial years, the country would have already started moving on the path of skill development.

7) **Healthcare Sector:** Another area where India needs to work on is the healthcare sector. To be able to cover lost ground in terms of per capita income, the country needs to ensure that not only health for all, ie Aayushman Bharat scheme is prevalent, but quality health is also available to its citizens. Yes, initiatives like National Digital Health Mission will play a catalyst role but improving the quality of healthcare provided and better existing infrastructure will optimize healthcare indicators such as mortality rate.

8) **Science-Based Industrial Parks:** In reaching the set target, NRIs can play a pivotal role with their talents and resources. India should create the required environment to attract them back home. Best practices on the lines of Taiwan's experiment of building exclusive townships can be seriously deliberated upon and executed with all facilities made available such as state of the art in housing, world-class schools for children, R&D facilities, banking, clearance process, healthcare, and entertainment avenues, etc.

9) **Administrative Reforms:** Perhaps one of the toughest to undertake as the task has to be achieved is using the very same bureaucracy. But the PM, with determination backed by stable government and goodwill of the people, can venture into implementing recommendations gathering dust over four decades. After all, the Government has been able to successfully build a faceless tax system, an unimaginable reform sometime back.

The concept of Atmanirbhar Bharat as envisioned rests on the five pillars of Economy, Infrastructure, System, Vibrant Demography, and Demand. With the endeavour of the Government being on building of businesses including MSMEs, creating new horizons for growth, and bringing about Government reforms that act as enablers, the long-term perspective is to Make in India for the World. Advocating of Vocal for Local will enable Indian companies to gear up their quality and production and be ready to engage in competition with businesses world over and tap new markets globally. India is no longer a closed economy and being Atmanirbhar is about two-way trade and for the country to be well seated and engaged in trade with the rest of the world.

It is all about instilling confidence in all stakeholders, ie investors, manufacturers, policy makers, economists, farming community, traders, and young citizens' eager to set forth and fulfil their aspirations. Atmanirbhar Bharat is about strengthening the economic fundamentals of the country and making India into a country worth emulating and becoming an economic superpower to be reckoned with. As stated by the Prime Minister, the very core of Atmanirbhar Bharat is to create wealth and values not only for Indians alone but also for the larger humanity.

Last but not the least, the measures stated above will pave the path for an 'Atmanirbhar Bharat' and 'Make in India' to 'Make for World' as declared by the Prime Minister in his Independence Day Speech 2020 from the Red Fort.

3.2

Giving Back to Society

The much-dreaded and unprecedented 'Black Swan' event, COVID-19, declared as a pandemic by the World Health Organization (WHO) has shaken countries and economies world over. India is no exception and has faced disruptions in social and economic life in terms of increased unemployment and compelled dislocation of migrant labourers. However, with the easing of regulations and unlock happening in phases, life had started limping back slowly and steadily towards normalcy. The announcement by the Ministry of Statistics and Programme Implementation (MoSPI), Government of India, of the provisional estimates for GDP for April–June quarter (Q1) 2020 had left many economists worried and clamouring for increased Government spending. Data available for Q1 FY2020–21 for India showed that the country had witnessed a contraction of 23.9%. The grim picture painted by GDP numbers had begun ringing alarm bells for policy makers and the Government machinery alike.

There was an outcry by economists for a stimulus package along the lines provided by Governments of advanced economies running into trillions of dollars. The Government of India ably responded to the need of the hour and provided a stimulus package to the tune of Rs. 20 lakh crores (equivalent to 10% of GDP) based on the five pillars of economy, infrastructure, system, vibrant demography, and demand in May 2020. However, many deliberations post this announcement were pointing towards the fact that the stimulus was inadequate for reviving the Indian economy, and the Government must pull out all stops to get the economy back on track. The point that was being missed out here was that the hands of the Government were tied due to the availability of limited fiscal space.

The question that all of us need to answer being: In times of an unprecedented situation such as a health pandemic, is it the whole sole responsibility of the Government alone to step forward and take action in

Resurgent India. Jagadish Shettigar and Pooja Misra, Oxford University Press. © Oxford University Press 2022.
DOI: 10.1093/oso/9780192866486.003.0032

such difficult times OR should Corporates and citizens join hands with the Government and work towards nation building especially during a crisis in hand? Should not the wealthy and citizens with deep pockets rise to the occasion and be a partner in the Government's efforts in bringing back the situation to normalcy?

The country is proud of citizens such as Sonu Sood—'the messiah of migrant labourers' whose image changed from a 'reel life villain' to a 'larger than life real life superhero'—a laudable example of a common citizen selflessly giving back to society. Pained by pictures flashing of migrant workers walking back hundreds of kilometres to the safe boundaries of their homes, the actor decided to take a step forward and lend a helping hand to thousands. From transporting back daily wage workers to their hometowns by arranging dedicated trains, chartered flights to providing meals to the underprivileged, this common citizen had taught a lesson to many people and corporates alike.

Stories have been heard of rich philanthropists like Bill Gates, committing USD100 million through the Bill and Belinda Gates Foundation to aid global research; Warren Buffet donating USD2.9 billion to four family charities and to the Bill and Melinda Gates Foundation; Giorgio Armani and 17 other Italian Billionaires donating USD28 million in Italy, Tata Group donating USD200 million, Azim Premji donating USD150 million, Mukesh Ambani donating USD66 million, and the list goes on.

Looking at it from the perspective of corporates, the last decade in India had witnessed an evolution of companies being cognizant of their Corporate Social Responsibility (CSR) and focusing on premeditated CSR initiatives towards nation building. There has been a growing awareness about CSR amongst stakeholders. CSR as a concept focuses on making a company socially answerable to the stakeholders, the public at large, and itself. Through CSR, companies can have an impact on all facets of society, ie social, environmental, and economic. As per the ruling of Section 135 of the Companies Act 2013, it is obligatory on the part of corporates to spend on a yearly basis a minimum of 2% of their average net profits on CSR activities. A KPMG report titled: India CSR Reporting Survey 2019 showed that CSR contribution towards socially responsible activities on the part of Corporates has been on the rise y-o-y, ie from Rs. 5115 crores in FY2014–15 to Rs. 8691 crores in FY2019–20. The Ministry of Corporate Affairs, Government of India, on 23 March 2020, was quick to announce that expenditure of CSR resources for the virus shall be taken under the head of eligible CSR activity. This created a win–win situation in the minds of many corporates who were keen to donate to relief measures and alongside fulfil legal requirements of the Companies Act.

From a perspective of creating a win for an organization committed to its CSR role, other than deriving tax benefit, it is seen that in today's socially conscious business environment, employees and consumers put a premium on working for and associating with companies that prioritize and are mindful towards their CSR role. How do external stakeholders, ie consumers and public at large, view a company is critical to its success? By building a positive image of a corporate unit from the viewpoint of being responsible and giving back to society, the concerned company can attract and influence both external and internal stakeholders such as consumers, shareholders, suppliers, and employees. To take an instance, Lego, has invested huge sums into addressing climate change and bringing down waste by including recycled packaging and using sustainable material, Starbucks has a socially responsible hiring process in place with gender diversity being the focus in its workforce, Google by spending on renewable energy sources and building ecologically sustainable office space, etc. has built an image perception in the minds of people. Investing in CSR activities helps build brand awareness and brand image. The 2016 Nielsen survey states that 56% of participants claim that a brand being acknowledged for its social value is one of the motivators for influencing consumer buying sentiments, 53% claimed that a brand with community commitment was a leading purchase driver and led to customer loyalty.

Companies that invest time and energy in CSR activities are perceived as having character and strong values. Consumers are known to trust brands that engage more with CSR initiatives. CSR gives a good feel of the brand to consumers and good and effective branding makes customers have a positive feeling for the brand. Horlicks 'Ahaar Abhiyaan' is about fighting malnutrition and the brand per se is all about improving nutrition levels for people. Mahindra's CSR initiative of constructing schools, associating with education programs for children of all age groups and giving medical facilities ties in with their brand philosophy of 'Rise'.

Thus during difficult times of the pandemic wreaking havoc on the lives of millions, it would be advantageous for companies and brands to align their CSR strategies towards improving the lives of the needy who had been adversely impacted by the virus and make it a win–win for both themselves and society at large. It is not important whether the initiative is large or small, it is the thought and motive behind these initiatives that are pertinent. From setting up free health check-up camps to distributing free masks and sanitizers to manufacturing ventilators to drones, lending assistance to the Government can go a long way in combating the pandemic situation and building the brand perception of Corporates.

Business conglomerates such as the Tata Group and Birla family are well known for their deep-rooted philosophy of giving back to society. The current health emergency brings to the forefront, Gandhiji's socioeconomic philosophy of 'Trusteeship'. The philosophy propounded by the Father of the Nation talks about ways and means by which wealthy people would be the guardians of trusts that worked for improving the welfare of the citizens. People with deep pockets in such times of emergency can be persuaded to partake in the Government's effort of working for the welfare of people and actively contributing to it.

India has already witnessed the fruits of Gandhiji's idea of trusteeship being a deeply influencing factor in the life of the founder of the Tata Group, Mr. J.R.D. Tata, who was widely known to base his personal and professional life on this value system. Mr. J.R.D. Tata's 'breadth of vision and genius for organization' coupled with his noble and benevolent nature formed the core of Tata Group's beliefs of giving back to society. This led to the conceiving of founding an institution of advanced scientific education and research such as the Indian Institute of Science (IISc) (originally Tata Institute of Science), the likes of which even the United Kingdom did not have, at the end of the 19th century. The Tata Trusts have also given India other fine institutions such as the Tata Institute of Social Sciences, the Tata Institute of Fundamental Research, the National Centre for the Performing Arts, along with working tirelessly for the upliftment of the underprivileged section of society, empowering of tribals, and the list goes on.

Another business house widely known for its philanthropy is the Birla Group which has Gandhiji's idea of 'Trusteeship' at its very core. The Birlas have been at the forefront of actively supporting the freedom struggle, constructing temples in practically every part of the country, building educational institutions of reckoning, being an integral part of social and economic development of communities with a focus on raising the country's human development index. Thus, it is important to recollect here that these corporate houses in crucial times had taken up the responsibility to selflessly give back to society as inspired by the Indian culture even in the absence of tax incentives and other benefits that were not provided by the Government then. In today's date too, we have business magnates such as Azim Premji venturing into grooming teachers to enhance the quality of primary education and thereby nobly contributing to nation building.

Given the health emergency and crisis situation, cash-rich corporates and wealthy individuals with deep pockets should co-create their CSR and philanthropic strategies as an effective response to the virus outbreak. The imperative thought in the minds of the corporates and wealthy, especially during these unprecedented times, should be of working towards the fact that attaining social goals is as significant as delivering shareholder value and profitability. No matter how big or small is the company, implementing socially responsible business practices helps strengthen the brand image and largely benefits the company.

In trying times of the pandemic, this was an opportune moment for corporates and wealthy individuals to take a leaf out of this concept of Gandhiji of 'Trusteeship' and imbibe it in their lives. For instance, they could lend a helping hand in grand-fathering vulnerable business units in terms of funding support, business strategy, etc. These cash-rich wealthy individuals could partner with State Governments in testing and treatment of the pandemic, especially the poor. They could work towards the rehabilitation of migrant labourers: right from providing psychological comfort to arranging transport, housing facilities, healthcare, etc. Adopting a backward district, especially in states like UP, Bihar, or North-Eastern States, is another avenue that could have been explored by the top 1% wealthy rich strata of India.

3.3

Behavioural Nudge

As forecasted and anticipated by experts and economists, Q1, 2020 results showed a major contraction in the growth of the Indian economy. On 31 August 2020, MoSPI, Government of India declared the provisional estimates for April–June quarter (Q1) 2020. It had posed a grim picture showing that the Indian economy had contracted by 23.9% in Q1 2020, the most drastic contraction witnessed over decades. The worrisome GDP numbers for India were corroborated by the IMF, chief economist, Gita Gopinath, who stated that as per IMF estimates, India's internationally comparable quarter-on-quarter (q-o-q) GDP shrank the highest amongst G20 countries at 25.6%.

The data by the National Statistics Organisation (NSO) showed that other than the agricultural sector, all other sectors had witnessed a contraction. The construction sector saw a sharp decline of 50.3%, manufacturing slipped by 39.3%, electricity, gas, and other utility services contracted by 7%. The worst hit was trade, hotels, transport, and communication, which contracted by 47.0%. The silver lining on the wall was the performance of the agricultural sector which was kept outside the ambit of the lockdown. A better than normal monsoons and essential services such as farming activities and transportation of foodgrains being permitted, the agricultural sector witnessed a growth of 3.4% in the June quarter. What was adding to the worry was that these GDP numbers did not take into account the impact felt by the country's vast informal workforce. The informal sector, once accounted for in the revised estimates, could manifest into a deeper contraction for the economy. However, keeping in mind the lockdown imposed, these numbers came as no surprise to anyone.

Looking ahead, data for economic indicators in August 2020 brought some cheer and a ray of hope for the Indian economy. Economists were deliberating in terms of the country witnessing a V-shaped recovery as

Resurgent India. Jagadish Shettigar and Pooja Misra, Oxford University Press. © Oxford University Press 2022.
DOI: 10.1093/oso/9780192866486.003.0033

the economy slowly and steadily unlocked and regulations were eased. The Purchasing Managers Index (PMI) for manufacturing for August 2020 rose to a six-month high of 52, pointing towards a turnaround in industrial activity (a figure above 50 is reflective of expansion). As per the Nomura India Business Resumption Index (NIBRI) there was an uptick in business normalization in August 2020 with other economic indicators showing a recovery. Power and fuel demand, railway freight, and mobility indices showed a marginal improvement while the passenger car segment had bounced back with vigour. The Google Mobility Index, which analyses visits to retail shops, workplaces, parks, etc., showed a 2% increase in visits to supermarkets, warehouses, farmers markets, specialty food shops in August 2020. However, rising unemployment numbers in August 2020 with urban and rural unemployment rising to 9.83% and 7.65%, respectively and the overall unemployment rate jumping to 8.35% from 7.43% in July 2020 had marred the bright picture being painted on the canvas.

As per IHS Markit, the PMI index indicated an expansion in August 2020 due to output and new orders expanding at its fastest pace since February 2020. An uptick in demand from domestic markets had given the push to production and input purchase. However, one cannot forget the fact that with the virus creating fear in the minds of people of not really being sure of what the future would hold, consumers were holding onto cash and not willing to indulge in discretionary spending behaviour. For the Indian economy to gather pace in its economic recovery path and give the requisite boost to demand, it was imperative that marketers would take notice of the absence of impulse buying behaviour of consumers and strategize accordingly. The pandemic had put a pause on consumers' urge to splurge and adversely impacted impulse purchases due to the fear of uncertainty lurking in their minds.

McKinsey in July 2020 had indicated that consumer sentiments were at a low and reflective of the uncertainty created by the virus. There had been a shift to mindful shopping including some trading down of value. RBI, in its Consumer Confidence Survey report published on 6 August 2020, stated that consumer confidence had plummeted in July 2020 with the Current Situation Index (CSI) showing an all-time low. The positive from the survey was that Future Expectations Index (FEI) was charting its way back into the positive territory.

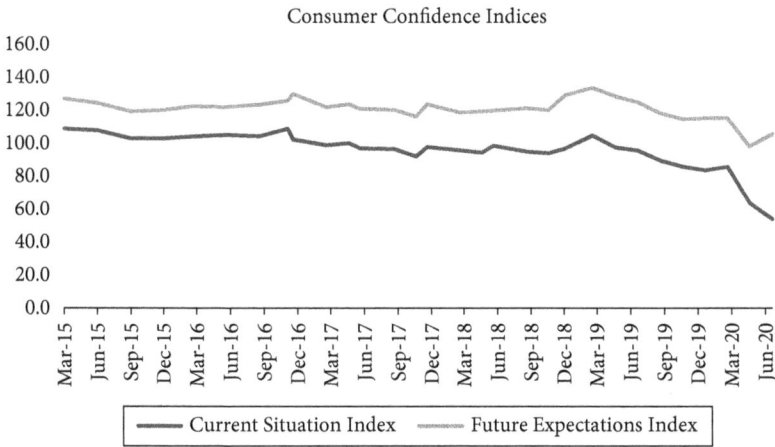

Source: Reserve Bank of India: https://m.rbi.org.in/Scripts/PublicationsView.aspx?id=19714

Thus, the novel coronavirus had led to a behavioural change in consumers and changed consumer preferences. With new hygiene and contagiousness concerns, people were unwilling to venture into shopping malls and marketplaces. Though the Google Mobility index showed a rise of 2% in August 2020, retailers were visionary enough and helped consumers navigate seamlessly between an offline and online experience and invest in an omni-channel world.

With consumers hesitant to step out of their homes to shop, there was an absence of the demonstration effect of customers. The demonstration effect denotes the consumption habits of individuals to imitate consumption trends adopted by others. Keeping up with the Joneses was a thought far away from the minds of consumers. Thus, the unprecedented situation created by the virus required organizations to go back to the drawing board and restrategize.

With the festival season coming up and keeping in mind that consumer behaviour was influenced deeply by cultural factors, brands and companies could have explored utilizing the 'Nudge theory' in wooing back customers. Nudges are physical cues that influence individuals to behave in a certain way, without categorically promoting any behaviour. Nudge principles have been actively utilized in commercial marketing earlier too. While the anticipation was that consumers would only be willing to step out of home post the vaccine being launched, marketers could have looked at rebuilding, restrategizing, and rethinking for the festival season.

With localized lockdowns and the virus surfacing back, Q2, 2020 was reflective of a slight uptick but hopes were pinned on Q3, 2020. The festive season slated in Q3, FY2020–21 was expected to bring cheer and respite from the pandemic-linked slumber. Brands were pinning much hope on the festive season and advertisement campaigns reflecting empathy and positive sentiments of the world being able to win over the virus could have helped win back customer trust and reshape consumer sentiments. Festive season beginning from August 2020 and extending until January 2021 was to be the time for brands to give the much-needed nudge to discretionary spending and drive back GDP numbers for the Indian economy.

Agreeably, rising unemployment numbers were a cause of worry and indicated that the formal sector had restrained from hiring while jobs in rural areas had remained stagnant. At this point of time, it was important to reflect on the negative impact that reverse migration had brought about on production activities. Sectors such as construction and manufacturing, which had shown a contraction of 50.3% and 39.3%, respectively, had also been hit drastically by labour shortages. One-third of the labour that had migrated back in April 2020 had still not returned to the cities and industrial areas. Yes, some corporate leaders did come up with out-of-box measures to bring back labour and employees by paying for their return flight and train journeys, offering housing facilities, etc., but the pandemic did force all to rethink on this account. The pandemic had reinforced the importance of unskilled and semi-skilled labour and labour shortage would drive up the minimum wages being paid. Wasn't it only fair that corporate magnets and the Government should have looked at providing the basic necessity of food, clothing, housing, and a minimum basic income to this section of society too?

As they say, an unprecedented situation requires out-of-line strategies and out-of-box thinking. While the Government was already working on providing stimulus measures to improve EODB for producers and ease of living, especially for the lesser strata of society, it was high time that corporate stalwarts in all fairness improved working and living conditions for its labour force. This would have helped bring back migrant workers, fuel up production and act as a booster on the supply side. Festival season and the nudge theory in conjunction would have helped bring back positive consumer sentiments and thus propelled the demand side of the economy. Thus, in a way with both demand and supply getting the requisite shot in the arm, Q3 2020 and Q4 2020 would have witnessed the Indian economy in the orbit of economic growth and moving fast on the track of a V-shaped recovery path.

3.4

Gramodaya

The Indian economy is constituted of approximately two-thirds of the population and 70% workforce residing in rural areas. India's per capita GDP in rural regions is known to have grown at a CAGR of 6.2% since 2000. Agriculture and its allied services are the prime sectors of rural economy and rural employment. The agricultural sector had shown an impressive growth of 5.9% in Q4 2020 despite the COVID-19 lockdown. This sector had outshone the performance of the overall Indian economy, which had a growth figure of 3.1% in Q4, 2020 due to contraction in the core sectors. As per CRISIL's forecast, the agricultural sector would depict a growth of 2.5% in 2020–21 as against the GDP numbers for India which were being projected at a contraction of 4.2%. The winds blowing favourably for the agricultural sector could be attributed to a 15% better than normal monsoon, availability of water in reservoirs for irrigation, increase in sowing acreage area of Kharif crop with planting expanding to 80% of the 100 million hectares resulting in an increase by 18.5% higher than last year's level, aggressive implementation of the MGNREGA scheme by the Government and various other welfare measures targeting the rural sector.

The COVID-19 pandemic negatively impacted not only the health and well-being of citizens but also the Indian economy had grinded to a halt due to the Lockdown leading to countrywide demand and supply chain disruption. However, going by estimates, the Indian rural economy had been resurgent and Bharat seemed to have been moving relatively faster on the path to recovery. Unemployment numbers given by Centre for Monitoring Indian Economy (CMIE) were indicative of the fact that the worst was over and unemployment was fast on the decline. Interestingly, rural employment numbers were leading the way with a 6.8% rural unemployment rate (nearing pre-COVID numbers of January 2020) as against urban unemployment rate of 9.7% as in the first week of August 2020.

Resurgent India. Jagadish Shettigar and Pooja Misra, Oxford University Press. © Oxford University Press 2022.
DOI: 10.1093/oso/9780192866486.003.0034

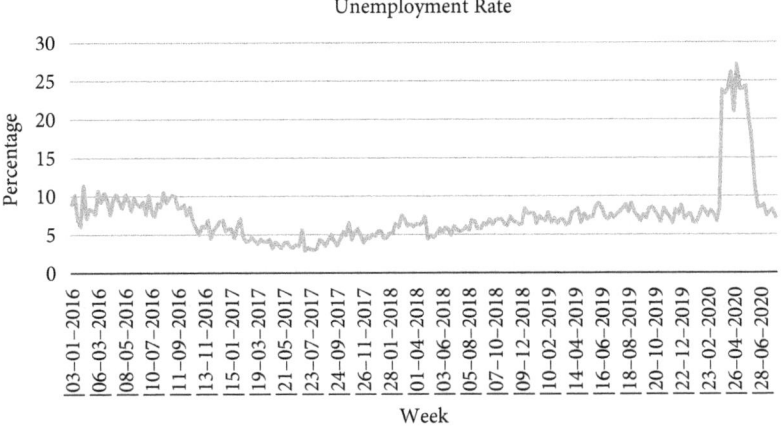

Source: CMIE

Month	Unemployment rate (%)		
	India	Urban	Rural
July 2020	7.43	9.15	6.66
June 2020	10.99	12.02	10.52
May 2020	23.48	25.79	22.48
April 2020	23.52	24.95	22.89
March 2020	8.75	9.41	8.44
February 2020	7.76	8.65	7.34
January 2020	7.22	9.7	6.06
December 2019	7.6	9.02	6.93
November 2019	7.23	8.88	6.45
October 2019	8.1	8.27	8.02
September 2019	7.16	9.62	6.00
August 2019	8.19	9.71	7.48

Source: Centre for Monitoring Indian Economy Pvt Ltd.

The Consumer Price Index-Agricultural Labourers (CPI-AL) and Consumer Price Index for rural labourers (CPI-RL) declined to 7.16% and 7.00% in June 2020. This could be attributed to the free supply of food grains by the Government of India under the PM Garib Kalyan Ann Yojana (PMGKAY), thereby lessening the burden on daily budgetary requirements of the rural labourers and putting more money in their hands to spend. Higher disposable income in the hands of the rural population led to a strengthened rural demand.

Stimulus measures such as increasing daily wages under the MGNREGS to Rs. 202 per day from Rs. 182; an additional allocation of Rs. 40,000 crores for this scheme (this was in addition to the Budgetary provision), increase in Minimum Support Price of foodgrains of 50% to 83% announced in June 2020, free foodgrain distribution of 5 kg free ration and 1 kg dal per month till November end 2020, Rs. 50,000 crores for implementation of public infrastructure works (and thereby providing livelihood) across six States and 116 districts being earmarked for the migrant workers returning to rural areas had increased disposable income in the hands of the rural population. This had fuelled up demand and a rise in consumption was being driven by this section of people.

FMCG manufacturers were confident of robust demand from the interiors and rural areas of the country. ITC Limited launched five new products in the wellness and hygiene segment, including a 50 paise hand sanitizer sachet targeting the rural consumer segment. Aspirations and consumer behaviour divide between the rural and urban areas were seen to have narrowed considerably over the years. The Indian rural market size for fast-moving consumer goods was estimated to cross the USD100 billion mark by 2025. As per Government directives, during the period of lockdown supply for essential items was not hampered. The IAMAI Nielsen report of 2019 stated that rural India had 10% more internet users as against urban India. Rather, during the period of lockdown, rural consumers were also seen to be embracing online purchases and driving consumption digitally. The lockdown propelled several brands involved in the sale of essential items to shift to digital media to continue to woo consumers and the proliferation of vernacular content only helped to deepen the engagement of rural Indians. As per experts, consumption levels in rural India were bordering at 85% of pre-COVID levels in May as against 70% in urban India.

Market leaders for two-wheelers in India, Hero MotorCorp's June sales were four times that of May 2020. The company ascribed this increase in demand to a rise in rural income. Data showed that tractor sales in the domestic market had registered a growth of 4% y-o-y (92,888 units in June '20 from 75,859 units in June '19), thereby reversing the auto slump which had plagued the Indian automobile industry for quite some time.

This was also indicative of growing economic activities in rural India. Rather, even as far as GST numbers were concerned, principally rural States, ie Madhya Pradesh and Chhattisgarh witnessed a whopping GST growth of 24% and 22% y-o-y in June 2020.

In addition to the stimulus being provided by the Government, factors such as more land being brought under cultivation (increase in planting by 18.5% higher than previous year's level), an increase of water stored in 123 reservoirs (55% more than previous year), farming activities being permitted during the lockdown and with reverse migration happening, ie migrant workers being involved in farming activities had led to a resurgence and positive consumer sentiments for rural India. A good rabi crop and 15% above normal rainfall resulting in increased acreage under sowing for the kharif crop augured well. Additionally, with the launch of Agriculture Infrastructure Fund of Rs. 1 lakh crores by the Prime Minister, Mr. Narendra Modi for setting up of cold chain, refrigerated transportation and other agri-entrepreneurs set-up being encouraged to be built by the Government, the farmers would be in a position to command better prices in the medium to long term. This would lead to more income in their hands, leading to further growth prospects. The Finance Ministry, in its Macroeconomic report for July 2020, also stated that the rural economy and the agricultural sector would play a key role in pushing India's growth forward.

Interestingly, even during the Global Financial Crisis of 2008, the rural consumer helped thwart the turbulence of global recession by increasing rural demand for FMCG and telecom products. The stimulus provided by the then Government in power through the National Rural Employment Guarantee Act (NREGA) and farm loan waiver of Rs. 60,000 crores put more money in the hands of the rural population in 2008. However, in July 2020, in addition to the Government stimulus mentioned above, structural reforms initiated by the Government in power added to the positive story being woven in Bharat. The three ordinances introduced by the Government under the Atmanirbhar Bharat scheme were announced in May 2020, with regards to the Agricultural Produce Marketing Committees Act, which would enable farmers to sell their produce outside the mandis, thereby breaking the monopoly of the middlemen and giving them the benefit of 'my crop, my right', amendment of the Essential Commodities Act, 1955 (lifting of restrictions on commodities such as cereals, pulses, onions) and Farmers (Empowerment and Protection) Agreement on Price Assurance and Farm Services Ordinance (providing a charter for farmers to engage in contract farming with large food multinational companies) would help them gain the benefits of higher prices for their produce. Not to forget, Rs. 1 lakh crores being set aside for the Agriculture Infrastructure Fund would help build the basic infrastructure of cold chain and refrigerated transportation, thereby enabling farmers to be in a position to command better prices in the medium to long term. These were structural reforms that would have gone a long way in rejuvenating India's rural ecosystem. This only cements the thought that with a little short-term pain, rural India would derive the benefits of long-term gain.

If all went well, what was needed in the immediate future was to be able to strategize for a bumper kharif crop too and avoid the 'paradox of plenty' situation for the farmers. With a large section of the migrant population staying back in rural areas post lockdown, states such as Uttar Pradesh, Bihar, Madhya Pradesh could have transformed this additional working population into an opportunity and reskilled them or alternately invited businesses and MNCs to set up industries across the hinterland. Such long-term measures would have led to a welcome fundamental shift in the rural-urban dynamics of India and would also be able to take care of disguised unemployment which is a malaise for rural India. Rather, UP had already taken the first step by proposing to set up a jewellery park near Agra to be able to harness the labour potential and provide local employment to returning silver artisans.

Initiatives undertaken by MNCs such as 'e-choupal' by ITC Limited, which enables rural India with technical know-how for an effective agri ecosystem and facilitates a transparent mechanism for price discovery, should have been encouraged. The Government should have consolidated and leveraged the Common Service Centre (CSC) pan India network which was already in place. Additionally, it should have also focussed on promoting cottage industries and providing better amenities in terms of health care, education, road network, communication, and power so that the rural population could also be in a position to access quality life on par with the urban sector. Besides helping in resolving the problem disguised in the agricultural sector, this would have also taken care of migration towards cities in search of a job. By setting up food processing units, small scale industries, building on the rural infrastructure and increasing employment opportunities in agri-allied activities, non-farm areas, and enabling healthcare facilities through 'Ayushman Bharat' and 'Housing for All' under the Pradhan Mantri Awas Yojana, the Government should vie towards decentralization from urban areas and metros and build a balanced regional developed India.

The Government's proposal of focusing on rural infrastructure should be implemented with all seriousness. In the past also such proposals were announced but failed to see the light of the day. For instance, the very first budget of the Vajpayee government talked about cold chains with PPP model. Similarly, under the UPA government, the then Railway Minister Lalu Prasad Yadav, proposed refrigerated wagons exclusively for the transportation of farm goods. If the Prime Minister's intention gets translated into action, this will go a long way in taking care of the interests of both farmers and consumers.

It is high time we remembered the Father of the Nation by targeting the concept of 'gramodaya'.

3.5
Functional Autonomy to Banks

A stable financial sector is a prerequisite for the smooth functioning of any business and provides confidence to investors and consumers. With the COVID-19 pandemic negatively impacting GDP of countries across the world and resulting in an ever-changing environment, risk prudence was reflective of being sagacious but risk aversion was also not advisable. In light of the pandemic, the 21st issue of the Financial Stability Report (FSR), July 2020 of the Reserve Bank of India, presented a grim picture of the status of Non-Performing Assets (NPAs) in India. The stress test conducted by the RBI was indicative of the fact that the challenging situation posed by COVID-19 could have resulted in the GNPA increasing to 12.5% by March 2021 as against 8.5% in March 2020. As per Standard and Poor's estimates (June 2020), GNPA could have risen to 13–14% for India.

Resurgent India. Jagadish Shettigar and Pooja Misra, Oxford University Press. © Oxford University Press 2022.
DOI: 10.1093/oso/9780192866486.003.0035

(a)   SCBs' GNPA Ratio

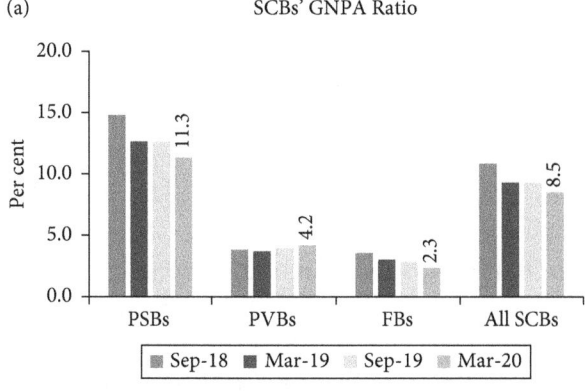

(b)   Growth in SCBs' GNPAs (y-o-y)

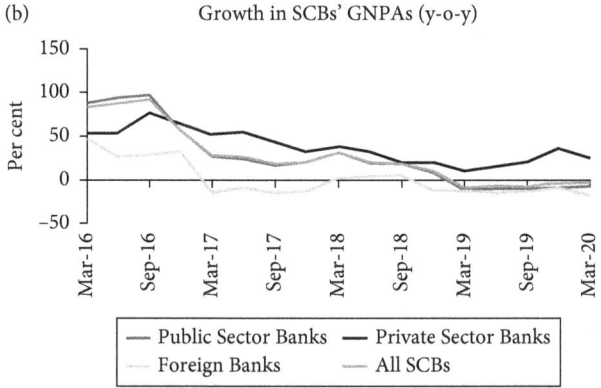

Source: RBI: https://rbidocs.rbi.org.in/rdocs//PublicationReport/Pdfs/6FSRCHAPTER269522
49FEDAA4019BC14F4FA93C89F2C.PDF

The FSR of the RBI is an evaluation of the risks associated with financial stability and measures the resilience of the financial system of the
country in light of the current changing environment and issues existing
in the financial ecosystem. The report is prepared by the collective evaluation of the Financial Stability and Development Council (FSDC) and
studies the issues concerning the development and regulation of the financial economy. The report highlighted the fact that in response to the
pandemic, an amalgamation of fiscal, monetary, and regulatory interventions had ensured a close to normal functioning of the Indian financial
markets. In addition to the pandemic, factors such as an overleveraged
non-financial sector, geopolitical tensions in reference to the US-China
trade war, and economic losses incurred due to the Lockdown imposed

resulted in the economy being abruptly brought to a halt and negatively impacting growth prospects of the country.

The FSR of July 2020 had stated that the capital to risks weighted assets ratio (CRAR) of scheduled commercial banks (SCBs) in March 2020 had declined to 14.8% as against 15.0% (September 2019) and GNPA had decreased from 9.3% to 8.5% for the same period. However, macro stress tests for credit risks were indicative of the fact that the GNPA ratio could rise to 12.5% (March 2021) from 8.5% (March 2020), keeping in mind the challenging economic scenario posed by COVID-19. The worst-case scenario as spelt out by the RBI was that the GNPA could even have risen to as high as 14.7% by March 2021. However, a positive ray of hope could be ascribed to the fact that with the improved capitalization of public sector banks, there could be a decline in contagion losses to the financial system.

The grim scenario can be attributed to the pandemic resulting in an economic downturn. The RBI, in response to this worrisome situation, had proposed for a three-month moratorium in March 2020 along with a freeze in ratings of customers who were availing of the loan so that it would not impact their credit scores. The moratorium period was further increased to 31 August 2020 as a part of the stimulus package. However, financial stalwarts such as Rajnish Kumar (SBI Chairman) and Deepak Parekh (HDFC Chairman) had opined that the RBI should not extend the interest moratorium beyond August 2020. Their advice was that banks be permitted for a one-time restructuring on loans. Data showed that while at the end of April 2020, 50% of the debtors had availed of this moratorium facility, the numbers had considerably improved since then. As of end June 2020, only 30% were shown to have availed of this facility. Interestingly, RBI, on 6 August 2020, announced that lenders would be allowed for one-time restructuring of loans of corporate and MSMEs, and the moratorium facility would not be extended beyond 31 August 2020. Thus, what was needed was a calibrated approach of stimulus to be provided by RBI to those sectors only which were still bearing the brunt of the pandemic and a blanket approach to all was not advisable as individuals and corporates were taking undue advantage and unnecessarily deferring payments.

India's banking sector plays a pre-dominant role in the financing of projects and working capital for businesses. Credit availability and smooth flow of funds to businesses aid economic growth. NPAs and the presence of weak recovery of credit in the system can undermine credit availability. However, not all NPAs are an outcome of wilful default. It is vital that banks identify bad loans as per standards applicable globally. An ineffective management, inappropriate handling of projects, managerial deficiencies, a poor credit appraisal system, lack of adequate resources could lead to a business venture failing and ending up as a non-performing asset. As per Former RBI chief Raghuram Rajan, factors such as explosive expansion without due diligence, slower GDP growth resulting in industrial demand falling short of projections, promoters and banks conspiring to hide the true NPA numbers by evergreening of loans and fraud and divergence of funds could be some of the factors which led to rising NPAs. Thus, what was needed was an enabling environment facilitating smooth entry and exit for firms. This would ensure that firms that were tending towards industrial sickness and being non-performing had policy measures to take recourse to and enabled them for a smooth exit option. As per the Industrial Disputes Act of 1947 and subsequent amendment in 1982, a firm with 100 or more workers (for States like Maharashtra, Madhya Pradesh, etc., the stipulation is of 300 or more workers) requires permission from the State Government for retrenchment, closures, and layoffs. For State Governments to grant approval for closure and retrenchment, political will and backing is required and is a must. Thus, for a business tending towards industrial sickness, exiting from the industry is a long and tedious process. For companies that are operating at their 'shut-down' points and not being able to also recover their variable costs, it is advisable for them to close operations. However, the lengthy process of initiating closure formalities discourages the promoter from closing down and he/she opts for the easier path of borrowing more from banks, thereby getting into a debt trap resulting in higher NPAs for the banking industry. To further add fuel to the fire, with regards to enforcing contracts under the EODB rankings, India ranks 163rd amongst 190 countries which is a reflection of the state of the Indian judiciary. Thus closing down operation is not an easy option for a sick business unit.

The need of the hour was for a policy amendment to the Industrial Disputes Act of 1947. Yes, the present Government did find an alternate solution by way of the Insolvency and Bankruptcy Code (IBC) of 2016—'a game changer, a transformational reform'. This Code is a one-stop solution for resolving insolvencies, thereby offering an economically viable solution. The IBC can be initiated by the debtors or creditors and has shown amazing results with regards to NPAs post its implementation. As per RBI's report titled Trend and Progress of Banking in India 2018–19, the amount recovered as a percentage of the amount involved had been much higher for IBC at 49.6% in 2017–18 and 42.5% in 2018–19 as compared to recovery by traditional bodies such as Lok Adalats and Debt Recovery Tribunals. Data is reflective of the fact that IBC has proved to be a deterrent and a masterstroke in curbing bad loans, be it of big industrial houses or small businesses. Rather, as per the rankings of the World Bank for 'Ease of Doing Business' India under the 'resolving insolvency' parameter leaped 56 places to 52nd rank in 2020 from 108 previously. The recovery rate in terms of cents on the dollar recovered for India had improved to 71.6 in 2020 as against 25.7 in 2016, and in terms of time period had improved to 1.6 years in 2020 as against 4.3 years in 2016 under the IBC. The restructuring and liquidation of bad loans have opened up new vistas for foreign and domestic investors to invest in distressed Indian assets. Resolving insolvencies in a time-bound manner creates a conducive environment for industrialists, attracts foreign portfolio investments, and boosts the economic growth of the country.

However, it also needs to borne in mind that in response to the blow dealt by the pandemic, the IBC proceedings under the stimulus announced in May 2020 had been suspended for one year so that Companies are not dragged into judiciary proceedings at this untoward point of time and debts related to the coronavirus would not be a part of the default category under IBC. Also, the minimum payment threshold for triggering bankruptcy proceedings had been increased to Rs.1 crore as against Rs. 1 lakh. While it is understandable that the calamity requires such out-of-the-box decisions but to keep NPAs in check, the Government should ensure that they are able to do away with these relaxations at the earliest and bring the IBC back into force as soon as possible. The same would be possible only once the country started gaining momentum and re-treading the path of economic growth. Revival of the economy would anyways act as an automatic stabilizer for NPAs.

Last but not the least, it must be kept in mind that the IBC is not an answer to all banking issues. Additional structural reforms in the financial ecosystem will be a catalyst to financial stability and boosting of business confidence. With Know Your Customer (KYC) norms in place, it is possible for banks to ensure that their customers are real. Bankers should be consistently monitoring and assessing risks associated with their customers through the KYC norms and taking action accordingly. Thus, bankers should be ever vigilant and try to minimize cases of wilful defaulters. Also, they should be given adequate functional autonomy so that they can ensure that NPAs are kept to a minimum. Rather, RBI's suggestion of reducing the shareholding of the Government in Public Sector's Bank's to 26% is worth serious deliberations. Importantly, political discretion in allocations should be discouraged, and all efforts should be aimed at curbing cronyism.

3.6

Petroleum Products Pricing

With petrol and diesel prices surging to a record high in India, the sky-rocketing prices were a cause of worry for the Government and common man alike. Higher fuel prices lead to increased travel costs and keeping in mind that oil is an essential raw material for the industrial and agricultural sectors both, it would also lead to increased cost of production, thereby having a supply-side inflationary impact on the economy and negatively impacting household budgets.

The reason for the spiralling price increase had been ascribed to output cuts by oil-producing nations and with India being the third-largest oil importer and importing 86% of its crude oil requirements, increased crude oil prices raised the base price. International crude oil prices had been on the rise and with a deal being struck between the OPEC countries and its allies for reduced oil production, ie reduced supply, fuel prices were on the rise. To further worsen the situation, Saudi Arabia had agreed to a voluntary cut of 1 million barrels per day produced, resulting in crude oil prices touching a high of USD63 per barrel. With the havoc being wreaked by COVID-19 across all nations worldwide, crude oil which was trading at USD71 in January 2020 had declined to USD21 in April 2020 due to low demand. However, now with economic recovery taking place (Nomura Business Resumption Index rising to 98.1 for India as of 14 February 2021) and oil-producing nations strategizing internally, prices had steadily been on the rise. In August 2020, crude oil was trading at USD43 per barrel, while in January 2021, it had been trading at USD53.

Looking at fuel prices from a different perspective, petrol and diesel prices in India consist of international crude oil price, ie the base price; import duty; refinery cost; freight cost, central excise; state value-added tax; marketing companies' margin and outlets' margin. Tracing back history, petrol and diesel, which were historically regulated by the Government and under the administrative price mechanism, had been

Resurgent India. Jagadish Shettigar and Pooja Misra, Oxford University Press. © Oxford University Press 2022.
DOI: 10.1093/oso/9780192866486.003.0036

dismantled over the years. The shift from administrative pricing to dynamic pricing was an outcome of two factors, ie first being that the benefits of the smallest change in international oil prices could also be put into effect by dealers and passed on to consumers and second being that under the Administered Price Mechanism while consumers were protected in bearing the actual burden of increased international crude oil prices, the brunt was being borne by the Oil Marketing Companies (thereby transforming Navaratna oil marketing companies into loss-making units). Apart from being a poor business decision forced on the oil PSUs, it also amounted to disrupting the role of market forces in the economic use of products, especially in the case of the use of petrol.

With regards to LPG cylinders, the Government was providing a subsidy on the sale of domestic and non-domestic LPG cylinders to consumers and for Rs. 769, approximately the price of the LPG cylinder, the subsidy amount falls anywhere between Rs. 420 and Rs. 465 for a 14.2 kg cylinder. It was heartening to see that citizens who could afford it voluntarily surrendered the subsidy benefit on the appeal of the Prime Minister.

The current point of debate seeing the light of the day was that India had one of the highest tax rates on diesel and petrol of approximately 60% of the total price. In addition to rising crude oil prices in the international market, the heavy load of taxes had raised fuel prices to an all-time high and it was the pandemic affected revenue stream collection which was impeding both the Centre and States from considering a duty cut. The Central excise duty is a specific duty while State value-added taxes are on an ad valorem basis (percentage of the product price), resulting in States benefiting from higher prices. Keeping in mind that higher fuel prices would stoke an inflationary impact on the economy, the RBI Governor had called for the reduction of indirect taxes to contain price levels at a reasonable level and Finance Minister, Ms. Nirmala Sitharaman had also stated that the steep rise was a vexatious issue.

So the relevant point that one needs to ponder on is: What would be the likely impact if petrol and diesel prices are brought under the ambit of GST?

It is a known fact that considering fuel is a major revenue collection source for both the Centre and States, initially, as a strategy to get all the States on board in view of the fact that GST implementation involved constitutional amendment (which meant the necessity of the state assemblies endorsing) and it was not a mere structural tax reform, fuel prices were kept outside the purview of GST. However, for sure all would agree that it is a narrow viewpoint that the Centre and States would lose a major source of revenue if petroleum products are included as a part of GST.

The above view needs to be deliberated upon through a wider perspective. Bringing petroleum products within GST means the cost of production coming down (even if the highest GST rate is applied of 28%), which in turn would lead to a higher profit margin resulting in higher dividend contribution by the PSUs and higher corporate tax by the private sector. The net result could very well be that of the government mobilizing higher revenue and it would be worthwhile for an appointed committee to deliberate on the pros and cons of the same. On the other hand, States' interests might also be protected as they are entitled to a share in the GST. Additionally, bringing petroleum products under GST will replace the current multiple tax structure and entail consensus amongst the state governments controlled by different parties apart from the central government.

Constituting a Regulatory Authority to strike a balance between the interests of the service provider and the users is a part of reform measures in any sector. Along with the decision to phase out APM for petroleum products, the government had also issued a notification for constituting the Petroleum and Gas Regulatory Board in 2006. As of today, the board is practically defunct with the exception of a single member rest of the positions, including the Chairperson is vacant. It is high time a full-fledged board takes over the responsibility of pricing petroleum products.

Not to miss the key point that the common consumers would end up paying a lower price. Being the devil's advocate, even if one was to compute petrol prices with a 28% GST, it could be in the range of Rs. 42.75 approximately as against Rs. 86.30 per litre. Thus, getting petroleum products into the purview of GST is going to be a win–win for all stakeholders and all concerned should build up consensus on the issue. For the ruling party, such a measure is bound to provide a political dividend.

3.7

Taxation Reforms

With the Prime Minister's call to make India—a self-reliant nation, one of the key pillars for achieving the same is a stable policy and regulatory environment. Investment decisions by the private sector are based on the state of the financial market, existing policy framework in the economy, prevalent tax regime, a well-functioning judiciary, and access to developed infrastructure. A simplified and stable taxation policy adds to EODB and can effectively promote economic growth through the effective utilization of available resources. Viewing taxes from the perspective of an avenue for mobilizing revenue to facilitate public expenditure would rather be a narrow outlook as against building a transparent taxation policy that is able to encourage and woo businesses and corporations to set up shop in India, thereby promoting domestic manufacturing and production, employment opportunities and propelling the country into the path of economic growth.

Tracing back history, it can be seen that the mindset of policymakers had witnessed a sea change since the beginning of the 1990s with a gradual fall in both direct and indirect taxes (ie maximum marginal tax on income from 97.75% has been brought down to 30% + surcharge rate; highest excise duty from 150% to.12.36% and customs duty from 300% to approximately 40%). On 1 July 2017, GST, an indirect, comprehensive, destination-based tax was implemented in India, subsuming practically all indirect taxes. The outcome of these major changes in the tax regime has shown positive results in terms of cost of production, leading to horizontal expansion of standard of living; price stability and acceleration in growth rates. The post-pandemic trend in terms of tax revenue collection has been an exception, but keeping in mind the unprecedented crisis that the virus has resulted in for countries across the world, it has sprung absolutely no surprises.

Resurgent India. Jagadish Shettigar and Pooja Misra, Oxford University Press. © Oxford University Press 2022.
DOI: 10.1093/oso/9780192866486.003.0037

Not to forget with the corporate tax rate being amended in 2019 and with the Government lowering the base corporate tax rate to 22% from 33% and to 15% from 25% for new manufacturing companies, it has provided the requisite stimulus to investments from across the globe especially in manufacturing thus revving up the growth engine and resurrecting sentiments in the minds of investors. It has resulted in increased cash flow to Corporate India which can be channelized towards debt reduction or incremental investments in increasing capacity. The changes in corporate tax rates are in tune with international standards resulting in higher re-investment and expansion; strengthening equity culture with more retail investors getting attracted due to improved dividend earning prospects.

Transparency in taxation is equally important and the current government with its approach of 'Minimum Government and Maximum Governance' and 'Reform, Perform and Transform' has been initiating measures in this context. The endeavour is to create a hassle-free tax return process through measures such as faceless and contactless payment and appeal and a taxpayer's charter. Digitization of tax administration and quick refunds and dispute resolution mechanisms have been put in place to restore trust and transparency between the taxpayer and tax collector and improve tax compliance. Reducing tax litigations remains high on the Government's priority list with schemes such as 'Vivaad se Vishwas' thereby providing a one-time opportunity for dispute resolution.

However, there are a couple of disturbing issues which are crucial from the point of facilitating a positive business environment. More so, when the incumbent government is seriously committed to improving EODB. The Vodafone retrospective taxation case which dated back to 2007 with the Government raising initial capital gains and withholding tax demand of Rs. 7990 crores during the acquisition of Hutchinson by Vodafone was one such example. The demand for retrospective tax by the Indian Government on Cairn Energy Plc. was being viewed as breach of the guarantee of fair and equitable treatment. It must be kept in mind that such issues would have endangered India's stance as an enticing investment destination as existing taxation policies are a crucial part of investment planning and with a country bringing in taxes from a retrospective perspective can create the perception of an unstable corporate regulation and taxation environment in the minds of the investor. Such cases could have a negative impact on the industry morale and dent the environment of faith created over the years by the Government.

Though the present government promised in the very first budget, FY15 not to go for retrospective tax, which creates a fresh liability for the investor, but the right to impose was retained. Examples of such tax disputes have been testing the Government's tax and investor protection policies in the international fora.

It must also be borne in mind that the basic objective of implementing GST in place of multiple taxes was not just to treat the entire country as a single market with a single tax rate. The larger perspective was to plug scope for leakage and zero tolerance for corruption. However, with four GST tax slabs, which provides ample bargaining scope for the business lobby and petroleum products, alcohol, etc., being kept outside the ambit of GST, the policy needs to be revisited. Countries such as New Zealand, Singapore, Australia follow a single and consistent tax rate on every purchase. Doing away with multiple GST tax slabs will ensure greater ease of compliance and avoid unnecessary confusion. The GST council in India should draw a roadmap to moving towards a single GST tax slab that can suitably create a balance between the vast variations in per capita income in India and generate adequate revenue sources.

Under 'one country one tax' principle, there should be no scope for keeping a few products outside the GST, and all products should be necessarily brought within the GST net. When tax revenue is to be shared with states as per the norms recommended by the Finance Commission, what is the issue for keeping petroleum products, liquor, and tobacco out of its purview is a question that needs to be pondered upon?

3.8

Making for the World:
Technology Is the Key

In light of the pandemic having adversely impacted countries world-wide and India's GDP contracting at 6.6% in FY2020–21 (a sharp 15.7% decline in the first half and 0.1% fall in the second half of the year), the Prime Minister's call for 'Make in India for the World' from the ramparts of the Red Fort in August 2020 had set the tone to boost domestic manufacturing and make India into a self-reliant nation. Translating the call by the PM would necessarily mean gearing up to be competitive in the international market in terms of quality, efficiency, and cost per unit of output produced. In both respects, upgradation of technology is the key to positioning India on the world map as a major manufacturing destination and the factory for the world. Improved technological know-how will help India manufacture quality products at competitive prices and thereby gain a strong foothold in global markets.

India's dependence on the international market is hardly 17–18% of GDP and the country often takes pride in not being an export-led economy, unlike countries such as Singapore, South Korea, or China. Of the four Ds, demography, deregulation, and demand may have provided a cushion from international crisis like the sub-prime crisis or South-Asian domino effect. However, in the long run, with a perspective of enhancing the quality of life for the aspirational younger population, growth acceleration is the only option. That would mean looking for market support beyond the boundary walls of the country.

Data shows that so far, India's track record in terms of export performance has been almost dismal with a share of merchandise exports amounting to 1.6% of the total world exports in 2018 and share of commercial service exports being 3.5% of total world figures. The Economic Survey 2019–20 aimed to raise the Indian export market share to

Resurgent India. Jagadish Shettigar and Pooja Misra, Oxford University Press. © Oxford University Press 2022.
DOI: 10.1093/oso/9780192866486.003.0038

approximately 3.5% by 2025 and 6% by 2030, but the country still has miles to cover to achieve the abovementioned target. Thus, to fulfil the PM's vision, the government should focus primarily on the upgradation of technology through an integrated approach keeping in mind both short-run as well as long-run targets. The strategy adopted could be both greenfield and brownfield.

In a greenfield approach, the government has taken the right step in the right direction through the New Education Policy focusing more on knowledge application as against rote learning method of education. It is a laudable move to promote certain selected universities and further develop as Centres of Excellence. Ideally, the Government should aim to catch brilliant minds at the very early stage of education, say primary school and once identified, it should be the responsibility of the State to incubate potential scientists irrespective of the socio-economic background of these young minds.

In the brownfield approach, the Government should target non-resident Indians performing well as scientists and technologists abroad-including places like NASA. Data shows that 7% of employees in NASA are Asian American and 1% are American Indian. Interestingly, international companies of the likes of Google, Microsoft, WeWork, IBM, MasterCard, Nokia, Palo Alto Networks, Adobe, Cognizant, Bata, etc., are being led by Indian-origin CEOs. Many of them might prefer and are looking for viable opportunities to return to their home country provided a conducive working environment is created in the Indian universities and laboratories—at least at the proposed centres of excellence. We may look at the success story of Taiwan's science-based industrial park—the Hsinchu Science Park, which is a special industrial zone meant to attract hi-tech industry and create a Silicon Valley of Taiwan. It is an exclusive township meant for the non-resident Taiwanese returning to the country. The township is complete with all facilities of international standard, be it schooling, entertainment, healthcare, housing apart from R&D, manufacturing, and governmental clearances.

With a view to attracting foreign investors to set up their manufacturing units in India and promoting local domestic manufacturers to set up or expand existing manufacturing units, recently, the government had identified thirteen sectors under the Production Linked Incentive (PLI) scheme. The aim of the PLI is to boost domestic manufacturing by creating a promising and conducive manufacturing ecosystem that will accelerate growth and increase employment opportunities, thereby having a multiplier effect on the economy. On similar lines, the government may identify futuristic knowledge areas such as Artificial Intelligence, Robotics, Blockchain, Clean Energy on the lines of 'Make in China 2025'. These knowledge hubs should aim at focusing on and targeting investments in research and development and technological innovation, thereby transitioning India from being a low-end manufacturer to a hi-tech manufacturing nation to reckon with.

It is equally important to examine why the Indian manufacturing sector is negligent of R&D efforts. The country's gross expenditure on research and development is 0.65% of GDP, significantly lower than the top 10 economies' spend of 1.5–3%. Increasing investment expenditure on R&D will be key for the country to become a USD5 trillion economy and increased investments both from the Government and private sector will be vital to achieving the same. Interestingly, India's rank amongst 131 innovating countries in the Global Innovation Index 2020 was 48th as against 81st in 2015. However, it was observed that the Indian Government did the heavy weight lifting on R&D as against the private sector.

The corporate sector should be made to understand the importance of research and development, especially under the buyers' market where the consumer is the king. From the Government side, whatever support is required that may be provided. The call of the day is to upgrade technology and 'innovate our way' into the future, which can be possible through a boost given to R&D by the Corporates and Government alike.

3.9

Patenting Crucial Medicines

With the onslaught of the second wave of the pandemic wreaking havoc on the lives of people across the world, especially India, there was a growing urgency to have 100% of the population vaccinated at the earliest. The challenge lay in the demand-supply mismatch, mainly due to the limited production capacity of vaccines. For India to achieve universal vaccination, the requirement was 1878 million doses at the rate of two doses per person for a population size of 939 million adults. There being only two manufacturers with a production capacity of 80–90 million doses per month which was foreseen to expand to approximately 160 million doses by July 2021, there was a demand-supply gap that needed to be bridged on a war footing.

To bridge this gap, there was a growing clamour to invoke the provision of Compulsory Licensing under the Indian Patent Act 1970, as was done a decade back for the treatment of cancer. In the case of a patented product, the Compulsory License provision allows the Government to grant manufacturing rights to other producers without the consent of the owner, especially during national emergencies. India's first Compulsory License was granted by the Indian Patent Office under the amended Indian Patent Act (2005), to the Hyderabad based drug manufacturer—Natco to manufacture and sell a similar version of the drug, Nexavar, (for which Bayer's had the patent right) for treatment of kidney cancer. The compulsory license was granted on the grounds that the life-saving medicine was not available at an affordable price and Bayer had not manufactured the drug to a reasonable extent in India.

In October 2020, India and South Africa had applied to the World Trade Organization to relax provisions in the international agreements which regulate Intellectual Property Rights (IPRs) for medicines and vaccines required for treatment and prevention of COVID-19, which was backed by the developing countries. Fortunately, some developed

Resurgent India. Jagadish Shettigar and Pooja Misra, Oxford University Press. © Oxford University Press 2022.
DOI: 10.1093/oso/9780192866486.003.0039

countries like the United States, Canada, and Russia had announced their support for waiving intellectual property provisions while European Union was opposed. Over 120 countries had backed the proposal while all 164 member nations of the World Trade Organisation (WTO) were to begin the negotiations. Under the prevailing circumstances with the pandemic devastating major part of the world economy, ie both lives and livelihoods, it might not have been a problem in getting the approval of WTO through majority voting.

As far as India was concerned, some were suggesting that through the open license method, vaccine technology could be transferred from Bharat Biotech to other manufacturers as the vaccine was invented with the support of ICMR. However, it is important to understand that ICMR's support can be compared to banks providing fund support to start-ups. Thus, this did not mean that one could take away the IPR of the vaccine manufacturer as Bharat Biotech is a separate entity, not a part of the government. Even amongst different PSUs or government departments, often legal disputes crop up as they are all individual entities.

However, in the prevailing pandemic condition, a humanitarian approach was needed and there might not be any complaints or opposition if traditional norms were violated, whether at the level of WTO or at the domestic front. On the flip side, would it not be better that a balanced approach was adopted, keeping in view not just immediate vaccine supply but also future requirements. To begin with, exceptions adopted to ensure universal vaccination are purely a temporary measure cushioning people at the most for approximately ten months. As per medical experts, another dose or two of an improved version of the vaccine would be subsequently needed, followed by a vaccine for life. Also, a vaccine for children below 18 years has just been developed. The fact is that the entire world was looking towards the scientists for their help and efforts. Thus, is it right to discourage scientific talent through a measure, whether at the WTO level or domestically? After all, medicine inventions involve talent, time, and energy of a scientist apart from money from the promoter.

It is equally important to understand and not negate the fact how the issue of IPRs was integrated into the trade agenda. In the pre-WTO era, developing countries, including India, allowed for the manufacturing of the patented product by other manufacturers by a change in the manufacturing process. Subsequently, these companies also started exporting cheap medicines manufactured through a change in process and making profits. The Trade-Related Aspects of Intellectual Property Rights (TRIPS) agreement thereby became critical in resolving trade disputes over the intellectual property at an international level. Hence, countries like the European Union which have reservations for relaxing IPRs, may be convinced with the assurance at WTO that the medicines for cure and prevention of the coronavirus would be used only for domestic use and not for exports. Additionally, there should be a provision for appropriate recognition for the original patent holder.

Thus, with regards to the relaxing of IPR provisions for vaccines for COVID-19 or for that matter, all crucial medicines, it is high time nations acted with a humanitarian angle at the WTO, but it is equally important not to disincentive research and development efforts. Also, the patented companies should be encouraged to explore technology transfer to facilitate the manufacturing of vaccines and medicines within a shorter time span and with some kind of royalty paid to them.

On the domestic front, attempts were made for the transfer of technology from companies like Bharat Biotech, involving additional manufacturers who have the potentiality with the required know-how. However, brand equity should be with Bharat Biotech with a sort of franchise arrangement. The company's R&D expenditure should be compensated through an appropriate pricing policy.

3.10
Need for Land Reforms

With the pandemic having adversely impacted the economic growth of countries worldwide and resetting the geopolitical agenda of nations, the central Government has recognized that this is an opportune time for rebooting, re-strategizing, redrawing, and reinventing the growth trajectory and re-positioning India in the World Economic Order. Even prior to the pandemic, many multinational corporations were keen to move out of China and had been scouting for viable alternate investment destinations. Given India's demographic dividend and cheap labour cost and more importantly, being a democratic society, the country should poise to be and work towards being the world's next manufacturing hub. However, one should not forget that in order to attract foreign investment and present the country as a credible alternative manufacturing location, the country needs to work on an important but unfinished agenda of Land Reforms.

To be able to woo Companies to move their operations into India, the country needs to upgrade its infrastructure, especially in terms of the two main parameters, namely, Enforcing Contracts and Registering Property. As per the EODB Rankings 2020, India has considerably moved up to 63rd place amongst 190 countries. However, on Registering Property, it is still ranked way below at 154th place.

The Registering Property index takes into account procedures a company has to undergo in purchasing a property, transfer of the property title to the name of the buyer, thereby enabling the buyer to be able to use the property for business transactions, providing as collateral security for a loan, etc. It also measures the time and cost required for completion of these procedures and takes into account the existing quality of land administration system prevalent in the economy ie reliability of infrastructure, transparency of information, geographic coverage, land dispute resolution, and access to property rights on an equal basis. Thus,

Resurgent India. Jagadish Shettigar and Pooja Misra, Oxford University Press. © Oxford University Press 2022.
DOI: 10.1093/oso/9780192866486.003.0040

the Government does have an incomplete task in hand which is warranting its urgent attention in terms of easing the process and time required for property registration and making the business environment conducive for an industrialist for registering property, resolving property disputes, etc.

The need of the hour for the Government is to bring about Land Reforms and work towards liberalizing the transfer of agricultural land to non-agricultural use, thereby maximizing land productivity output for the country.

Land reform measures that the country without further ado needs to focus on are: the creation of a land record repository, digitization, and integration of all records relating to titles and encumbrances, formalizing cadastral maps of all plots of land, defining a structured timeline for timely resolution of property disputes and making public land disputes data, etc.

Land reforms in India are a State subject. Ownership or title to a plot of land in the country is largely a presumptive title rather than a conclusive title. A conclusive title is unassailable and conclusive ownership of the property, while in the case of a presumptive title, it is the onus of the property owner to prove and verify the property's ownership and past history. NITI Aayog has prepared a draft model Land Title Act, 2019. The draft model recommends conclusive land titles and providing of State guaranteed ownership. Conclusive land titling will prove to be a game-changer and open up doors for farmers and help them gain easy access to credit, considerably reduce land associated litigations, enable transparent land transactions and make the process of land acquisition for infrastructure development smooth and efficient. Since land is a State subject, it is important that the Central Government persuades all States to come on board and agree to the draft legislation, which has been in the pipeline and waiting to see the light of the day for some time now.

The Central Government under the Ministry of Rural Development and State Governments/Union Territories administration are in the process of implementing the Digital India Land records implementation programme 2.0, wherein the endeavour is to digitalize the land records and land registration is to be maintained in a computerized database. Along with the same, a scheme for mapping of land parcels in rural inhabited areas using Drone technology is also underway and the objective is to ensure that phase-wise manner of mapping of land parcels across the country should be completed by 2024. However, gaps such as the absence of a nationwide template, ie standardized national registry of land records, record of rights being undertaken is primarily for agricultural land while responsibility for urban land lies with urban departments, etc. are still existing. It is imperative that the country has an integrated system or repository of land records for urban and rural areas which comprehensively cover agricultural, infrastructure, residential, and industrial land.

Another avenue that the Government needs to work on and bring changes to is that of land leasing. Until now, land leasing, especially that of agricultural land, has been done on an informal level due to legal restrictions prohibiting agricultural tenancy in some States resulting in adversely impacting agricultural efficiency, equity, agricultural productivity, and rural transformation. An institutional framework for leasing of land is required to be put in place which will bring transparency and ensure land ownership right and tenancy right for landowners and tenants, respectively, enable tenants to access bank credit and incentivize them to make investments in land improvement, allow mutually agreeable stipulations between the landowner and tenant for the lease agreement, etc. A model Land Leasing Act 2016 has been formulated by the NITI Aayog; however, based on inputs from all stakeholders, the same needs to be further worked upon and institutionalized.

Data shows that hardly 1% of the land mass is used for non-agricultural economic activities. Keeping in view substantial contribution to the economy in terms of GDP, employment generation, and contribution to exchequer, its requirement of land deserves a facilitating approach from both central and state governments. In this context, governmental authorities may consider offering the land not in use of agricultural activities to non-agricultural use on easy terms with a smooth and transparent process. Even with another 1–2% increase in landmass under non-agricultural use, returns for the country in terms of employment generation, increased production, and higher growth can be massive and can meet the requirements for infrastructure, industrial, and residential use.

In today's date, with the Right to Fair Compensation and Transparency in Land Acquisition, Rehabilitation and Resettlement (LARR) Act, 2013 in place, due to stringent measures and norms, it is seen that the private sector has stopped making land acquisition under the 2013 Act and investment in infrastructure by the private sector and capital expenditure is on a decline. A win–win solution for both the owners of the land and buyers has to be devised, thereby making the process easy and simple for acquiring land for urbanization and industrialization. Though the Modi government tried to speed up the availability of land for its dream projects like smart cities and bullet trains by bringing ordinance, the attempt was scuttled due to lack of support in the upper house. With the ruling party expected to be placed comfortably from November 2020, it was hoped to introduce the land bill again.

Besides, the government seriously considering releasing surplus land with the public undertakings under the National Monetisation Plan is a step in the right direction. In fact, a substantial part of the land owned by many PSUs and port authorities is illegally occupied by others and is in no way associated with the concerned public units-often with the active backing of local criminals in nexus with political leaders. It is the right time the Modi government initiates stringent measures to free land for productive use.

Thus, with an aspirational goal of India becoming a USD5 trillion economy by 2025, the imperative need today is to unleash the power of land and reap fruits by bringing about the much-needed Land Reforms, which are waiting to see the light of the day. Land Reforms which have been on the anvil for some time now, can very well be the next big game-changer for India.

3.11

Land Acquisition
for Atmanirbhar Bharat

The Prime Minister, Mr. Narendra Modi in his May 2020 address to the nation outlining the Rs. 20 lakh crores package gave a call for Atmanirbhar Bharat, which is making the country into a self-reliant economy. He had also given sufficient hints about India playing an important role as an integral part of globalization. In simple terms, this means an investor-friendly environment attracting both domestic and foreign investment. Keeping in view the vision envisaged, it is imperative that the country adopts long-term structural reforms that have been waiting to see the light of the day. The Land Acquisition Act, 2013 has certainly been a stumbling block against a large number of investment proposals getting transformed into a reality. Hence the government needs to address the issue and initiate corrective reform measures in order to reshape India's growth trajectory.

The Right to Fair Compensation and Transparency in LARR Act, 2013 was put in place with effect from 1 January 2014 by the then Government in power. Due to rigorous land acquisition norms enforced by this bill, a large number of projects were stalled or delayed. This had resulted in a downward trend in investments in infrastructure. As per the data given in Sept 2020 by the Ministry of State Road Transport and Highways, 210 national highway projectshad been delayed due to land acquisition issues amongst other reasons. Ministry of Statistics & Programme Implementation, which monitors infrastructure projects worth Rs. 1.5 trillion and above, stated that of the 1636 projects until October 2019, 563 projects were delayed due to a time overrun. Land acquisition issue is one of the reasons ascribed to for this time overrun. A report in May 2019 stated that land remains one of the top reasons why projects are stalled in India.

Resurgent India. Jagadish Shettigar and Pooja Misra, Oxford University Press. © Oxford University Press 2022.
DOI: 10.1093/oso/9780192866486.003.0041

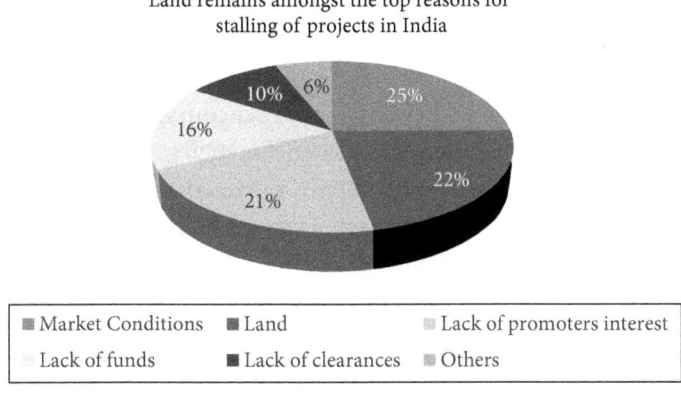

Land remains amongst the top reasons for
stalling of projects in India

■ Market Conditions   ■ Land   ▨ Lack of promoters interest
▨ Lack of funds   ■ Lack of clearances   ▨ Others

Source: Goldman Sachs, CMIE

As Land is a State subject, the Central and State Governments need to work hand in hand and solve land acquisition issues to expedite the process of acquisition of land and make it a smooth and seamless procedure for investors. A win–win solution for both the owners of the land and buyers has to be devised, thereby making the process easy and simple for acquiring land for urbanization and industrialization. The Government needs to adopt international best practices in land acquisition to spur growth in investment in infrastructure by domestic and foreign investors. In fact, the Economic Survey 2019–20 categorically pointed out the need for amending the LARR 2013.

The Right to Fair Compensation and Transparency in LARR Act 2013 replaced the Land Acquisition Act, 1984, which empowered both central and state governments to acquire private land for the public good. Despite the fact that the term 'public good' was not defined in clear-cut terms, all successive governments have been upholding the spirit that is to facilitate promotion of development where beneficiaries were general public, not private individuals. However, the process of land acquisition became controversial when the Special Economic Zone (SEZ) Act started getting implemented in 2005 with proactive involvement of the state governments in acquiring land for a large number of SEZs by private promoters.

The SEZ was conceptualized in India through the EXIM Policy for 2000–01 mainly to promote hassle-free industrial development and accelerate exports. The, then Government was keen to emulate success stories of the Silicon Valley, science-based industrial park of Taiwan and Chinese SEZ model, especially in attracting FDI in manufacturing for exports and had planned to set up only 18 SEZs across the country. The concept to speed up industrial development by encouraging of setting up of SEZs with easy access to many special benefits such as priority clearances, tax holiday, uninterrupted power supply, easy credit support, to mention a few, was noble. However, State Governments being overzealous in setting up SEZs and forcibly acquiring land helping private promoters (often distorting spirit behind 'public purpose') resulted in ruffling too many feathers. With 423 SEZs getting governmental approval against the original plan of setting up 18 SEZs, what was supposed to be 'special' practically turned out to be general economic zones.

Proposed chemical hub at Nandigram and Singur where Tata Nano manufacturing unit was to come up became classic controversial SEZs wherein farmers exhibited stiff resistance against the acquisition of three-crop fertile agricultural land—in a clear violation of the central SEZ guidelines. Not to forget the ambitious project of 8000 hectares of Mumbai SEZ project at Raigad district in Maharashtra also had to be shelved due to landowners refusing to consent to sell their landholding. Practically every state experienced such resistance against forcible land acquisition. Naturally, such incidents led to a panic reaction by the UPA Government as farmers were resisting the distorted implementation of the SEZ policy guidelines and were not agreeable to give up their landholdings—especially at a time when the 2014 parliamentary elections were nearing. LARR 2013 Act was thus passed by the Parliament, basically a political strategy rather than a step to rescue farmers—let alone a well thought of economic agenda. The, then government could not foresee the fact that while the Act resulted in the balance being tilted in favour of the farmers, it became a stumbling block for investors.

The new law, LARR 2013, with all its shortcomings, was perceived as being more participative and humane in nature and offering enhanced compensation to landowners along with resettling and rehabilitating displaced families. As per this law, 80% of the land in the case of private sector projects is to be acquired via negotiations, with the Government stepping in only for the balance of 20%, while for Public–Private Partnership (PPP) projects, 70% is to be acquired through negotiations.

On the flip side, from the investors' viewpoint, this Act is perceived as being cumbersome, unwieldy, taking too much time, and resulting in escalation of cost, thereby making its enactment difficult. Reports state that the 2013 Act is procedure heavy and on an average, the acquisition process takes 4.5 years to complete as there are numerous steps involved. It entails a social impact assessment to be done, consent of landowners to be obtained and resettlement and rehabilitation plans to be drawn up, leading to delays in implementation at the ground level. Secondly, as per the Act, if the acquisition is being made for a 'public purpose', then the consent of majority landowners is not required. However, there is considerable ambiguity around the term 'public purpose'. These drawbacks have resulted in seven States, bypassing the law and implementing their own Acts.

An example of a close to successful model of land acquisition has been that of Amravati. The acquisition of land for building the capital for the newly carved state at Amravati was made through a land pooling scheme under which for every acre given by landowners for development projects, the farmer would be entitled to 1000 square yards for a residential plot that has been developed and 450 square yards of a commercial plot in a developed state. This scheme resulted in farmers having voluntarily offered approximately13,300 hectares of land to the Andhra Pradesh Development Authority. Based on the widely acclaimed success of this scheme, the Central Government could probably look at land pooling as a model for the country to emulate.

With the Government vying to make India the world's next manufacturing hub and unleashing the true potential of land as a factor of production and attracting investors is the call of the day. In order to attract foreign investment and present the country as a credible alternative manufacturing location, the country needs to work on making the process of land acquisition a smooth and seamless process and ensure that it is not a hindrance to attract foreign investors into the country and dissuade domestic investors from setting up their factories in India.

The Modi government tried to speed up the availability of land for its dream projects like smart cities and bullet trains by bringing the ordinance in December 2014 and making it simpler for acquiring land in five key sectors, ie defence, infrastructure, industrial corridors, power, and affordable housing. However, the attempt was scuttled due to a lack of support in the upper house. With the ruling party expected to be placed comfortably from November 2020, it was hoped that the Central Government would bring back this long-term tough measure on the discussion table and introduce the investor-friendly land bill again.

3.12

Labour Reforms

India is projected to have the highest working population between 2022 and 2034 with 4.75 million youth entering the workforce every year. Investor and employee-friendly labour laws will be key to harnessing the potential of this large workforce. Indian labour laws in sync with and conducive to promoting the evolving business regulatory environment can help reshape India's growth trajectory and stimulate India's growth aspirations. Investment-friendly labour laws can be the pillar and facilitate an EODB environment and put the country on the path of economic development.

A simplified and modernized labour regulation and labour reforms have been the need of the hour to take care of the archaic Indian labour laws which have been acting as deterrents in attracting investment, especially foreign direct investment. Though policymakers realized the importance of labour reforms more than two decades ago, no government has been able to proceed with the same. The previous NDA government headed by Shri Atal Bihari Vajpayee did get the approval of the lower house, however, the move was struck down by the upper house where the government did not have the required majority.

Not to miss the fact that with the pandemic having adversely impacted the economy, the unemployment rate had increased to as high as 23.52% in April 2020. With a V-shaped economic recovery taking place, unemployment numbers had improved to 6.9% in February 2021. In such a scenario, labour reforms will only help to kickstart the virus-hit economy. Thus, now that the present government is in a position to get crucial laws passed with a little persuasion of its allies and friendly parties, the government should initiate steps to reform the outdated labour laws, which have acted as an impediment to attracting domestic and foreign direct investment.

Resurgent India. Jagadish Shettigar and Pooja Misra, Oxford University Press. © Oxford University Press 2022.
DOI: 10.1093/oso/9780192866486.003.0042

Agreeably, in September 2020, with the Parliament passing the three labour bills, the Government has been able to take a major step forward in the right direction. These three bills complete the codification of 29 labour laws into four codes, with the Rajya Sabha passing the Industrial Relations Code 2020, the Occupational Safety, Health and Working Conditions Code, 2020 and the Social Security Code, 2020. These codes aim to safeguard the interest and strike a balance between the well-being and interest of workers and employers.

However, it would only be right to state that the work with regards to the extant antiquated and complicated labour laws is only half done and there are crucial issues that warrant attention from the viewpoint of building a positive business environment. The Industrial Disputes Act, 1947 is one such archaic labour law that is badly in need of reformative measures, especially when we are thinking in terms of 'Make in India for the World'. The clarion call of the Prime Minister of a self-reliant nation necessarily means enhancement of competitive manufacturing strength and attracting foreign direct investment, more so, at a time when investors are in a mood to desert China.

The Industrial Disputes Act, 1947, which states that commercially unviable units cannot exit the business without the approval of the concerned state government if the number of workers is more than 100 (with an exception of Maharashtra where the limit is 300), has been a major stumbling block for investors. Based on inputs received and to make the business environment more industry-friendly, states like Rajasthan, Gujarat, Haryana, and Madhya Pradesh have also raised the bar for commercially unviable units to close shop without permission from the state government to 300 workers as against 100 workers. Due to apprehensions of employees losing means of livelihood, normally, State Governments do not approve the closure of units. In this process, capital gets locked in unproductive assets and continuing production only means acquiring losses beyond fixed costs which further worsens the situation leading to the manufacturing facility eventually becoming a sick unit.

As the units keep working only on paper, employees necessarily continue to be on the roles of the company and are hence being paid. In the absence of units generating income, workers need to be paid obviously through financial support from the banks with which the Company enjoys goodwill. The situation gets further enmeshed as the loan taken by the Company cannot be serviced, leading to an ensuing problem of proportionate increase in NPA of the friendly bank. Also, investors are unable to relocate the capital in an alternate business.

In fact, 'free entry and exit' is an integral part of the economic reforms of the country. Though free entry with delicensing of investment since 1991 has been facilitated, exit option for both domestic and foreign investors is yet to be provided, without which reform measures remain half-baked. Though the incumbent government cleverly provided an exit route at the initiative of lenders through IBC since 2016, however, that has also been pushed into cold storage due to pandemic hit recession.

Contract labour is another provision under labour laws that requires amendment. During the period of limited opportunities, which encouraged the culture of retiring from a company where one starts earning job protection was the need. However, under the changed economic situation of availability of unlimited opportunities sticking to the same job beyond a couple of years is considered a sign of competitive weakness within. Hence, the law, which was very much a necessity till the eighties, has become archaic and outdated. In fact, today, retaining talent is a challenge for employers. Why would any employer want to terminate services of performing employees as the latter contribute to the profit kitty of the former? The term 'human relations' has now replaced 'industrial relations'.

The Prime Minister's ambitious target of a five trillion economy cannot be achieved by relying mainly on domestic investment, which also needs to be accelerated. In an uncertainty of capital getting locked in for a very long period of time, ie more than a decade to get the sickness determined, how can anybody expect to tap potential foreign direct investment that too at a time when China is losing out? Once the government settles down after the States assembly elections, attention should be refocused on this long pending reform measure without getting deterred by the resistance of a small section of vested interests.

3.13

Judicial Reforms

In light of the pandemic, a conducive business environment and building a scenario of facilitating investments are pre-requisites for economic revival and moving India back into the trajectory of economic growth. Also, for India to transition from 'Make in India to Make for World', the need of the hour is to attract domestic and foreign investments into the country. Keeping the same in mind, the Government has been working on all avenues to improve its ranking on the EODB index to attract domestic and foreign investments. With India being ranked 63rd place, in the EODB, 2020, the country is still short of the goal set by the Prime Minister of being in the top 50 nations. One of the key parameters on which India has been faring low and needs to put its act together is that of Enforcing Contracts.

On the index of enforcing contracts, India ranked 163rd place in EODB 2020. This indicator measures the cost and time involved for the resolution of a commercial dispute and the quality of the judicial processes, thereby evaluating the efficiency and quality of the existing judicial system operating in the country. Data for the Indian economy shows that there are approximately 3.97 crores court cases pending (September 2020) with the Indian judiciary. In the period January end 2020–September 2020, the Supreme Court witnessed an increase of 3.6% pending cases, while High Courts and District Courts (along with subordinate courts) had a 12.4% and 6.6% rise in the number of pending court cases.

Resurgent India. Jagadish Shettigar and Pooja Misra, Oxford University Press. © Oxford University Press 2022.
DOI: 10.1093/oso/9780192866486.003.0043

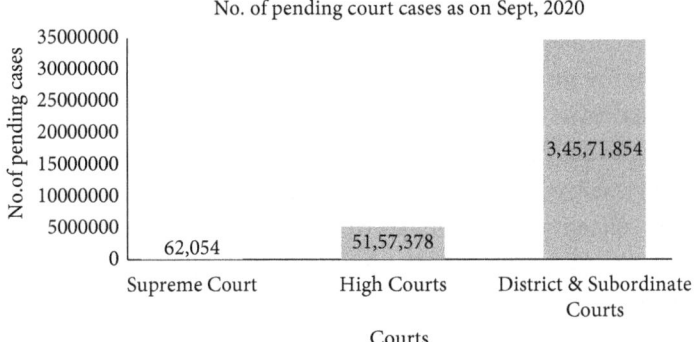

No. of pending court cases as on Sept, 2020

Source: Written reply in Rajya Sabha, September 2020

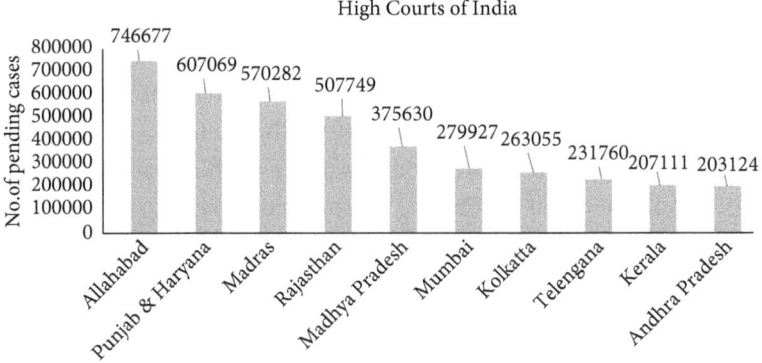

High Courts of India

Source: Written reply in Lok Sabha, September 2020

At the district and subordinate court level, the state of Uttar Pradesh ranked the highest at 81.86 lakh cases, followed by Maharashtra (42.21 lakh cases), Bihar (30.94 lakh cases), and West Bengal (23.39 lakh cases). Of these unresolved court cases, approximately 70% were civil cases, while the balance 30% were criminal cases. On average, it takes approximately four years or 1445 days to enforce a contract in India clearly being reflective of the fact that the Indian judicial process is highly cumbersome and unwieldy. Thus, huge pendency of cases exists at all levels and even though the Modi government since 2014 has done away with 3500 archaic laws, it still has considerably unfinished work that needs to be looked into.

In a nation where investors find it difficult to resolve business-related issues at different stages such as supply chain, payment due, procurement or auctioning by government agencies, taxation, land acquisition, the environmental issue does not bode well for the inflow of foreign investments. The relevant point being when issues fail to get resolved mutually amongst the involved business partners, the dispute is taken to the judiciary or the related tribunals. Investors cannot afford to waste precious time and unnecessary delays in the process might lead to cost escalation in projects, higher interest outgo to banks, contested tax revenue, failure to meet domestic and international commitments—which might even lead to loss of market forever and consequently reduce investment levels in the country.

An efficient judiciary instils confidence in investors and signals the commercial viability of transactions. An attempt was made by the Vajpayee government to speed up the process by limiting the number of hearings for each case. Unfortunately, the then Law Minister, late Mr. Arun Jaitley, had to face stiff resistance by the practicing lawyers throughout the country. The key to enforcing contracts is an efficient judicial system and it is imperative that the judiciary and Government work on it.

Lawyers, counsels, and the Government spend a considerable amount of time on delaying of the judicial process. Unnecessary adjournments are sought for inane reasons such as the lawyer or complainant are of the view that the appointed bench would not be favourable for their petition. Adjournments should be an exception rather than a norm as is the case today. Data shows that the complainant ends up spending approximately 30% of the value of the contract as legal and associated fees. That's far too long, far too expensive by any stretch of the imagination.

Interestingly, the Government is the biggest litigant across the country and 46% of the lawsuits filed are by various Government departments. Officials fearing to bear the brunt of being called out for wrongly favouring opposite parties in a litigation opt for the safe option of filing for an appeal as against an amicable settlement of disputes. Thus, the need is for the Government to categorically spell out the criteria under which appeals should be applied for which will subsequently help unclog the judicial system and speed up the process of justice. Rather, disputes relating to inter-governmental departments or public undertakings should be resolved through the intervention of political leadership if the bureaucratic intervention fails so that courts are not unnecessarily burdened with cases.

Indian courts are known to operate at 50% of their sanctioned capacity (February 2020). The twin problems of the chronic shortage of judges and inexperience are crippling the Indian judicial system, and the executive and judiciary in joint consultation need to find a quick and competent solution. In spite of the backlog of pending cases, as per the 2020 working day's calendar, the Supreme Court works for only 190 days and Mumbai and Delhi high courts had 210 days as their working days. Even after seven decades of independence, this archaic practice of the British era continues. Is it justified?

Alternative dispute method of resolution or out-of-court settlement is another avenue that seriously needs to be given a thought to. Arbitration is used world-over to reduce the pressure on the judicial system and speed up the judicial process. India did try to adopt and incorporate the Alternative Dispute resolution mechanism by the Arbitration and Conciliation Act, 1996, however, it has not proved to be effective and has not been able to provide timely solutions. It is a known fact that even in today's date, corporates avoid their arbitration in India and prefer to opt for Singapore or London for the arbitration process.

Another idea worth contemplating is that of time-bound settlement of cases and setting up of Corporate Courts exclusively to deal with business-related issues at lower and higher levels of the judiciary with the scope of appealing only to the Supreme Court where a separate bench may be constituted. This will lead to speedy adjudication of business cases.

Last but most importantly, embracing the latest technological innovations for improving the judicial courts' competence levels and digitization of the judicial system is long overdue. The pandemic with the enabling of virtual hearings has shown that this is a measure that can be easily incorporated and will yield results of a geometrically progressive magnitude. Thus, the judicial system should find a long-term solution towards adopting technologically advanced solutions aimed at improving the efficacy of the judicial system.

Improved management and disincentivizing of delays, reducing government litigations (limiting appeals made by Government departments), increase of judiciary capacity in lower courts, thus lessening the burden on the higher courts, increase in workings days for the judiciary, facilitating arbitration, use of technology and building a robust infrastructure to improve the efficiency of courts are some of the initiatives that need to be taken for this parameter to improve and the country to be a sought after global manufacturing hub for investors. Thus, it is important that the country draws up a blueprint for judicial reforms and works on it on a war footing.

3.14

Administration Reforms

The role of the Government of any country is to primarily facilitate economic growth and provide common citizens and industry alike with increased access to basic services, thereby building an environment conducive to and promoting ease of living consistent with equity and social justice. The key constituents of any governance model are economic reforms, decentralization, accountability, and respect for citizens' rights and transparency and with the current Government clearly spelling out its focus on 'Minimum Government, Maximum Governance' it should be working towards achieving the same.

The role of any Government is extremely important in facilitating and promoting economic development. Administrative reforms, which are a continuous requirement in any society, are all the more needed when society experiences game-changing reforms. An attempt to set up an Administrative Reforms Committee had been made in the past to reform administration by constituting expert committees such as the First Administrative Reforms Commission (ARC), which was set up in 1966 for reviewing the public administration system existing in India. The Commission recommended measures for making administration fit to implement the Government's social and economic policies and be responsive to the people of India. Thereafter, the second ARC was constituted in 2005 and was assigned the task of preparing a blueprint for revamping the public administration system. However, recommendations given by such committees have largely been kept in cold storage.

While the Government has no business to be in business, its role as a facilitator for promoting industry is key. India has traversed long since 1991, the year of liberalization, privatization, and globalization of the country. However, despite economic liberalization especially delicensing it has been witnessed that since the big-ticket reforms in 1991, a number of clearances are still required to set up a manufacturing unit or

Resurgent India. Jagadish Shettigar and Pooja Misra, Oxford University Press. © Oxford University Press 2022.
DOI: 10.1093/oso/9780192866486.003.0044

even constructing a warehouse. In the EODB Index, India, contrary to the game-changing reforms initiated, still ranks 63rd. The Government is pulling out all stops to be within the top 50 and the administration needs to especially focus on parameters such as Enforcing Contracts and Registering Property.

On parameters such as Starting a Business, Dealing with Construction Permits, and Registering Property, the country stands at 136th, 27th, and 154th position, respectively. While the country has streamlined the process of construction permits and reduced the time and cost of obtaining these permits, it still has some way to go. This results in increased costs for investors due to the delays involved. Moreover, the meter on interest payments on bank loans starts running from the day the loan is granted. Delays in the clearance process entail an increase in the cost of production, which ultimately would be passed on to consumers resulting in cost-push inflation.

Time-bound clearances are the need of the hour. For example, the Ministry of Environment and Forests had a commitment of 210 days to complete all formalities for environment clearance for projects. However, time-consuming procedures frequently escalate project costs and can be intimidating for any investor, be it a domestic or foreign investor. Despite the stated commitment, files are held up, and earlier companies would have to wait for as long as two years to obtain their environmental clearances. Reforms in this account have been initiated, and the timeline for obtaining the environmental clearance was changed to 150–170 days.

On the flip side, it is also worth mentioning that the Central and State Governments are putting in all efforts to streamline and improve the governance process, an example of which is the state of Gujarat, known for its development-oriented governance. The State had given all-out support for the setting up of the Tata Nano factory in Sanad and eased the process from land acquisition to all clearances being provided within a period of 72 hours.

Thus, the key point here is that the Government, in its key role of being the planner and facilitator of business, needs to initiate bureaucratic reforms. With the Government serious about making India into an Atmanirbhar Bharat—self-reliant nation, administrative reforms are crucial. To make India into a manufacturing hub and tap both domestic and foreign investments, policies, and procedures should build an investment-friendly environment at the earliest, especially to tap investments exiting China. Yes, schemes such as PLIs are steps in the right direction but the country still has some miles to go.

A total overhauling of the present bureaucratic system is the need of the hour. The present Indian Administrative Services should be replaced by specialist cadres such as Indian Economic Service, Indian Welfare Service, Indian Security Service, Indian Foreign Service—with matching educational qualifications.

Additionally, a scope for lateral entry should be made to enable harnessing the potential of private-sector employees who have excelled in their respective fields. Upto the Joint Secretary level cadre can get promoted on merit-cum time basis. Beyond that level, government cadres should compete with non-cadre experts from outside. Lateral entry is a well-established norm world over and countries such as the United States, the United Kingdom, Australia, New Zealand have institutionalized the practice as a permanent part of their system. This would catalyse better governance, build efficiency in the system and provide a cutting-edge experience in public administration.

There should be time-bound clearances in place, which should also see the light of the day through effective implementation. Each process should have pre-committed time within which the fate of the file should be declared with a valid reason if it is a red signal. There should be monitoring mechanisms through a dashboard to keep a watch on different administrative ministries.

To build confidence amongst all stakeholders, be it investor, industry, consumer, etc., bureaucratic accountability and transparency is needed. In case of failure to explain the delay in the process, the concerned officer should be held responsible for the provision for penalty.

Last but not the least, it is important to free bureaucrats from undue political influences. Though bureaucracy is supposed to implement the political ideology of the party in power, all instructions from political bosses should be on record and no instructions outside the law or set norms should be accepted, even if it is through written order. It is equally important to protect the cadre if they are expected to work without fear or pressure. Transfer before the expiry of the minimum service period at a post/assignment should be exceptional, ie only in case of proven guilty. Transfer should not be a tool in the hands of political bosses but on the basis of set norms.

3.15

Cooperative Federalism

With India having a federal system of governance in place, both the Centre and States have the freedom to operate and function in their allotted spheres of jurisdiction. Under the federal structure, responsibilities are distributed between the Centre and States, and division of powers is given in the Seventh Schedule of the Constitution in the three lists, ie Union List, State List, and Concurrent List. Developmental responsibilities such as healthcare, land policies, law and order are with the States, while the Centre is responsible for defence, foreign affairs, atomic energy, banking, insurance.

Tracing back history, during the first two decades of independence, it was seen that with a single party ruling both Centre and the States, there was no major coordination problem. However, for the last three decades, States are being governed by different political parties while the Centre is governed by mostly coalition governments which otherwise means weak in command. To enable smooth administration, it is important that the Centre and States work in coordination with each other.

With the NDA coming into power in 2014, and even though it is a coalition government, the leading party has a majority on its own, even then the Prime Minister has been repeatedly articulating the relevance of 'Cooperative Federalism'. However, a sort of cold war has been going on between the Centre and the States ruled by the opposition parties. This could be due to the fact that the States are not happy with an assertive, strong, and stable government. Rather than making use of the opportunity to develop the States under their control, policy initiatives by the Centre are often viewed as imposing. For smooth governance, it is key that different state governments understand the importance of working together with the central government.

Keeping aside political differences once in the government, Central and State Governments should work hand in hand so that developmental, as

Resurgent India. Jagadish Shettigar and Pooja Misra, Oxford University Press. © Oxford University Press 2022.
DOI: 10.1093/oso/9780192866486.003.0045

well as welfare measures, are effectively implemented without any unnecessary hurdles. Irrespective of who has initiated the project, citizens give credit for its implementation. The successful implementation of Aadhar and with the present Central government extensively using this concept though conceived by the previous government is a classic example. Such is also the case with a number of flyovers that have seen successful completion in Delhi.

Not to forget, the evolving consensus amongst all the states for introducing the GST, which required ratification of the constitutional amendment by all state assemblies, is a landmark development in the process of strengthening cooperative federalism. It is worth recollecting here that the issue which was in cold storage for almost 17 years, ultimately saw the light of the day in July 2017 though some amount of compromise was made in the process. This 'one nation, one tax' has subsumed most of the other indirect taxes and brought uniformity in terms of tax administration in the country. With the implementation of GST, the central finance minister is no longer an authority to decide on indirect taxes. On the other hand, the GST council, headed by the Central finance minister and all State finance ministers as members, takes a decision on a consensus basis.

However, there are many areas where the Centre and the opposition-ruled State governments are at loggerheads. One major case of political hypocrisy is the stand on the farm laws. In reality, practically every national party is committed to reforms in the agricultural sector. Going by the articulations of the political leaders both inside and outside the Parliament, everybody realizes the importance of undertaking agricultural reforms that are in the overall interests of farmers and have been long overdue. The farm laws, which have been widely proclaimed to be a 'game-changer' for the Indian agricultural sector, sought to build a scenario of 'One India, One Agricultural Market' for the benefit of farmers. These laws encouraged and provided for barrier-free trade outside the areas designated as market yards and aimed to build a viable environment for farmers to be able to sell their produce to the highest bidder, ie 'my crop, my right' thereby resulting in higher income for farmers. However, the position taken by the opposition is in complete contradiction of their stand while in power.

Rather, narrow politicking by many political parties at times stoops to such low levels that poor people are even deprived of benefits of many welfare measures. To take an example, the Ayushman Bharat scheme, which aims to provide free health coverage of Rs. 5 lakhs to over 10 crores households or 50 crores Indians, was considered to be bigger than even Obamacare. The scheme should have been welcomed by all with a viewpoint of taking care of poor people's health who otherwise are left to the mercy of God, however, even in such a purely humanitarian act, certain States decided not to implement the scheme lest the credit goes to the current Prime Minister. Similarly, certain states refused to pass on benefits under schemes like PM Kisan, which entitle poor farmers to a direct cash transfer. The relevant question here being: Why should innocent poor people be deprived of benefits of welfare measures because of dirty politics?

Not to forget, the onslaught created by the pandemic—whether natural or lab-created has resulted in creating havoc and economies world over have been adversely impacted. India has been no exception to the downsides of this black swan event. With rising cases having resulted on manifold pressures on hospital beds, oxygen supply, and the need for accelerated universal vaccination resulting in demand outbidding supply, poor health infrastructure, naturally, was in focus. The moot point being: Who is responsible for this pathetic situation? Data shows that India has 1.4 beds per 1000 people, 1 doctor per 1445 people; 1.7 nurses per 1000 people as against WHO's norm for doctors being 1:1000 and nurses being 3:1000. Unsatisfactory health infrastructure cannot be an outcome of short-term negligence but is the result of the indifferent attitude of successive governments over seven decades.

Undoubtedly the pandemic should have been an issue for all stakeholders to come together and unitedly take on the crisis as Team India. Instead, opposition-ruled states started putting undue pressure on the Centre and had not been cooperating in effective implementation of healthcare measures or were leading to confusion or questioning credibility of the vaccine first and were then blaming the Government for its inadequate supply. Vaccine wastage as much as 30% in states like Rajasthan and Jharkhand at a time when the Centre was knocking at all possible sources was a preposterous situation for the Government to be faced with.

There are many other such policy measures that require coop-eration and seamless coordination between the Centre and States. Transformation of the New Education Policy, refining of GST, ambi-tious, smart city projects, and of course the much-desired reforms in labour laws, land acquisition act, etc., are a few of them which warrant urgent attention, coordination, and action by both Central and State Governments. Taking a cue from successful implementation of GST, the Central and State Governments could probably formulate a joint council to bring about the much needed reforms in land acquisition, labour, ag-riculture, etc. This would help in opinion building across all political par-ties and States and all the envisaged bottlenecks can be suitably addressed beforehand by a consultative approach. Politics could be played in terms of competence and transparency in implementation. There should not be any scope for dirty politics, especially on issues relating to the standard of living of ordinary citizens or national security or natural calamity and seamless coordination between the Centre and States under the realm of Cooperative Federalism should be the primary focus of all governing parties.

3.16

Challenges before the Government

The Prime Minister's vision of building the country into an Atmanirbhar Bharat is certainly motivating and an attempt to instil confidence amongst all stakeholders, be it investors, policymakers, intellectuals, workers, farmers, and, above all, aspiring youths. With the focus on building India into a self-reliant nation, many innovative policy measures have been initiated in order to lead the country towards the ultimate goal. However, one must bear in mind that policy decisions can get transformed into reality only with the support of a conducive macroeconomic environment that includes both economic and non-economic factors. A stable macroeconomic scenario prevalent in the country gives the required impetus and improves business confidence and consumer sentiments.

Fortunately, the country is blessed with a stable government led by a visionary leader committed to lead the country towards becoming an economic powerhouse backed by initiatives such as the asset monetisation plan, PM Gatishakti plan, etc. With the Government being in the majority, it is also in a position to get crucial bills passed by the Parliament. However, the road towards the ultimate goal is not going to be a smooth ride. There would be many hurdles that would have to be crossed.

Keeping the same in mind, for democratically elected governments world over appropriate timing is crucial for effective implementation of policy measures. No incumbent government in a democratic setup enjoys the luxury of initiating harsh economic reform measures during the end of their term as they have to start gearing up for the electoral battle. Normally, the mid-year of the term is the most suitable period. In that sense, 2021–22 was the year that should have emboldened the government to venture into tough measures. However, a pandemic battered recessionary economy, which had led to a humanitarian and economic crisis worldwide, has deprived the Modi government of this luxury. Also, with the government having strategically repealed the three farm laws, it

Resurgent India. Jagadish Shettigar and Pooja Misra, Oxford University Press. © Oxford University Press 2022.
DOI: 10.1093/oso/9780192866486.003.0046

has definitely dented the government's investor-friendly image and also put a question mark on the economic reform measures in the near future at least till 2024 parliamentary elections.

The relevant point here being: Controversial, but much-needed reform measures such as the Land Acquisition Act and Labour Reforms which are crucial for attracting investment, both foreign and domestic investments will have to wait till the post-2024 poll. Similarly, one cannot imagine the government mustering courage to initiate other crucial reform measures such as Judiciary reforms and Administrative reforms prior to the next Parliamentary elections. Rationalization of GST is important to bring transparency in governance and strengthen the ethical fabric of the business. It is important to rectify distortion in the present form of GST. Unless the incumbent government returns to power that too with comfortable strength, such tough measures cannot be initiated.

Also, not to forget that Cooperative federalism is crucial in the implementation of many economic measures. Both the Centre and State Governments need to work together, hand in hand, for the successful execution of long-overdue reforms, which are vital in building the country into an Atmanirbhar Bharat. Under the prevailing non-cooperative attitude by some States, it might not be easy for the Central Government to carry forward reform measures.

In light of the fact that during the second and third wave of the virus, the Indian economy had been adversely affected more on the demand side and localized lockdowns while reducing mobility and minimizing economic activities had not majorly impacted and led to supply-side disruptions, consumption demand is crucial for reviving the economy. With all efforts being focused towards containing the spread of the virus wave, universal vaccination will play a key role. It would build the requisite sentiments amongst consumers, and people will be encouraged to venture out to market places. Instilling consumer confidence will also give the much-needed boost to discretionary spending and increase consumer demand. Increased demand will lead to increased production and improve capacity utilization thereby, setting in motion the demand–supply cycle.

Though the Indian economy is not export-led, however, it is important to bear in mind that nearly one-fifth of India's GDP depends on external markets. More than 90% of the economies were pandemic hit which also included the country's major export destinations. While in May 2021,

India's trade deficit stood at an eight-month low of USD6.32 billion, exports were above the USD30 billion mark for three months in a row, reflecting a positive trajectory for this sector. However, with the pandemic recurring in waves across the world and an uncertain future staring at us, the country still needs to be on the lookout for consistent and stable demand from the rest of the world.

Not to miss the fact that implementation of ambitious infrastructure projects as spelt out in the Union Budget for FY2021–22 and FY2022–23 means huge resource support. With the fiscal deficit going out of control and the second and third wave of the virus reversing gains made post the graded unlock in 2020, the required fiscal stimulus is still a far cry. Rather, the fiscal deficit target which was slated to be 6.8% in Union Budget 2021–22 has already been revised by the Government in February 2022 to 6.9%. With Q3FY22 numbers resulting in GDP growth rate for FY22 being revised downwards to 8.9% from 9.2%, the revised fiscal deficit numbers might have to be further re-worked on. On the other hand, with the RBI going all out to strengthen the macroeconomic stability of the country and help improve the economic and investment climate, these are a few of the challenges without tackling of which it might not be easy to fulfil the target of India becoming an Atmanirbhar Bharat.

Last but an important point being with the Government focusing on ambitious supply side measures as announced in the Union Budget 2022–23, though these are welcome steps in the medium and long term but without demand boosting measures investors might not get enthused. Also, with geopolitical tensions getting aggravated due to the Russia-Ukraine war in February 2022, the Government and RBI need to keep a keen eye on its ramifications for the Indian economy in terms of crude oil prices, supply chain disruptions leading to increased commodity prices, chip shortages, etc. The capital market might not be in a position to facilitate the Government's disinvestment programme including the IPO from LIC. The repercussions of the war could result in higher inflationary pressures, increased current account deficit and growth rates having to be revised downwards for FY23. However, there is nothing more exciting and satisfying than reaching the target by overcoming hurdles and crossing bumpy roads and with a well-structured path charted out, the journey towards India being a self-reliant nation backed by well-defined reforms is going to be an exciting but an achievable one.

References

- Economic Survey 2020–21
- Statement on Developmental and Regulatory Policies, RBI https://www.rbi.org.in/Scripts/BS_PressReleaseDisplay.aspx?prid=49582
- Governor'sStatement—22May2020https://www.rbi.org.in/Scripts/bs_viewcontent.aspx?Id=3859
- Industrial Outlook Survey of the Manufacturing Sector for Q4: 2019–20, RBI https://www.rbi.org.in/Scripts/PublicationsView.aspx?id=19437
- Database of Indian Economy, RBI, https://dbie.rbi.org.in/BOE/OpenDocument/1608101729/OpenDocument/opendoc/openDocument.faces?logonSuccessful=true&shareId=1
- Ministry of Statistics and Programme Implementation
  o http://www.mospi.gov.in/data
  o http://mospi.nic.in/
  o http://mospi.nic.in/iip
  o http://mospi.nic.in/sites/default/files/iip/iipjan20.pdf
  o http://mospi.nic.in/sites/default/files/iip/iip_feb20.pdf
  o http://mospi.nic.in/sites/default/files/iip/IIP_PR_Mar_120502020.pdf
  o http://mospi.nic.in/sites/default/files/press_release/PRESS%20NOTE%20PE%20and%20Q4%20estimates%20of%20GDP.pdf
  o http://www.mospi.gov.in/sites/default/files/press_releases_statements/nad_Statement22_1dec14.xls
  o http://www.mospi.gov.in/sites/default/files/press_releases_statements/Statement_13_3Mar2020.xls
- Ministry of Commerce and Industry, Department of Commerce https://commerce.gov.in/writereaddata/UploadedFile/MOC_637251634305315092_Press%20Release%20April%202020.pdf
  o https://commerce.gov.in/writereaddata/uploadedfile/MOC_637036322182074251_Annual%20Report%202018-19%20English.pdf
  o https://commerce.gov.in/writereaddata/UploadedFile/MOC_636988184002556003_Press_Release_June_2019.pdf
- Ministry of Petroleum and Natural Gas
  o http://petroleum.nic.in/more/indian-png-statistics
  o http://petroleum.nic.in/documents/reports/annual-reports
  o http://petroleum.nic.in/sites/default/files/ipngstat_0.pdf
  o http://petroleum.nic.in/sites/default/files/AR_2018-19.pdf
- NSDL
  o https://www.fpi.nsdl.co.in/web/Reports/Yearwise.aspx?RptType=5
- IMF

- o https://www.imf.org/external/datamapper/NGDP_RPCH@WEO/OEMDC/ADVEC/WEOWORLD
  o https://www.imf.org/en/publications/weo
  o https://www.imf.org/en/About/FAQ/imf-response-to-covid-19#Q4
- Money Control
  o https://www.moneycontrol.com/news/business/economy/abhijit-banerjee-on-rs-20-lakh-crore-package-5319971.html
  o https://www.imf.org/en/Publications/WEO/Issues/2020/04/14/weo-april-2020#Introduction
  o https://www.moneycontrol.com/news/business/personal-finance/coronavirus-impact-making-sense-of-the-global-market-crash-5062681.html
  o https://www.moneycontrol.com/news/business/economy/rbis-targeted-long-term-repo-operations-all-your-questions-answered-5139191.html
- World Economic Forum
  o https://www.weforum.org/agenda/2020/03/stock-market-volatility-coronavirus/
  o https://www.weforum.org/agenda/2020/05/preventing-a-covid-19-food-crisis/
- EIA—U.S. Energy Information Administration https://www.eia.gov/dnav/pet/hist/LeafHandler.ashx?n=pet&s=rbrte&f=a
- Ministry of Home and Family Welfare
  o https://www.mohfw.gov.in/
- Data Hub
  o https://datahub.io/core/oil-prices
- Causality between public expenditure and Economic growth, P. Srinivasan, (2013)
  o https://papers.ssrn.com/sol3/papers.cfm?abstract_id=2376143
- Recent Global Recession and Indian Economy, Rajiv Kumar Bhatt, (2011) http://www.ijtef.org/papers/105-D10003.pdf
- Does Stock Market Development Cause Economic Growth? A Time Series Analysis for Indian Economy, Soumya Guha Deb and Jaydeep Mukherjee, (2008) https://memberfiles.freewebs.com/99/21/62292199/documents/irjfe_21_12.pdf
- Financial Deepening, Foreign Direct Investment and Economic Growth: Are They Cointegrated, Rudra Prakash Pradhan, (2010) http://citeseerx.ist.psu.edu/viewdoc/download?doi=10.1.1.1024.564&rep=rep1&type=pdf
- https://en.wikipedia.org/wiki/Essential_Commodities_Act#:~:text=The%20Essential%20Commodities%20Act%20is,fuel%20(petroleum%20products)%20etc.
- https://en.wikipedia.org/wiki/Economic_impact_of_the_COVID-19_pandemic_in_India
- https://www.investopedia.com/terms/c/crude-oil.asp
- https://timesofindia.indiatimes.com/business/india-business/cabinet-decisions-for-farmers-msmes-poor-key-points/articleshow/76135314.cms
- https://www.livemint.com/news/india/15-ways-to-define-india-s-slowdown-1565715613762.html
- https://www.thehindu.com/business/explained-why-are-oil-prices-in-negative-terrain/article31394425.ece
- https://www.rbi.org.in/Scripts/BS_PressReleaseDisplay.aspx?prid=50949
- https://rbidocs.rbi.org.in/rdocs/PublicationReport/Pdfs/6CHAP2JAN21783500073F0A40159E3E0A7CFAF1A1F7.PDF

- https://www.indiabudget.gov.in/doc/Budget_at_Glance/budget_at_a_glance.pdf
- https://www.india.gov.in/spotlight/union-budget-2020-2021
- https://www.indiabudget.gov.in/economicsurvey/
- https://www.imf.org/-/media/Images/IMF/Publications/WEO/2020/April/Arrows.ashx
- www.imf.org
- https://www.bseindia.com/index.html
- https://www.nseindia.com/
- https://unemploymentinindia.cmie.com/
- https://pib.gov.in/PressReleasePage.aspx?PRID=1635572
- https://www.indiamacroadvisors.com/
- file:///D:/Macroeconomics/Covid19/BCG-India-Perspective-COVID19-25May.pdf
- https://www.indiamacroadvisors.com/page/category/economic-indicators/inflation-prices/consumer-price-index/
- http://gstcouncil.gov.in/gst-revenue
- https://m.rbi.org.in/Scripts/PublicationsView.aspx?id=19714
- https://rbidocs.rbi.org.in/rdocs//PublicationReport/Pdfs/6FSRCHAPTER269522
  49FEDAA4019BC14F4FA93C89F2C.PDF
- https://www.cmie.com/
- https://www.dipam.gov.in/dipam/asset-monetisation
- https://nrega.nic.in/netnrega/home.aspx
- https://www.rbi.org.in/scripts/FS_Overview.aspx?fn=2752
- https://www.ppac.gov.in/content/149_1_pricespetroleum.aspx
- https://www.nasa.gov/offices/odeo/workforce-data
- https://home.kpmg/in/en/home/insights/2020/02/india-s-csr-reporting-survey-2019.html#:~:text=the%20prescribed%20format.-,India's%20CSR%20reporting%20survey%202019%20analyses%20and%20brings%20together%20findings,of%20the%20Companies%20Act%2C%202013
- https://www.mca.gov.in/content/mca/global/en/home.html
- https://www.adityabirla.com/media/stories/gd-birla-a-visionary-who-transformed-india
- https://www.tatatrusts.org/upload/pdf/report-tata-group-and-the-sdgs.pdf

Author's Profile

Dr Jagadish Shettigar

Dr Jagadish Shettigar has a doctorate in Economics from IIT-Delhi and has got over four and a half decades of varied experience in teaching, research, and industry. As an academician, he has his grip strengthened over basic theories of Economics, especially State of Indian Economy, Global Business Environment, and Public Finance. During his stint at the Apex Chambers of Commerce and Industry, such as ASSOCHAM and FICCI, he became familiar with ground-level problems of the industry in terms of ease of doing business. As a member of the Prime Minister's Economic Advisory Council (1999–2004), he learnt the skill of striking a balance between economic logic and limitations in terms of popular perspectives, especially while initiating harsh economic reforms, such as disinvestment, rationalization of subsidies, and user charges. Dr Shettigar has been a keen observer of domestic as well as global economic situations and has been articulating his opinion through newspaper articles and TV debates/interviews since 1991. He worked as Professor in Economics at Birla Institute of Management Technology from September 2007 to March 2021 and has been appointed as Professor Emeritus since May 2021.

Dr Pooja Misra

Dr Pooja Misra, Associate Professor in Economics, has a work experience of 25+ years in academics and the corporate industry. Dr Misra is currently the Chairperson, Economics, Birla Institute of Management Technology, Greater Noida. She has spent 12+ years in the industry with organizations such as American Express, Standard Chartered Bank, and Lazard Creditcapital. She opted for the academic world in 2008 and holds a post-graduate degree in Masters in Business Economics from the University of Delhi. She has completed her PhD in Management from Gautam Buddha University. Her research interests include macroeconomic dimensions of an economy, compensation, and current trends in the business environment. An in-depth exposure to economic concepts and theories coupled with insights of the prevalent economic and business environment gives her the edge in formulating her viewpoints and voicing her thoughts around public policy. Dr. Misra is a recipient of the ET Now Woman Leadership Awards of 2019.

Index

For the benefit of digital users, indexed terms that span two pages (e.g., 52–53) may, on occasion, appear on only one of those pages.

Tables and figures are indicated by *t* and *f* following the page number

Lightning Source UK Ltd.
Milton Keynes UK
UKHW020627100922
408587UK00001B/1